Competition Law in Slovenia

Competition Law in Slovenia

Second Edition

Andrej Fatur
Klemen Podobnik
Ana Vlahek

This book was originally published as a monograph in the International Encyclopaedia of Laws/Competition Law.

Founding Editor: Roger Blanpain
General Editor: Frank Hendrickx
Volume Editors: Francesco Denozza & Alberto Toffoletto

Wolters Kluwer

Published by:
Kluwer Law International B.V.
PO Box 316
2400 AH Alphen aan den Rijn
The Netherlands
E-mail: international-sales@wolterskluwer.com
Website: lrus.wolterskluwer.com

Sold and distributed in North, Central and South America by:
Wolters Kluwer Legal & Regulatory U.S.
7201 McKinney Circle
Frederick, MD 21704
United States of America
Email: customer.service@wolterskluwer.com

Sold and distributed in all other countries by:
Air Business Subscriptions
Rockwood House
Haywards Heath
West Sussex
RH16 3DH
United Kingdom
Email: international-customerservice@wolterskluwer.com

ISBN 978-94-035-2690-4

e-Book: ISBN 978-94-035-2691-1
web-PDF: ISBN 978-94-035-2692-8

The Authors

Dr Andrej Fatur obtained his bachelor's degree in Law from the University of Ljubljana Law School, Slovenia, in 1997, and continued his education at the University of Ljubljana with postgraduate studies in Civil and Commercial Law. During that time he spent a trimester at the University of Amsterdam as a research scholar. He obtained his MSc in 2000 by defending a thesis on international antitrust law. In 2004, he obtained an LLM *(cum laude)* in International Trade and Business from Fordham University, New York. He was awarded PhD from King's College London; the thesis under the supervision of Professor Richard Whish dealt with subject of high-tech network industries and competition law. During his research as a PhD student, he was awarded Fulbright and Chevening scholarships and was a visiting tutor at the University College London of EU Competition and Regulatory Law on undergraduate and postgraduate levels. He delivered papers on international conferences and published several academic works on EU competition law, including recent book on Information and Communication Technology Network Industries and EU Competition Policy published by Hart Publishing in 2012. As for Dr Fatur's professional career, he was a judicial clerk at the Appellate Court of Ljubljana from 1997 to 1998 and in 2005 a Dean Acheson stagier in the Cabinet of Judge Borg Barthet at the Court of Justice of the EU. He worked as a senior associate at a commercial law firm in Ljubljana from 1998 to 2005. In 2009 he served as a legal counsel at the Bank of Slovenia, which he left to establish his own law firm in early 2010 where he is now a principal attorney practising competition and corporate law. Since 2012, he is a member and since 2016, also a Chairman of the Supervisory Board of the second largest Slovenian bank, NKBM. He is a member of the Slovenian Bar since 2001 and of the New York bar since 2004. Beside Slovenian, the author speaks English, Croatian, and Serbian, and additionally he has working knowledge of French.

Dr Andrej Fatur is the author of the following chapters of the present monograph: Part I, Chapters 1, 2, 3 and 4; and Part II, Chapter 2. The work was done with valuable research assistance by Fatur Menard Law Firm colleagues, Helena Belina Djalil and Dino Zadnikar.

The Authors

Professor Klemen Podobnik obtained his bachelor's degree in Law from the University of Ljubljana, Faculty of Law in 1994. After several short-term research and education oriented visits (University of Amsterdam School of Law, Kingston University Law School) he continued his education at Columbia Law School in New York, where he obtained his LLM in 2000. He then returned to his *alma mater* University of Ljubljana, where he defended his doctoral thesis on issues of democratic efficiency as main goals of modern competition law and policy with honours in 2002 and was awarded the title of Doctor of Laws. He began his academic career in 1996 when he joined the Faculty of Law of the University of Ljubljana as junior researcher. He was awarded tenure as university docent in 2004 and started a multifaceted teaching career, dealing with such diverse courses as Competition Law, European Law, Corporate Law, Intellectual Property Law, International Trade Law, Transport Law and Media Law. His main research agenda, however, remained firmly focused in the field of antitrust. As of 2015, he is a university professor of Civil and Commercial Law. He has co-authored the *Commentary on Slovenian Prevention of the Restriction of Competition Act* in 2009 and has become a fixture on the lecturing circle in the field of competition law in Slovenia. He has also proven himself internationally, drafting and coordinating projects such as the European Commission training action *Education and Training of National Judges in the Field of EU Competition Law* organized by the Institute for Comparative Law at the Ljubljana Law School where Dr Podobnik has been active as a researcher since 2004. He chaired the European Competition and Consumer Day plenary session in 2008. As an out-house expert, he was intensely involved with legislative procedures in the fields of competition law, cooperating closely with the Office for protection of competition of Slovenia, he co-authored and co-led a long-term research project on competition and competitiveness for the Ministry of Finance of Slovenia, authored a seminal expert opinion and programme for modernization and reform of Slovene competition legislation in 2006. He closely cooperated with the Austrian Academy of Sciences as a member of the research team on the project titled *The Implementation and Application of EC Competition Rules in Austria, Czech Republic, Hungary, Poland and Slovenia*. He has also served as out-house competition law expert to major companies in Slovenia (*Mobitel, Pošta Slovenije, Interbrew, Petrol, Europlakat, Telekom Slovenije*) and served as President of the Expert Council of the Consumer Protection Office of Slovenia from 2004 to 2011. Beside Slovenian, the author speaks English, French, Croatian, and Serbian, and additionally he has working knowledge of German.

Professor Klemen Podobnik is the author of the following chapters of the present monograph: Part I, Chapters 3, 4 and 5; Part II, Chapters 1 and 3; and Part III, Chapters 2 and 3.

Associate Professor Dr Ana Vlahek obtained her bachelor's degree in Law from the University of Ljubljana, Faculty of Law, in 2003 defending with honours her thesis on the reform of EC competition law. She continued her education at the University of Ljubljana with postgraduate studies in Civil and Commercial Law including short-term research and education visits to Cambridge, Cologne and Salzburg. In 2005, she was also an intern at UNCITRAL in Vienna. She obtained her PhD in 2009 by defending a thesis on derivative transfer of movables in the European legal environment. Since 2003 she has been employed at the University of Ljubljana Law School, first as teaching assistant, and subsequently as university docent and associate professor of civil and commercial law, and university docent of European law. She has published several academic articles and has delivered papers at national and international conferences; her major interests being European law, competition law, property law and contracts. Within competition law, she is specialized in antitrust private enforcement. She is a co-author of the *Commentary on Slovenian Prevention of the Restriction of Competition Act* and has been involved in its *travaux préparatoires*. She has been dealing with competition law as a lecturer at graduate and postgraduate studies in the Faculty of Law of the University of Ljubljana, as well as within several projects, such as projects within the European Commission training action *Education and Training of National Judges in the Field of EU Competition Law* that have been organized by the Institute for Comparative Law at the Faculty of Law in Ljubljana where Dr Vlahek is employed as a researcher. She was also a member of the Austrian Academy of Sciences' research team performing the European Commission project titled *The Implementation and Application of EC Competition Rules in Austria, Czech Republic, Hungary, Poland and Slovenia*. Beside Slovenian, the author speaks English, German, Croatian, and Serbian, and additionally she has working knowledge of French.

Dr Ana Vlahek is the author of the following chapters of the present monograph: General Introduction; Part I, Chapter 5; and Part III, Chapters 1 and 4.

The Authors

Table of Contents

List of Abbreviations

ADA-1	Administrative Dispute Act of 2006
CJEU	Court of Justice of the European Union
CFI	Court of First Instance (until 1 December 2009; now the General Court)
CO	Code of Obligations od 2002
CPA	Public Agency of RS for the Protection of Competition (Slovenian Competition Protection Agency)
CPrA	Civil Procedure Act of 1999
CPO	Competition Protection Office (until 1 January 2013; now CPA)
CrC-1	Criminal Code of 2008
EC	European Community
ECA-1	Electronic Communications Act of 2012
ECJ	European Court of Justice (until 1 December 2009; now CJEU)
ECtHR	European Court of Human Rights
ESCCA	Enforcement and Securing of Civil Claims Act of 1998
EU	European Union
FLRJ	Federal People's Republic of Yugoslavia
GAPA	General Administrative Procedure Act of 1999
Ger.	German
Lat.	Latin
LLPCOA	Liability of Legal Persons for Criminal Offences Act of 1999
MOA-1	Minor Offences Act of 2002
PECA	Post and Electronic Communications Agency (renamed Agency for Communication Networks and Services of the Republic of Slovenia on 22 January 2014)
PCA	Protection of Competition Act of 1993
PRCA	Prevention of Restriction of Competition Act of 1999
PRCA-1	Prevention of Restriction of Competition Act of 2008

List of Abbreviations

Regulation 1/2003	Council Regulation (EC) No. 1/2003 of 16 December 2002 on the implementation of the rules on competition laid down in Articles 81 and 82 of the Treaty (Text with EEA relevance), OJ L 001, 04/01/2003 P. 0001 – 0025
Regulation 139/2004	Council Regulation (EC) No. 139/2004 of 20 January 2004 on the control of concentrations between undertakings (the EC Merger Regulation) (Text with EEA relevance), OJ L 24, 29.1.2004, 1–22
RS	Republic of Slovenia
SCPA	Slovenian competition protection authority (i.e. the CPO until 1 January 2013, the CPA as of 1 January 2013; this abbreviation is in principle used where the statement applies to both the CPO and the CPA and does not necessarily refer specifically to the CPO or the CPA)
SFRJ	Socialist Federal Republic of Yugoslavia
SIT	Slovenian tolar (official currency in the Republic of Slovenia as of 8 October 1991 until the introduction of the EUR on 1 January 2007)
Sl.	Slovenian
TFEU	Treaty on the Functioning of the European Union

General Introduction

§1. General Background of Slovenia

1. Slovenia[1] is a small European country whose territory stretches in between the Alps in the northwest, the Adriatic Sea in the southwest, the Pannonia plane in the northeast, and the Dinarides in the southeast. Located at vital transport crossroads Slovenia has a strategic location between the Balkans and Western Europe. The currency is the euro (EUR) that has been introduced on 1 January 2007 replacing the Slovenian tolar (SIT).

2. Slovenia has a population of 2,084 million with 51.2% of women and 48.8% of men. About 93% of the population are Slovenian citizens while 6.9% are foreigners of which only 33.9% are women.[2] In the first quarter of 2019, the natural increase was negative, while a positive net migration of nearly 15,000 persons was recorded.[3] The main ethnic group is Slovene (more than 80%), while other nationalities living in the country are Serbs, Croats, Bosnians, Macedonians, Montenegrins, Hungarians, Italians, Albanians, Roma, and others. The official language in Slovenia is Slovene. In those municipalities where Italian or Hungarian national communities reside, Italian or Hungarian is also the official language. The majority of Slovenes are Roman Catholics, although there are dozens of other registered religious communities, spiritual groups, societies and associations.[4] Under the Slovenian Constitution, the state and religious communities shall be separate, and religious communities shall enjoy equal rights and pursue their activities freely. There are currently 212 municipalities in Slovenia being the basic local self-government communities. Some of them have the status of a city municipality.[5] Population density is approximately 102.7 persons per square km.[6] The mean age

1. Based on and partly cited from Kramberger & Vlahek, *Property Law, Slovenia*, 15–24, and from Podobnik & Vlahek, *Chronology of Development of Private Law in Slovenia*, 283–286. Statistical data was gathered from the webpages of the Statistical Office of the Republic of Slovenia (available in English): http://www.stat.si/.
2. Data for 1 Apr. 2019. Seehttps://www.stat.si/statweb.
3. Seehttps://www.stat.si/StatWeb/en/Field/Index/17.
4. According to the 2002 census, the religious affiliation were as follows: Roman Catholic 57.8%, Muslim 2.4%, Orthodox 2.3%, other Christian 0.9%, unaffiliated 3.5%, other or unspecified 23%, none 10.1%. See http://www.slovenia.si/slovenia/country/people/religion/.
5. See http://www.stat.si/StatWeb/pregled-podrocja?idp=69&headerbar=17.
6. Data for 1 Apr. 2019. Seehttps://www.stat.si/StatWeb/en/Field/Index/17.

of the population is 43.4 years, and 19.8% of the population is over 65.[7] Life expectancy for men is 78.32 years and for women 83.98 years.[8]

3. Slovenian territory or its parts formed part of many European states and other entities, and were – consecutively or even concurrently – under several different political, economic and legal regimes, such as the Holy Roman Empire, the Illyrian Provinces, the Habsburg Monarchy, the Austrian Empire (and subsequently Austria-Hungary), the State of Slovenes, Croats, and Serbs (Sl. Država Slovencev, Hrvatov in Srbov – Država SHS), the Kingdom of Serbs, Croats, and Slovenes (Sl. Kraljevina Srbov, Hrvatov in Slovencev – Kraljevina SHS), the Kingdom of Yugoslavia (Sl. Kraljevina Jugoslavija), the Democratic Federal Yugoslavia (Sl. Demokratična federativna Jugoslavija – DFJ), the Federal People's Republic of Yugoslavia (Sl. Federativna ljudska republika Jugoslavija – FLRJ), and of the Socialist Federal Republic of Yugoslavia (Sl. Socialistična federativna republika Jugoslavija – SFRJ)). A part of western Slovenia belonged to Italy between the two world wars and was reunited with Slovenia in 1947 (partly – as regards parts of the Free Territory of Trieste – de facto in 1954 while formally in 1975).

4. After the Second World War Slovenia was one of the six constituent republics of Yugoslavia (in SFRJ named Socialist Republic of Slovenia, Sl. Socialistična republika Slovenija – SRS; in FLRJ named People's Republic of Slovenia, Sl. Ljudska republika Slovenija – LRS). The republics had their own executive, legislative, and judiciary bodies in addition to the federal ones. The political system in Yugoslavia (called 'self-management', Sl. samoupravljanje) was, at least after the constitutional changes in 1953, different from that of the countries under the Soviet rule. Yugoslavia was not a member of the Warsaw Pact and played a leading role in the Non-Aligned Movement. Despite state-owned industry, Yugoslavia was not subjected to full-blown central planning after 1965; enterprises were left with significantly more autonomy than in the Stalinist states and were market oriented; the regime of 'social ownership' replaced one of 'state ownership' that was introduced after the Second World War on the basis of different measures, such as nationalization; the enterprises were (supposed to be) managed by workers rather than by state officials, etc.[9] The political and economic changes in Eastern Europe in the 1990s were thus arguably not that difficult to implement in Yugoslavia.

5. The amendments to the Slovenian Constitution of 1989 and 1990 paved the way to democratization and independence of Slovenia. The prefix 'socialist' was erased from the official name of the republic in 1990. The plebiscite on independence was held on 23 December 1990. Around 88.5% of the population with the right to vote, and 95% of those actually voting, voted for independence. In April 1991, the first free elections were held seeing the centre-right coalition win. As in the six-month period after the Slovenian plebiscite, no agreement was reached among the former republics to form kind of a loose confederation, the plebiscite

7. See https://www.stat.si/StatWeb/en/Field/Index/17/104.
8. See https://www.stat.si/StatWeb/en/Field/Index/17/95.
9. Cf. Pleskovic & Sachs, *Political Independence and Economic Reform in Slovenia*, 192–193.

decision was implemented in the constitutional act adopted by the Slovene National Assembly. Independence was declared on 25 June 1991. An armed attack by the Yugoslav army on Slovenia followed. After a ten-day war in June and July 1991 between the Yugoslav army and the Slovenian territorial defence and police forces, the Yugoslav army gradually left its positions in Slovenia.[10] Starting with Croatia in June 1991, Slovenia had been internationally recognized by several states and international organizations in 1991 and 1992, the most important being the recognition of Germany and the EC in December 1991 and January 1992. In May 1992, Slovenia became the 176th UN Member State. It joined the EU in May 2004 and adopted the euro in January 2007.

6. The legal and political organization of the Republic of Slovenia is determined by the Constitution of the Republic of Slovenia of 23 December 1991 (amended seven times to date – in 1997, 2000, 2003, 2004, 2006, 2013 and 2016).[11] The Republic of Slovenia is a democratic republic. It is a social state governed by the rule of law. Slovenia is a territorially unified and indivisible state of all its citizens and is founded on the permanent and inalienable right of the Slovene nation to self-determination. In Slovenia, power is vested in the people. Citizens exercise this power directly and through elections, consistent with the principle of the separation of legislative, executive, and judicial powers. The head of state is the President of the Republic of Slovenia who represents Slovenia and is the commander-in-chief of its defence forces. The Government, led by the Prime Minister, exercises the executive power. Legislative tasks are performed by the National Assembly with ninety representatives elected directly at universal elections. The second house of the parliament is the National Council of the Republic of Slovenia representing employers, employees, farmers, crafts and trades, independent professions and non-commercial activities as well as local interests. It has forty members who are elected by electoral bodies at indirect elections held within interest groups or local communities. The Constitutional Court of the Republic of Slovenia (which was founded already by the Yugoslav constitution of 1963) evaluates the conformity of the acts of the National Assembly and other bodies competent to create law, with the Constitution, ratified international treaties, and the general principles of international law. It also decides on the petitions of individuals claiming violations of their human rights by the decisions of state authorities.

7. Slovenia is a member of the European Union (EU) (since May 2004)[12] and the European Economic Area (EEA) (since May 2004), the Eurozone (since January 2007) and the Schengen area (since December 2007), the Organization for Security and Cooperation in Europe (OSCE) (since March 1992), the United Nations (UN) (since May 1992), the Council of Europe (since May 1993), the World Trade

10. The Brioni Accord which was signed in 1991 by the representatives of Slovenia, the SFRJ and the EC provided for a three-month moratorium on Slovenian independence activities. In the meanwhile, the Presidency of the SFRJ reached a decision to withdraw the army from Slovenia what was in full on 25 Oct. 1991 when the last Yugoslav army soldiers left Slovenia.
11. Sl. *Ustava Republike Slovenije (URS)*, Official Gazette RS, No. 33I/91, with further amendments, available at (in English): http://www.us-rs.si/en/about-the-court/legal-basis/.
12. Almost 90% of the voters at the referendum held in March 2003 voted for joining the EU.

Organization (WTO) (since November 1994), the International Monetary Fund (IMF) (since January 1993), the World Bank (since February 1993), the North Atlantic Treaty Organization (NATO) (since March 2004), and the Organisation for Economic Co-operation and Development (OECD) (since July 2010).

§2. Economic System

8. After the Second World War, the economy in Slovenia[13] developed rapidly, particularly in the fifties when the country was strongly industrialized. The processing industry was evolving fast, various new consumer goods were offered on the market and first traces of consumerism could be detected. Agriculture was lagging behind, and people started migrating to the cities seeking job opportunities. In the sixties, the industrial growth fell by one half due to the economic and political crisis induced by the discrepancies of the system of self-management. State funds which amounted to somewhat 75% of all funds in Yugoslavia were invested mainly in the primary sectors of industry – coal mines, ironworks and cement factories. Undertakings lacked resources for adequate progress, imports grew, exports declined and the Yugoslav dinar was devaluated. Eventually, social and economic reforms strengthening decentralization and productivity were implemented enabling Slovenia to start moving towards the market economy. Processing industry within electrics, chemicals, paper and food, was at its peak leaving aside the traditional Slovenian textile, wood and leather industries. The percentage of citizens active in agriculture fell under 20%. At the end of the sixties, Slovenia had also intensified its presence in international trade developing ties mainly with the Member States of the European Economic Community and with the socialist countries (barter trade only), less with the developing countries, which did not go hand in hand with the ideology of the central communist regime which tried to suppress the commodity exchange with the West. Another economic crisis hit Yugoslavia at the end of the seventies and in the eighties due to the devaluation of the currency resulting from the intensified trade deficit and low work efficiency, due to sunk investment coupled with unnecessary bureaucratization of industry and trade. In addition, a large foreign debt enabled a non-proportional standard of living. Foreign currencies and oil were lacking, the unemployment rate had risen, and Yugoslavia almost went bankrupt. The gap between the ideas of economic stabilization based on market economy and trade liberalization on the one hand, and the ignorant persistence with the centralized economy on the other, was insurmountable. Tensions between the republics were amplified – those more economically developed (Slovenia,[14] Croatia) opted

13. Figures and statistics presented are sourced from the webpages of the Statistical Office of the Republic of Slovenia (available in English): http://www.stat.si/; Nešović & Prunk, *20. stoletje*, 202–212, 236–239; Pleskovic & Sachs, *Political Independence and Economic Reform in Slovenia*. This chapter is partly based on and extensively cited from Podobnik & Vlahek, *Chronology of Development of Private Law in Slovenia*, 286–287.

14. Slovenia was the republic with the highest GDP in Yugoslavia. It preserved a high level of economic development based on highly educated, skilled and organized workforce. Although it comprised less than 10% of Yugoslavia's total population, it accounted for approx. 20% of Yugoslavia's GDP and around 30% of its exports in 1990. That year, its income per capita was over USD 6,100, while the

for more autonomy and fair distribution of resources adequate to the productivity of each of the republics, while the others led by the regime itself insisted on the solidarity principle condemning the allegedly selfish attempts of the northern republics. With deteriorating economic position, recurrent riots, growing nationalism and contradictory ideas of how to manage the state lacking efficient economic and political reforms, Yugoslavia was at its breakdown.[15]

9. In the 1990s after its independence, Slovenia has experienced a stable political and economic transition from the centralized socialist regime of self-management to a democratic social order and market economy. The Constitution of 1991 guarantees free economic initiative. It states that the conditions for establishing commercial organizations shall be established by law, and that commercial activities may not be pursued in a manner contrary to the public interest. Unfair competition practices and practices which restrict competition in a manner contrary to the law are prohibited.[16] By introducing its own currency in October 1991 it achieved monetary independence which enabled it to avoid the hyperinflation present in the rest of Yugoslavia in 1992.[17] Private initiative flourished, new businesses were launched, the services sector evolved. It has, however, not been immune to transition anomalies. The processes of privatization,[18] denationalization and implementation of structural reforms were delayed due to political disagreements on their implementation, and the economy has long suffered from a high level of state control. In the last decade in times of political and economic instability in Slovenia, a large part of Slovenian politicians and population have been opting for retention of state control (in particular of focal (though often ineffective enterprises) by referring to a so-called national interest.[19] Joining the EU in 2004 and adopting the euro in 2007 as well as implementing reforms to improve the business environment, have enabled the opening of Slovenian market and greater foreign participation in Slovenian economy, but have not had all the desired effects. High taxes, administrative barriers, politicization of civil service, inefficient court system,[20] inflexibility of the labour market coupled with the fact that Slovenia is a small market have all tended to refrain foreign capital from investing to Slovenia.[21]

---

average income in other Yugoslav republics was USD 2,800. Slovenia's prosperous economy and strong market ties to the West have also been an important factor in the process of gaining independence.

15. See also Kovač & Možina, *Commercial and Economic Law Slovenia*, para. 16.
16. Article 74 of the Constitution.
17. Pleskovic & Sachs, *Political Independence and Economic Reform in Slovenia*, 191. See also Juhart, *Currency Regulation*.
18. See Grilc & Juhart, *Slovenia, Privatization;* Gregorič & Brezigar Masten & Zajc, *From Social to Private Ownership Firms* ... ; Brezigar Masten, Gregorič & Zajc, *Power Struggle: Cooperation or Competition?* ... .
19. See also Kovač & Možina, *Commercial and Economic Law Slovenia*, para. 16.
20. See Dimitrova-Grajzl, Grajzl & Zajc, *Understanding Modes of Civil Case Disposition* ... ; Gregorič & Zajc & Simoneti, *Agents' Response to Inefficient Judiciary* ... .
21. See also Bugarič, *Law and Development in Central and Eastern Europe* ... , 135, 141–142, 145; Bugarič, *Courts as Policy-Makers: Lessons from Transition* ... Bugarič, *The Europeanization of National Administrations in CEE*; Možina & Kovač, *Commercial and Economic Law Slovenia*, para. 16.

10. As of end of 2008, the world economic crisis has had additional negative impact on Slovenian economy which slid into recession due to decrease in domestic consumption initiated by budget expenditure restrictions, inability to implement economic reforms, etc. The construction sector, for example, having increased (too) rapidly prior to the crisis and led to soaring infrastructure investments, collapsed in 2010 and 2011 leaving thousands of workers unemployed and projects unfinished. Businesses have been insolvent to a great extent, payment indiscipline is at its peak. Controversial management buyouts, unsecured politically motivated bank loans and similar corruptive activities, too, have been detected in the last few years and are to date in the centre of daily reports leaving citizens somewhat disappointed with the functioning of the state. The euro crisis and the inability to tackle with the recession have also contributed to growing distrust in the financial system and to lower consumption.

11. In 2018, GDP in Slovenia was EUR 45,755 million, GDP per capita EUR 22,083.[22] Volume growth of GDP in the second quarter of 2019 was 2.5%.[23] In 2018, Government debt amounted to EUR 32,232 million (70.1% of the GDP).[24] In August 2019, average annual inflation rate was 2.3%, average consumer price index 101.7 and monthly change of consumer confidence indicator – 2 percentage points.[25]

12. Since independence and during the transition, the tertiary sector (amounting to approximately 65%–70% of the GDP) has rapidly increased while the percentage of industry sector has fallen to only around 30% while the primary sector amounts to only around 2%.[26]

13. In June 2019, Slovenia's export of goods amounted to EUR 28.13 billion, while import of goods amounted to EUR 30.25 billion. Around three-quarters of export and three-quarters of import are with EU Member States. Most exported and imported goods are products from the manufacturing section. Slovenia exports mainly motor vehicles, trailers and semi-trailers, electric and electronic equipment, machinery, refined petroleum and pharmaceuticals. Its main export partners are Germany, Italy, Austria, France, Croatia and other regions of former Yugoslavia.[27] It

22. See https://www.stat.si/StatWeb/en/Field/Index/1/29.
23. See https://www.stat.si/StatWeb/en/Field/Index/1.
24. See https://www.stat.si/StatWeb/en/Field/Index/1/86.
25. See https://www.stat.si/StatWeb/en/Field/Index/2/35.
26. https://www.indexmundi.com/slovenia/gdp_composition_by_sector.html.
27. See https://oec.world/en/profile/country/svn/. Today, ex-Yugoslav republics are important trading partners of Slovenia. Because of the conflicts that arose in the former Yugoslavia in the nineties, Slovenia was cut from these markets resulting in almost 40% reduction in exports to those areas. As already before the war, Slovenia's export was oriented to the Western countries (68%), the adjustment was not that insurmountable. Pleskovic & Sachs, *Political Independence and Economic Reform in Slovenia*, 208–209.

imports mainly cars and delivery trucks, chemicals, refined petroleum and packaged medicaments, its main import partners being Germany, Italy, Austria, China and South Korea.[28]

14. In 2017, there were nearly 200,000 enterprises registered in Slovenia (88,762 legal persons – mostly limited liability companies and associations, and 106,994 natural persons – mostly individual private entrepreneurs that have in the last couple of years been subject to more favourable administrative and tax rules as before and were thus encouraged to start their business in this legal form).[29]

15. Slovenia has a well-educated populace (in academic year 2018/2019, 46.1% of Slovenian young people aged 19–24 participated in tertiary education)[30] that often lacks job opportunities due to the crisis that has been present on the Slovenian labour market since the second half of 2008. In recent years, younger people (despite having university degrees and even PhDs) have had difficulties obtaining employment, especially on the basis of full-time indefinite term contracts. In the second quarter of 2019 the unemployment rate was 4.2%.[31] Average monthly gross earnings amounted to EUR 1,737.42 and net to EUR 1,119.08.[32] In 2018, the percentage of population below the at-risk-of-poverty threshold was 13.3%.[33] It is worth stressing that Slovenia has one of the lowest Gini indexes in the world.[34] Share of households with Internet connection is 87%.[35]

§3. Legal System

16. The highest legal source[36] in Slovenia is the Constitution. All rights and obligations have to be determined either in the Constitution or in the acts adopted by the National Assembly representing the first level of secondary legislation, while

28. See https://oec.world/en/profile/country/svn/.
29. https://pxweb.stat.si/SiStatDb/pxweb/sl/20_Ekonomsko/20_Ekonomsko__14_poslovni_subjekti__01_14188_podjetja/1418803S.px/table/tableViewLayout2/.
30. See https://www.stat.si/StatWeb/en/Field/Index/9/111 and https://www.stat.si/StatWeb/en/News/Index/8155. The number of children in basic education has been growing since 2010/11 when the population of pupils was the smallest in independent Slovenia (161,046). Smaller generations born 10–15 years ago are leaving for upper secondary schools (nearly 18,000) and bigger generations of 6-year-olds are entering basic education (nearly 22,000). This trend is expected to reverse soon due to falling fertility and thus smaller generations of today's pre-school children. Almost all of primary school leavers (in Slovenia, primary school of 9 years is obligatory for children between the ages of 6 and 15) continue their education immediately (there are currently around 73,000 pupils enrolled in upper secondary education), while around 80% of secondary school leavers decide to continue with tertiary education. Today there are twice as many students in tertiary education as there were at the beginning of the 1990s.
31. The highest unemployment rate in independent Slovenia was 15.5% in December 1993.
32. See https://www.stat.si/StatWeb/en/Field/Index/15.
33. See https://www.stat.si/StatWeb/en/Field/Index/10/39.
34. See https://data.worldbank.org/indicator/SI.POV.GINI?end=2015&locations=SE-FI-DK-GB-CZ-SK-SI&start=2015.
35. https://www.stat.si/StatWeb/en/Field/Index/10.
36. Partly based, structured and cited from Kramberger & Vlahek, *Property Law, Slovenia*, 15–24.

executive regulations that are issued by the Government or the ministers can only determine the implementation and enforcement of such rights and obligations.

17. Laws and other regulations must comply with generally accepted principles of international law and with treaties that are binding on Slovenia. Ratified and published treaties are to be applied directly. The law of the European Union applies in accordance with the general principles of EU law.[37]

18. Slovenia belongs to the civil law legal family. The main sources of law are written acts adopted by the National Assembly. Case law of Slovenian courts is an important interpretative instrument, but is – in contrast to case law of the CJEU which is an important source of EU law applied in Slovenia as of 1 May 2004 – officially not a binding source of law, save the so-called legal opinions and principled legal opinions adopted at plenary sessions of the Supreme Court of RS, which are binding on all the panels of the Supreme Court but not on the lower courts.[38] Legal theory also has considerable influence on Slovenian law and court practice.[39]

19. The courts in Slovenia are divided into courts of general jurisdiction (forty-four local and eleven district courts as first instance courts[40]) and courts of specialized jurisdiction (courts for labour and social matters,[41] and the Administrative Court of RS[42]). There are four general high courts as courts of appeal in Slovenia located in Ljubljana, Maribor, Celje and Koper (some of them have exclusive jurisdiction in some matters (the High Court in Ljubljana in insolvency cases and the

37. See Art. 3a/3,4 of the Constitution. See also Craig & de Búrca, *EU Law*; Tridimas, *The General Principles of EU Law*.
38. Despite this lack of a formal binding power of case law, the courts are obliged to be aware of the case law in similar cases. They should either take the same position or provide reasonable legal argumentation if they decide to depart from it. For further details, see Štajnpihler, *Precedenčni učinek sodnih odločb pri pravnem utemeljevanju*, 90–114; Galič, *The Role of the Supreme Court …* .
39. Štajnpihler, *Sodna praksa kot dejavnik pri sodnem odločanju: sociološki vidik.*
40. Located in Ljubljana, Celje, Maribor, Kranj, Murska Sobota, Koper, Nova Gorica, Krško, Novo mesto, Ptuj and Slovenj Gradec. Local courts are organizational units of district courts of the relevant territory (save the Local Court in Ljubljana which is an autonomous organizational unit). In competition-related matters, only the district courts have jurisdiction irrespective of the general rules on the division of jurisdiction between the district and the local courts. For reasons of specialization and unification of case law, some of these courts have exclusive jurisdiction in some maters (not, however, in competition law related matters). The organization of the courts is regulated by the Courts Act, Official Gazette RS, No. 19/94, with further amendments. For further details, see Galič, *Civil Procedure, Slovenia*, 67–77, and Pogorelčnik Vogrinc, *Der Zivilprozess in Slowenien*, 27–29. The new Slovenian Collective Actions Act, Official Gazette RS, No. 55/17, that applies also to claims resulting from breaches of Slovenian and/or European antitrust, sets out specific rules on jurisdiction in proceedings with collective actions and collective settlements: only the district courts in Ljubljana, Maribor, Celje and Koper have jurisdiction at first instance (whereas collective labour disputes are assessed only at labour courts in Ljubljana, Maribor, Celje and Koper).
41. The first instance Labour and Social Court is located in Ljubljana, while additional first instance labour courts are in Maribor, Celje and Koper having their external offices also in Nova Gorica, Brežice, Kranj, Novo mesto, Murska Sobota, Ptuj and Slovenj Gradec.
42. The Administrative Court is located in Ljubljana having its three external offices in Maribor, Nova Gorica and Celje. In competition matters, however, the Administrative Court rules only at its seat in Ljubljana.

High Court in Koper in land registry cases)), while a specialized Higher Labour and Social Court is located in Ljubljana. The highest court in Slovenia is the Supreme Court of the RS also located in Ljubljana. It has jurisdiction in a variety of matters as a first, second and third instance court, the most important being the assessment of cases in third instance extraordinary remedies' proceedings.[43] Between April 2008, when the PRCA-1 entered into force giving jurisdiction to the Supreme Court of RS to review as the first (and at the same time the last) instance court the decisions of the CPO (replacing previous PRCA giving jurisdiction to the Administrative Court of RS), and August 2013 when Act amending Courts Act gave jurisdiction back to the Administrative Court of RS, the Supreme Court had a vital role in competition law matters.[44] As of August 2013, the Supreme Court acts again only as an appellate administrative court in competition law cases.

20. Judicial statistics for 2018[45] show that 891 judges and further 3,265 judicial staff are employed in Slovenia. According to EU Justice Scoreboard, Slovenia has dropped from the first to the second place in the average number of judges per capita.[46] On average, more than 80% of first instance and around 75% of second instance judges are women while around 60% of the Supreme Court judges are men.[47]

21. In 2018, approximately 838,000 cases were filed with the courts while almost 200,000 cases were transferred as unsolved from 2017. Of all of these cases approximately 853,000 cases were solved in 2018. The percentage of unsolved cases dropped by 9% in comparison to 2017 and by 51% in comparison to 2013.[48] In 2018, the average time for solving a case was 2.7 months (5.4 months at the Administrative Court and 5.6 months at the Supreme Court).[49] The Supreme Court solved 90% of the cases in commercial matters in 14.7 months and 90% of the cases in administrative matters in 22.5 months, while the Administrative Court took 20.6 months to solve their cases.[50] Around 90% of the commercial cases at the high courts were solved in 13.5 months, at district courts in 25.6 months.[51] There is unfortunately no detailed official statistics available that would enable to detect only competition law-related cases. EU Justice Scoreboard 2019 does, however, offer some insight into the time-management of Slovenian courts in competition cases in 2010, 2015, 2016 and 2017: it shows that in competition cases, the average time of solving a case has lowered putting Slovenia in eighteenth place in the EU, but it is

43. For further details, see Galič, *Reshaping the Role of Supreme Courts …* , in particular 299–305.
44. For further details on the functioning of Slovenian courts, see the official website of the Judiciary of the Republic of Slovenia: http://www.sodisce.si/ (available also in English), as well as Galič, *Civil Procedure, Slovenia*, 49–56.
45. Official statistics available at (in Slovene): http://www.sodisce.si/sodna_uprava/statistika_in_letna_porocila/.
46. See http://www.sodisce.si/mma_bin.php?static_id=2019053010295563.
47. *Ibid.*
48. See http://www.sodisce.si/mma_bin.php?static_id=2019053010295563 and https://podatki.gov.si/dataset/sodna-statistika-bilten.
49. *Ibid.*
50. *Ibid.*
51. *Ibid.*

not clear from the data which 'competition cases' are being covered (only administrative ones or also private enforcement cases, etc.).[52] A general overview of the time-frames of handling competition law cases, be it within administrative review proceedings or damages and other private enforcement cases, can also be detected from the analysis of case law referred to in Part I, Chapter 5, §2, II B 2 of this monograph.

22. One of the focal difficulties of Slovene judiciary in the past decades has been a massive judicial workload resulting in backlogs what often made the court system inefficient and forced individuals to lodge requests for supervision of trials or to motion for setting of deadlines according to the Protection of Right to Trial without Undue Delay Act of 2006,[53] or to even sue Slovenia in Strasbourg at the ECtHR claiming that their right to trial within reasonable time had been violated.[54] Debates over judicial reform in Slovenia arose only after a very significant accumulation of court backlogs in the mid-1990s.[55] The resulting long delays were a consequence of an overall increase in the demand for court services spurred by the disorganization that naturally followed the implementation of liberalization and stabilization unaccompanied by institutional improvements, particularly in the resource-starved court system.[56] According to Slovenian leading experts of civil procedure, violations of the right to trial within reasonable time are not that often a result of inadequate measures of a judge in a particular case but rather of the mere fact that the case did not yet get on the agenda due to backlogs.[57] The Government of RS tried to tackle the problem by introducing the so-called Hercules project in 2001 that enabled the reassignment of judges to other courts of the same or lower instance with more workload,[58] and the so-called Matra flex project that implemented a system of measuring judges' work efficiency and courts' workload. In 2005, a large-scale project called Lukenda[59] was introduced to improve the overall functioning of Slovenian courts

52. *Ibid.*
53. Sl. *Zakon o o varstvu pravice do sojenja brez nepotrebnega odla šanja (ZVPSBNO)*, Official Gazette RS No. 49/06, with further amendments. For further details, see Galič, *Civil Procedure, Slovenia*, 44–46; Galič, *Legal Remedies for the Protection of the Right to Trial within a Reasonable Time in Slovenia*.
54. Between 2005 and 2009, for example, Slovenia paid damages for breaching the right to trial without undue delay in 2.644 cases amounting all together to EUR 5,572,004. Data available at (in Slovene): http://www.rs-rs.si/revizije-in-revidiranje/arhiv-revizij/revizija/odprava-sodnih-zaostankov-1419/.
55. Dimitrova-Grajzl et al., *Court Output, Judicial Staffing, and the Demand for Court Services* ..., 3.
56. *Ibid.*
57. Galič, *Civil Procedure, Slovenia*, 46.
58. *Ibid*, 44–45.
59. The project was called *Lukenda* due to an ECtHR case initiated by a Slovenian plaintiff Mr Lukenda who instituted court proceedings for a higher disability allowance that were not progressed for almost a decade (*Lukenda v. Slovenia*, No. of the application 23032/02; judgment dated 6 Oct. 2005). The ECtHR found that the Slovenian legal system does not provide for adequate and effective legal remedies against the violation of a right to trial within reasonable time. After the decision of the ECtHR in this case, the Slovenian Constitutional Court also rendered a judgment in which it declared that Slovenian legal system does not provide for adequate remedies against the violation of the right to trial without undue delay. Following the decisions of the ECtHR and the Constitutional Court, Slovenian legislator adopted a new law – the Protection of the Right to Trial without Unnecessary Delay Act. Galič, *Civil Procedure, Slovenia*, 44.

by 2010, focusing mainly on the increase in judicial staff.[60] As the goal was not reached in the anticipated time, the Government prolonged its implementation until the end of 2012, but the project was not finalized until that date either. The Government then drafted a document Justice 2020 Strategy that based its actions also on the previous projects and aimed to reform judiciary between 2014 and 2020 in order to contribute to solving the crisis in the Slovenian economy and creating competitive conditions for economic growth and prosperity. The reforms have already resulted in reduction of backlogs.[61] The trust in the courts' decision-making that has in recent years been perceived as inefficient and of low quality expertise wise is nevertheless is also slowly being regained.[62]

§4. Historical Background of Antitrust Law

23. While the first competition legislation in the independent Republic of Slovenia was enacted only in 1993, the origins of the Yugoslav competition legislation in force also in the Slovenian territory can be traced back to 1935, when the first Decree on Cartels[63] came into force in the Kingdom of Yugoslavia.[64] It was accompanied by several other acts, such as ordinances on the implementation of the decree, on the registration of cartels, on the cartel court, and on the supervision of cartel prices. The Decree was a modern version of the Czechoslovak cartel legislation.[65] In principle, the cartels were allowed as long as they were not abused. They had to be registered in the cartel register led by a minister who could initiate proceedings and prohibit the cartels if abused, i.e., if a cartel agreement violated or threatened the interests of national economy, general national welfare of the state or other public interests.[66]

24. Within the centralized economy and social ownership of the communist Yugoslavia there was no real place for free business enterprise and competition. However, during the relatively independent market activity that was allowed after 1954, the Yugoslav legislator enacted quite some legislation stressing the importance of competition, e.g., Regulation of 1955 on Trade and Trading Enterprises and

60. See Galič, *Civil Procedure, Slovenia*, 44–46; Dimitrova-Grajzl et al., *Court Output, Judicial Staffing, and the Demand for Court Services …* .
61. See http://www.sodisce.si/mma_bin.php?static_id=2019053010295563.
62. *Ibid.*
63. Sl. *Uredba o kartelih*, Official Gazette of the Kingdom of Yugoslavia, Nos 190-L, 18. VIII. 1934, and 291 – LXX, 14. XII. 1935.
64. Before the end of the First World War, Austrian anti-monopoly regime was in force in the Slovenian territory. In parts under Italy, Italian laws were in force. For further details, see Zabel, *Tržno pravo*, 141–145.
65. No explanation as to why it was based on Czechoslovak law is available.
66. For further details, see Zabel, *Tržno pravo*, 142–143.

Craft,[67] Law of 1962 on Regulation of Business Relations on the Market,[68] Law of 1967 on Trade in Goods,[69] Law of 1974 on Suppression of Unlawful Competition and Monopoly Agreements,[70] Law of 1976 on Business Practices,[71] and Law of 1990 on Trade.[72]

25. According to this legislation, unfair competition, monopolistic agreements[73] and abuse of dominance were prohibited.[74] Reading its provisions isolated from the reality of the Yugoslav market would lead to a conclusion that competition was inherent to it. The reality was somewhat different. Because of the characteristics of a centralistic planned economy, the competition matters were dealt with from a particular, one might even say perverted, viewpoint.[75] As competition was not perceived as the apparatus of economic development and Yugoslav economy was founded on a conception of huge industrial cartels and distribution chains, and banned private entrepreneurial initiative, the prohibition of horizontal as well as vertical restraints of competition was perceived unnecessary and even unwanted.[76]

26. The first competition legislation in the independent Slovenia was the Protection of Competition Act of 1993 (PCA of 1993),[77] enacted on the basis of Slovenian Constitution of 1991 that prohibits unfair competition practices and practices which

67. Official Gazette FLRJ, No. 37/55.
68. Sl. *Zakon o ureditvi poslovnih razmerij na trgu*, Official Gazette FLRJ, No. 53/62. For further details, see Rosina, *Monopolski dogovori in zloraba dominantnega tržnega položaja.*
69. Sl. *Zakon o blagovnem prometu*, Official Gazette SFRJ, No. 1/67. For further details, see Rosina, *Monopolski dogovori in zloraba dominantnega tržnega položaja;* Rosina, *Sporazumi o vertikalni delitvi trga in izključitvene pogodbe.*
70. Sl. *Zakon o zatiranju nelojalne konkurence in monopolnih sporazumov*, Official Gazette SFRJ, Nos. 24/74 and 72/86.
71. Sl. *Zakon o temeljih poslovanja*, Official Gazette SFRJ, No. 43/76.
72. Sl. *Zakon o trgovini*, Official Gazette SFRJ, No. 46/90.
73. According to Art. 3 of the Law of 1974, for example, monopolistic agreements were '*agreements of two or more Basic Organizations of Associated Labour on trade conditions aiming at restricting or preventing free competition and enabling one or more organizations to achieve a monopolistic or otherwise privileged position with regard to other organizations or consumers*'. According to Art. 12, such agreements had no legal effects. For details, see Zabel, *Uvod v gospodarsko pogodbeno pravo*, 311–318.
74. According to Art. 4 of the Law of 1974, for example, '*monopolistic or other privileged position*' was relevant for the determination of a dominant undertaking. According to Art. 11, '*abuse of the undertaking's advantage*' was prohibited. The following two practices were set out as examples of the abuse: '*refusal of sale, or sale under the conditions and in the manner by which the Basic* Organization *of Associated Labour takes its advantage being the only or the predominant producer*' and '*buying products under the conditions and in the manner by which the Basic* Organization *of Associated Labour takes its advantage being the only or the predominant buyer*'. For details, see Zabel, *Uvod v gospodarsko pogodbeno pravo*, 318–320.
75. Cf. Podobnik, *Framing a New Competition Law for Slovenia.*
76. *Ibid.* For details on the so-called self-management agreements and social agreements, see Zabel, *Uvod v gospodarsko pogodbeno pravo*, 164–169; Rosina, *Samouporavni sporazumi in družbeni dogovori o cenah.*
77. Sl. *Zakon o varstvu konkurence (ZVK)*, Official Gazette RS, No. 18/93; entered into force on 24 Apr. 1993.

restrict competition in a manner contrary to the law.[78] PCA of 1993 covered restrictive business practices as well as unfair competition, prohibited speculative practices, dumping and subsidization, and regulatory restrictions of competition.[79] Although it was extensively based on German competition law (reflecting thereby also EU competition law),[80] the PCA of 1993 also followed the non-programmatic provisions of the old Law of 1974 that regulated the trade behaviour of market participants in the former SFRJ and retained its provisions on illegal speculation, dumping, unfair competition, etc., next to the provisions regulating restrictive practices and concentrations.

27. In 1999, a new modern Prevention of Restriction of Competition Act (PRCA of 1999, PRCA)[81] was enacted and was in force from 1999 till 2008. It divided the regulation of competition in the Republic of Slovenia into two legal frameworks, where the new Prevention of Restriction of Competition Act regulated restrictive practices while the remaining part of PCA of 1993 covered unfair competition.[82] A new Act on State Aid Control was enacted in 2000.[83] Although the PCA of 1993 already aligned some of its substance to the competition regime of the EU, the true qualitative leap came about with the enactment of PRCA of 1999, which is perceived as one of the first and most important legislative projects in Slovenia's nascent negotiation for accession to the European Union. As opposed to PCA of 1993 which set out only some of the basic competition law concepts and was not detailed enough to enable efficient regulation and implementation, PRCA of 1999 regulated extensively both substantive and procedural issues of restrictive practices (both those of undertakings and those of the state) as well as concentrations of undertakings.

28. According to the provisions of the Association Agreement between the RS and the European Communities and its Member States,[84] the Slovene side was obligated to harmonize its legislation with the acquis communautaire before it could apply for full membership of the EU. The harmonization of competition legislation was Slovenian overriding priority in its negotiations with the EU. In its Negotiating Position on Chapter 6 (Competition and State Aids),[85] Slovenia acknowledged that

78. Article 74/3 of the Constitution.
79. For further details on the PCA of 1993, see Zabel et al., *PCA of 1993 Commentary*.
80. Grilc & Juhart, *Slovenia, International Franchising*, 5; Grilc, *Competition law*, 4–5.
81. Sl. *Zakon o preprečevanju omejevanja konkurence (ZPOmK)*, Official Gazette RS, No. 64/07, with further amendments; entered into force on 14 Jul. 1999.
82. Additional parts of the PCA of 1993 have become obsolete with the enactment of modern consumer legislation.
83. Sl. *Zakon o nadzoru državnih pomoči (ZNDP)*, Official Gazette RS, No. 1/00, with further amendments. It was replaced by the Monitoring of State Aids Act (Sl. *Zakon o spremljanju državnih pomoči (ZSDrP)*, Official Gazette RS, No. 37/04) in 2004 aligning state aid regulation to the EU framework.
84. Available at (in English): http://www.uradni-list.si/files/RS_-1997-013-00051-MP~P002-0000.PDF#!/pdf.
85. Available at (in English): http://www.arhiv.svrez.gov.si/fileadmin/svez.gov.si/pageuploads/docs/negotiating_positions/6.pdf.

its legislation on the control and prevention of competition was only partially harmonized with that of the EU. Slovenia also undertook to pass the Law on Prevention of Restraints on Competition no later than 30 June 1999. In addition, Slovenia would pass a number of acts necessary for the full implementation of the Law by December 1999. Slovenia was thus obviously aware of the importance of the field of competition and was determined to comply fully with the demands set forth by the EU. The revision of existing legislation and the drafting of new legislation covering an area as complex as competition proved to be a tremendous task.[86]

29. The presently valid act regulating competition in Slovenia is the Prevention of Restriction of Competition Act of 2008 (PRCA-1 or PRCA-1 of 2008).[87] It represents a conceptual and systemic change in the area of competition law and policy in Slovenia as it is a truly modern piece of legislation, mending all the imperfections of the previous acts, as identified by academia and users alike. The new act closely follows the concepts set forth in the EU modernization regulations (i.e., Regulation 1/2003[88] and Regulation 139/2004[89]) as well as in the Commission's soft-law and thus strives for the creating and strengthening of a new competition culture in Slovenia.

30. The PRCA-1 regulates restrictive practices, concentrations of undertakings, regulatory restrictions of competition and measures to prevent restrictive practices and concentrations, which significantly restrict effective competition, where they cause or might cause effects on the territory of the Republic of Slovenia. To this end it lays down the authority responsible for the protection of competition, its powers and the procedures before it. Although in principle, the PRCA-1 regulates only national antitrust and national law on concentrations, some of its provisions have been inserted into its text directly on the basis of the requirements set out in Regulations 1/2003 and 139/2004.[90] The PRCA-1 is thus to a certain extent also an implementing measure of EU competition legislation.[91]

86. Cf. Podobnik, *Framing a New Competition Law for Slovenia.*
87. Sl. *Zakon o preprečevanju omejevanja konkurence* (*ZPOmK-1*), Official Gazette RS, No. 36/08, with amendments; entered into force on 26 Apr. 2008; English version of the Act is available at: http://www.varstvo-konkurence.si/fileadmin/varstvo-konkurence.si/pageuploads/ZPOMK-1-EN_consolidated_2013.pdf (nota bene: the text is a consolidated version of the original text of 2008 and its 2009, 2011, 2012 and 2013 amendments, but not of its latest amendment of 2014, 2015, and 201 7).
88. Council Regulation (EC) No. 1/2003 of 16 Dec. 2002 on the implementation of the rules on competition laid down in Arts 81 and 82 of the Treaty (Text with EEA relevance), OJ L 001, 4 Jan. 2003 P. 0001–0025.
89. Council Regulation (EC) No. 139/2004 of 20 Jan. 2004 on the control of concentrations between undertakings (the EC Merger Regulation) (Text with EEA relevance), OJ L 24, 29 Jan. 2004, 1–22.
90. As also expressly set out in Article 2 of the PRCA-1.
91. See, for example, Arts 4, 12, 25, 35, 40, 42, 43, 48 and 63 of the PRCA-1 regulating substances set out in Arts 3, 5, 6, 11, 13, 15, 16, 20, 22, 35 of Regulation 1/2003, and in Arts 1, 4 and 13 of Regulation 139/2004.

31. To date, the PRCA-1 has been amended eight times, once in 2009,[92] twice in 2011,[93] once in 2012,[94] once in 2013,[95] once in 2014,[96] once in 2015,[97] And once in 2017. In 2009, provisions on the protection of confidential data and on disclosure of data, as well as provisions on leniency were amended. The 2011 and 2012 amendments established and regulated a novo the Public Agency of RS for the Protection of Competition that has replaced on 1 January 2013 the Office of RS for the Protection of Competition that had been the Slovenian competition authority since 1994.[98] In 2013, the amendments to Courts Act restructured the system of court assessment of the CPA's decisions (taking jurisdiction from the Supreme Court and giving it back to the Administrative Court as was the regulation of the PRCA prior to its revocation by the PRCA-1 in 2008) although the Constitutional Court (assessing such regulation in 2013 on motion by the Supreme Court itself) had not found the system in force at the time (giving jurisdiction for review directly to the Supreme Court with no further remedies available) in breach of the Constitution.[99] The 2014 amendments entering into force on 10 May 2014, followed the Constitutional Court's decision of 11 April 2013 finding the CPA's dawn raid proceedings unconstitutional,[100] and set out a court order as a basis for performing investigation by the CPA in the absence of the undertaking's assent to it. A duty of the CPA to publish on its website all national courts' decisions revisiting the CPA's decisions save the confidential data was also added into the PRCA-1. The Slovenian legislator also changed Articles 81 and 82 TEC to 101 and 102 TFEU although the Lisbon Treaty renamed and renumbered TEC already in December 2009. The 2015 amendment to the PRCA-1 annulled the Protection of Competition Act of 1993 and (surprisingly and without any consultation with the academia) transferred provisions on unfair competition into the PRCA-1.[101] In 1999 when the new PRCA of 1999 was enacted, unfair competition remained regulated in the CPA of 1993. As most of the provisions of the CPA of 1993 have become obsolete leaving only provisions on unfair competition regulated in the CPA of 1993, the legislature has obviously decided to transfer its content into the PRCA-1 arguing that it is the law most appropriate to integrate unfair competition. It is, however, explicitly stated in the PRCA-1

92. *ZPOmK-1A*, Official Gazette RS, No. 40/09, entered into force on 13 Sep. 2009.
93. *ZPOmK-1B*, Official Gazette RS, No. 26/11, entered into force on 23 Apr. 2011, and *ZPOmK-1C*, Official Gazette RS, No. 87/11 entered into force on 3 Nov. 2011.
94. *ZPOmK-1D*, Official Gazette RS, No. 57/12, entered into force on 28 Jul. 2012.
95. *ZS --K* (Act amending the Courts act), Official Gazette RS, No. 63/13, entered into force on 10 Aug. 2013.
96. *ZPOmK-1E*, Official Gazette RS, No. 33/14, entered into force on 10 May 2014.
97. *ZPOmK-1F*, Official Gazette RS, No. 76/15, entered into force on 24 Oct. 2015.
98. See Bugarič, *Neodvisne regulativne agencije v Evropi ...* .
99. Constitutional Court decision No. U-I-40/12-3 of 11 Apr. 2013, published on 6 May 2013.
100. *Ibid.*
101. New Arts 63a and 63b were inserted into the PRCA-1. Art. 63a prohibits unfair competition, provides for a definition of unfair competition, and lists the acts of unfair competition harming or potentially harming other undertakings on the market. Art. 63b regulates the protection of market participants having sustained loss as a result of unfair competition.

that the CPA has no power whatsoever within this field.[102] Finally, the 2017 amendments[103] took place as a consequence of implementing the new Directive 2014/104/EU of the European Parliament and of the Council of 26 November 2014 on certain rules governing actions for damages under national law for infringements of the competition law provisions of the Member States and of the European Union.[104] Apart from implementing the directive, the law added new and amended some of the existent definitions; deleted the provisions on the agency's duty to report to the Government and the National Assembly and the Government's approval of the agency's working and financial programmes; and amended the existent rules on the cooperation between the Slovenian courts and the competition authorities. The so-called ECN+ Directive, i.e. Directive 2019/1 of the European Parliament and of the Council of 11 December 2018 to empower the competition authorities of the Member States to be more effective enforcers and to ensure the proper functioning of the internal market has not yet been implemented in the Slovenian law (the implementation deadline is set to 4 February 2021).[105]

102. Article 12/3 PRCA-1. Only judicial remedies are available as set out in Art. 63.b of PRCA-1.
103. *ZPOmK-1G*, Official Gazette RS, No. 23/17, entered into force on 20 May 2017.
104. For further details as to the directive, see Pt. I, Ch. 5, §2, II B 1of this monograph.
105. *OJ L 11, 14.1.2019, 3–33.*

Part I. Structure of Antitrust Law and Its Enforcement

Chapter 1. Sources of Antitrust Law

§1. NATIONAL SOURCES

32. The basis for the legal arrangement of the protection of competition in the Republic of Slovenia is provided in Article 74/3 of the Constitution of RS, which prohibits unfair competition practices and practices which restrict competition in a manner contrary to the law.[106] The general provisions of the Constitution guaranteeing, inter alia, private property, free initiative, freedom of work and free enterprise, are also of relevance.[107]

33. Systematic protection of competition is regulated in the PRCA-1 of 2008 which is fully harmonized with the EU competition legislation. In addition to the PRCA-1, the basic principles of the protection of competition are also contained in the provisions of legislation governing particular sectors, such as public procurement, telecommunications, banking, insurance, energy and media.

34. When Slovenia entered the European Union in 2004, the PRCA of 1999 was amended to cover proceedings for breaches of Articles 81 and 82 TEC (now Articles 101 and 102 TFEU) and the EU Merger Regulation.[108]

35. This implies direct application of EU competition law by the SCPA (and other relevant bodies) as well as by Slovenian courts. The direct application of national law and EU law is parallel when the inspected behaviour of the undertakings under Article 6 (agreements restricting competition) or Article 9 (abuse of a dominant position) of the PRCA-1 may affect trade between Member States. Accordingly, Article 25 of the PRCA-1 (single procedure) provides that in case of the institution of proceedings alleging the infringement of Articles 101 or 102 TFEU, the SCPA shall simultaneously institute proceedings alleging the infringement of the provisions of Articles 6 or 9 of the PRCA-1. Moreover, if during such

106. Grilc & Podobnik, *Das Wettbewerbsrecht in Slowenien*, 1006.
107. *Ibid.*; Grilc & Juhart, *Slovenia, International Franchising*, 4–5; Grilc, *Competition Law*, 3–4.
108. Article 2 of the PRCA-1. See Vlahek in Grilc et al., *PRCA-1 Commentary*, 46–51.

single proceedings it is determined that there are no grounds for instituting proceedings pursuant to Articles 101 or 102 TFEU since trade between the EU Member States has not been affected, the SCPA shall issue a decision terminating the proceedings in this part.[109]

36. The national courts are equally obliged to apply EU law provisions, as well as follow and apply the case law of the Court of Justice and the General Court of the EU even though the notion of precedent is somewhat foreign concept in Slovenian judicial system.[110]

§2. International Sources

37. Apart from the law of the EU (see supra Part I, Chapter 1, §1), no other legal sources that were not adopted in Slovenia apply in Slovenia within competition law.

§3. Secondary Sources

I. Regulations

38. The PRCA-1 being a systemic competition legislation provides the legal basis for adoption of more detailed regulations by the Government of RS in three areas: (i) block exemptions (Article 8 of the PRCA-1); (ii) merger notification (Article 43 of the PRCA-1); and (iii) leniency (Article 76 of the PRCA-1). At present, there are two applicable regulations adopted on the basis of the PRCA-1: the Decree Defining the Contents for the Notification Form for the Concentration of Undertakings,[111] and the Decree on the Procedure for Granting Immunity from Fines and Reduction of Fines in Cartel Cases.[112] The latter one sets out the rules for leniency applications as well as the rules for handling of such applications. The aim of those rules is to increase transparency and legal certainty in the handling of leniency applications.

39. Apart from the above-mentioned regulations issued by the Government of RS, no other generally binding secondary legal sources exist under Slovenian competition law.[113]

109. See also Bratina in Grilc et al., *PRCA-1 Commentary*, 286–294.
110. See General Introduction, §3 of this monograph.
111. Official Gazette RS, Nos 36/09, with further amendments.
112. Official Gazette RS, Nos 112/09, with further amendments.
113. In the past, the Government of RS issued two additional regulations on the basis of the PRCA: (i) Decree on block exemptions which regulated the permissible horizontal and vertical restrictive agreements (Official Gazette RS, Nos 69/02 and 06/03); and (ii) Decree defining the contents and elements required for the notification form for the concentrations of undertakings (Official Gazette RS, No. 4/00). Both regulations are no longer in force.

II. Guidelines

40. There exist no formal Guidelines under Slovenian competition law.[114]

§4. Sources' Relation and Hierarchy

41. According to provisions of the Slovenian Constitution, the inter-relationship between various sources of law and their hierarchy is clear.

42. Article 153/1 of the Constitution (Chapter VII on Constitutionality and Legality) sets out the general principle of hierarchy and conformity of legal acts in RS by providing that laws, executive acts and other general legal acts must be in conformity with the provisions of the Constitution.

43. Article 8 of the Constitution introduces the general principle of supremacy of international law and provides that laws and other legislation must be in line with the generally accepted principles of international law and with binding international treaties. Ratified and published international treaties shall be applied directly. Accordingly, the Constitution gives firm ground for direct use of international law and for conclusion that ratified international treaties are hierarchically above the national laws.

44. The interrelationship between national law and international law is further defined in Article 153 which provides that laws must be in conformity with generally accepted principles of international law and with international treaties ratified by the Slovenian parliament. Regulations and other general legal acts must also be in line with other ratified treaties and with the Constitution and the laws.

45. Individual acts and actions of state authorities, local community authorities and bearers of public authority must be based on a law or regulation adopted pursuant to the law.

46. To clarify the provision of Article 8 on the supremacy of international law and to underpin the accession of Slovenia to the EU (and the NATO), a new article – Article 3a was introduced into the Constitution in 2003. This article gives the RS a possibility to transfer an execution of a part of its sovereign rights to those international organizations, which are based on the respect of human rights and fundamental freedoms, democracy and the principles of the rule of law. The legal acts adopted within such international organizations shall be applied in the RS in accordance with the legal regulation of these organizations. Such transfer of the sovereignty rights can be executed only on the basis of an international treaty ratified by the two-third majority of all members of the Slovenian Parliament.

114. In the past, the Ministry for Economy issued Instructions on the method and conditions for defining the relevant market (Official Gazette RS, Nos 83/00 and 69/02). These guidelines are no longer in force.

47. On the basis of Article 3a of the Constitution and with the ratification of the accession agreement with the EU, the RS partly gave up its sovereignty, and the acts adopted within the area of competence of the EU take precedence over the constitutional or any other national legal provisions.

§5. Role and Authority of Precedents

48. The legal order in the RS is based on the continental law system, and thus the statutes represent the primary source of law. Therefore, precedents are not deemed an official source of law in the Slovenian legal order. The judge in the RS is not compelled to take into consideration any decisions taken in similar cases by the court of the same level or by the higher level, and consequently judicial decisions as such do not create binding new law. Any judgment of the court has effect only *inter partes*. However, taking into account the principle of legal certainty, courts and administrative bodies must assess similar situations equally.[115]

49. Additionally, it can be noted from the developments in jurisprudence that the precedents, while not formally binding, have been a useful tool for the interpretation of the legal rules and their role is increasing. In practice it can often be noticed that previous jurisprudence, especially of the higher courts is being quoted either in submissions of the parties or even in judgments.

50. The jurisprudence of the CJEU has a significantly different role. The CJEU has been given the extraordinary status of the prime developer of EU law. This role of the CJEU derives somewhat from the specific constitutional structure of the EU and its unorthodox division of powers amongst the various EU institutions. Given the direct application of EU law to the competition law cases in the RS (at least to those assessed under Articles 101 or 102 TFEU), national courts are required to follow the jurisprudence of the CJEU. However, in practical terms, there still seems to be a significant lack of know-how amongst the judiciary regarding the basic principles of EU law as well as the application of the CJEU's case law.

51. The SCPA is the key institution responsible for the enforcement of the competition policy in Slovenia. It issues its decisions at the first instance in administrative proceedings. Analysis of the SCPA's decision-making shows that EU law is regularly taken into consideration even when cases have solely national competition law dimensions. Review of the SCPA's decisions is currently carried out by the Administrative Court of RS and the Supreme Court of RS.[116]

115. For details, see General Introduction, §3 of this monograph.
116. For further details as to review proceedings, see Pt. III, Ch. 4, §3 of this monograph.

Chapter 2. Scope of Application

§1. Territorial Reach

52. The question of territorial reach is at the core of every competition law case, as it designates the use of applicable laws and what dimension the case has – just national or cross-border/EU.

53. Article 1 of the PRCA-1 states:

> This act regulates restrictive practices, concentrations of undertakings, unfair competition, regulatory restrictions of competition and measures to prevent restrictive practices and concentrations that significantly impede effective competition, where they cause or might cause effects in the territory of the Republic of Slovenia, and individual rules on compensation for breaches of competition law.
>
> This Act determines the authority responsible for the protection of competition, the competences of this authority and the proceedings conducted by this authority.

54. According to this preliminary provision, the territorial reach of the PRCA-1 covers all the territory of the Republic of Slovenia. Consequently, it applies to all undertakings in the territory of Slovenia: undertakings that are established, domiciled or have their affiliated company in the Republic of Slovenia, as well as those that are established, domiciled or have their affiliated company outside the Republic of Slovenia, but their acts cause or might potentially cause effects on the territory of the Republic of Slovenia.[117]

§2. Special Sectors

55. Certain sectors of economy bear quite distinctive characteristics, either due to their very nature or due to the significance the state attributes to them or both. These sectors have always been more heavily regulated. However, competition law principles are also applicable in these areas – to name the most important ones: banking, public media, postal services and electronic communications, insurance, energy, food, rail transport and financial sector.

56. Accordingly, concurrent jurisdiction exists between the SCPA and the following sectoral regulators: Bank of Slovenia (banking),[118] Ministry of Culture (media),[119] Agency for Communication Networks and Services of the Republic of Slovenia (Sl. AKOS) (named Post and Electronic Communications Agency (PECA, Sl. APEK) until 22 January 2014) (postal services and electronic communications,

117. See also Podobnik in Grilc et al., *PRCA-1 Commentary*, 103.
118. English website available at: www.bsi.si/en/.
119. English website available at: www.mk.gov.si/en/.

rail transport),[120] Insurance Supervision Agency (insurance),[121] Energy Agency (energy),[122] and Securities Market Agency (Sl. ATVP) (mergers and acquisitions).[123] While there is a general legal duty under Slovenian administrative legislation for public authorities to assist each other, in general, there is no close cooperation between the SCPA and the majority of the sectoral regulators. In some sectors (banking, insurance, media), however, there are additional legal requirements in sectorial regulation regarding mergers, and the approval of the merger by the SCPA is only a part of merger control procedure.

57. The closest cooperation exists between the SCPA and the PECA. The PECA is an independent government agency – the regulating body within the scope of postal, telecommunication and management of frequencies activities, and control of the requirements to electromagnetic compatibility. Majority of powers of the PECA are regulated in Electronic Communications Act (ECA).[124] The PECA carries out the analysis of the relevant markets in the scope of telecommunications products and services. The PECA's analysis aims at ascertaining whether the relevant market is effectively competitive, which in turn means that the PECA regulates telecommunications markets *ex ante*, while the SCPA acts *ex post. Ex ante* regulation is therefore used in those segments of the market that have characteristics of a natural monopoly, where general competition law is not sufficient to tackle the market failure as is usually the case with ex-national telecommunications incumbents. These operators with significant market power have such an overwhelming economic power that they impede the entry of potential competition on some segments of the telecommunications market. In order to prevent potential abuses of market power by these operators, the PECA may issue various regulatory measures primarily covering third-party access to their facilities.

58. Article 214 of the ECA-1 explicitly deals with the cooperation between the PECA and the SCPA. The two authorities are obliged to exchange data and information, which they require for performing their tasks taking due account for their confidentiality. Such exchange of data and information has to be limited according to what is appropriate and proportional to the purpose of exchange. Furthermore, when analysing the conditions of the relevant markets and determining significant market power under the provisions of the ECA-1, the PECA shall cooperate with the SCPA without prejudice to the exclusive authority of the PECA to adopt a decision in this area.

---

120. English website available at: www.akos-rs.si/akos-ang.
121. English website available at: https://www.a-zn.si/en/.
122. English website available at: https://www.agen-rs.si/web/en.
123. English website available at: http://www.a-tvp.si/eng.
124. Sl. *Zakon o elektronskih komunikacijah (ZEKom-1)*, Official Gazette RS, No. 109/12, with further amendments. The ECA-1 provides also for the conciliation proceedings aimed at reaching a consensual settlement between the parties in dispute. For further details, see Galič & Hodges, *Consumer ADR in Europe*, Slovenia, 198–199.

59. Article 209 of the ECA-1 also deals with the relationship between the PECA and the European Commission, BEREC as well as with other Member States' regulators. Accordingly, it prescribes mandatory consultations when a proposed measure concerns (i) determining a relevant market, market analysis procedure and/or the imposition, amendment or revocation of certain obligations under the chapter on ensuring competition, if the measure may affect trade between the EU Member States.

60. An additional indicator of good cooperation and efficient working relationship between the two authorities is the Protocol on cooperation between the SCPA and the PECA[125] of 1 September 2009, which established a Coordination group for electronic communications with members from both authorities enabling the experts of both regulators to join forces with the aim of ensuring effective competition on the market of electronic communications. Such cooperation will also result in a unified approach, practice and effectiveness, also with implementing 'good practices' from other EU Member States. In practice, the SCPA has consulted with the PECA in the majority of the cases concerning telecommunications or postal markets, most notably in the abuse of dominant position proceedings against incumbent telecommunications operator Telekom Slovenije, such as *Telekom Slovenije/ABM* (ISDN)[126] and *Mobitel II* (*Itak Džabest*).[127]

61. The PECA's powers with regard to postal services are regulated in the Postal Services Act,[128] which prescribes that the conduct of the PECA must be transparent and must prevent discrimination between operators and users of postal services. The liberalization of postal services market was implemented gradually since 1997 and has been fully effective since 3 August 2009 with the adoption of the new Postal Services act based on the principles of the Postal Service Directive.[129] In accordance with Article 3 of the Postal Services Act, the Republic of Slovenia ensures universal postal services in public interest under the same conditions to all of its users on its territory. Consequently, the PECA has the power to appoint (by issuing a decision either on the basis of analysis of the current state of affairs or by public tender) such universal service provider(s) and monitor its performance and quality. Until 2023, such universal service provider will be Pošta Slovenije d.o.o., former national postal incumbent.[130]

---

125. Available at (in Slovene): http://www.varstvo-konkurence.si/fileadmin/varstvo-konkurence.si/pageuploads/Protokol_UVK_in_APEK.pdf.
126. CPO's decision No. 3073-9/2002-50 of 22 Oct. 2007, available at (in Slovene): http://www.varstvo-konkurence.si/fileadmin/varstvo-konkurence.si/pageuploads/ijz017.pdf.
127. CPO's decision No. 306-14/2009-239 of 13 Feb. 2012, operative part of the decision is available at (in Slovene): http://www.varstvo-konkurence.si/ostali-dokumenti/arhiv-odlocb/odlocba228/.
128. Sl. *Zakon o poštnih storitvah (ZPSto-2)*, Official Gazette RS, No. 51/09, with further amendments, available at (in English): https://www.akos-rs.si/files/APEK_eng/Legislation/postal-services-act-zpsto2.pdf.
129. Directive 2008/6/EC of the European Parliament and of the Council of 20 Feb. 2008 amending Directive 97/67/EC with regard to the full accomplishment of the internal market of Community postal services, OJ L 052, 27 Feb. 2008 P. 0003–0020.
130. See (in Slovene): https://www.akos-rs.si/univerzalna-storitev.

62. The most important provision regarding facilitating competition in the Postal Service Act is Article 32 granting access to the facility of the universal service provider to other interchangeable postal service providers. Consequently, universal service provider must, upon a demand of a interchangeable postal service provider, enable access to its facilities and enter into a contract covering (i) the mode and conditions of access, (ii) the price of access, which must be cost based, (iii) the mode of calculation and (iv) payments. When it comes to pricing policy and conditions of access, the universal postal service provider must not discriminate amongst interchangeable postal service providers. At the same time, any interventions of the PECA as a regulator in this regard must be transparent, proportional and non-discriminatory. Additionally, the general pricing of postal services is also prescribed in Postal Services Act and any changes to the prices must be approved by the PECA.[131]

63. Further, the PECA also monitors the competition on the railways services market of passengers and cargo traffic. In case the PECA discovers violations of competition, it acts in accordance with its powers under the Railway Transport Act[132] and other relevant legislation. Due to the EU plan to form a unified European market of services in railway transport, its liberalization is a precondition. The market of services in railway transport has been gradually opening for cross-border competition in two steps. By January 2007, EU transporters have been granted the right to access to railway infrastructure for performing all services in international cargo transport in all Member States under the same and just conditions. Next to the above-mentioned monitoring of competition, the PECA also monitors this right to access.[133]

64. The role of the Bank of Slovenia in the scope of competition law is focused mainly on giving consent to merger of two or more banks or to division of a bank.

65. The Ministry of Culture is the regulating body responsible for media, having the right to give its consent regarding concentration of ownership of printed media, radio or TV. The threshold for its consent is 20% of ownership/management/voting rights in the capital or assets of the media publisher. Such consent, which is based on the information obtained from the Securities Market Agency or in case of radio and television, on the opinion of the Broadcasting Council, is a precondition for the validity of the transaction.

66. Insurance Supervision Agency is a regulatory body of the insurance market entrusted with consent when merger of insurance companies is in question. According to Article 107 of the Insurance Act,[134] Insurance Supervision Agency may not give its consent to the merger if the SCPA has refused its consent to the merger or

131. See: http://www.akos-rs.si/price-regulation.
132. Sl. *Zakon o železniškem prometu (ZZelP)*, Official Gazette RS, No. 92/99, with further amendments.
133. See: http://www.akos-rs.si/railway-service-market.
134. Sl. *Zakon o zavarovalništvu (ZZavar-1)*, Official Gazette RS, No. 93/15, with further amendments.

has forbidden the merger. In the event of a merger taking place the new undertaking must apply for the insurance license, since such license(s) is a precondition for entering the insurance market.

67. The Energy Agency (EA) is a national energy regulatory authority with the responsibility to supervise the implementation of the provisions of the law and regulations of the European Union concerning electricity and natural gas markets. The EA's monitoring tasks are expanding from the regulated activities to the overall monitoring of electricity and natural gas markets activities. An important role has been given to the EA also in ensuring the competitiveness of the energy markets. Article 387 of the Energy Act[135] explicitly deals with the cooperation between the EA and the SCPA. The two authorities are obliged to exchange data and information, which they require for performing their tasks. Such exchange of data and information has to be limited according to what is appropriate and proportional to the purpose of exchange. Furthermore, the EA annually reports to the Slovenian Government and the National Assembly on potential dominant position on the market for electricity and natural gas and on actions restricting competition in energy markets in Slovenia.[136] The latter report also entails the review of all ownership changes in the undertakings and measures taken on the state level, with which the state (i) ensures adequate number of market players or (ii) encourages cross-border exchange and competition.[137]

68. In the scope of competition law, the Securities Market Agency gives its consent on obtaining qualified shares in brokerage companies, funds, management companies and stock exchange and central securities clearing corporations. Further it gives its consent regarding takeover offers and exercises control over procedures under Takeover Act.[138]

§3. State-Owned Enterprises and Public Utilities

69. The term 'state-owned enterprises' includes:

- companies incorporated under the Companies Act[139] and in which the RS has a financial investment;
- public companies and institutions incorporated under the Public Utilities Act[140] in which the Republic of Slovenia has a financial investment, assets under management or another form of financial asset belonging to the state;

135. Sl. *Energetski zakon (EZ-1)*, Official Gazette RS, No. 17/14, with further amendments.
136. Article 404 of the Energy Act.
137. See: http://www.agen-rs.si/en/.
138. Sl. *Zakon o prevzemih (ZPre-1)*, Official Gazette RS, No. 79/06, with further amendments, available at (in English): https://www.a-tvp.si/Documents/ENG/ZPre/Takeover_Act_ZPre-1_EN.pdf.
139. Sl. *Zakon o gospodarskih družbah* (*ZGD-1*), Official Gazette RS, No. 42/06, with further amendments.
140. Sl. *Zakon o gospodarskih javnih slu žbah (ZGJS)*, Official Gazette RS, No. 32/93, with further amendments.

– other persons incorporated under public law (public institutions, agencies, funds) in which the state has its assets under management.[141]

70. State-owned enterprise is defined as a legal entity, operating independently on the market, and with the profit motive as its primary motivation. It is usually organized in the form of a joint-stock company or a limited liability company. An analysis showed that such enterprises are usually predominant in public services, energy, transport, telecommunications and financial sector. The operating results of these companies present a substantial share of gross domestic product, employment and the market value and are thus often referred to as 'natural monopolies'.[142]

71. The PRCA-1 covers both private as well as public undertakings. Article 3/1 in connection with Article 4/1 of the PRCA-1, defines 'an undertaking' as an 'entity engaging in economic activities, regardless of its legal form and ownership structure'.

72. 'Economic activity' is defined as 'any activity performed on the market for payment'. Accordingly, public entities and other legal entities subject to public law and performing economic activities are also subject to the PRCA-1. An 'undertaking' also means an association of undertakings that is not directly engaged in an economic activity but affects or may affect the behaviour on the market of undertakings as defined above. While in most cases it is not problematic to decide whether a particular entity or person is an undertaking and might be party to the anti-competitive agreement or infringe competition law, the legal definition of an undertaking under the PRCA-1 is very broad and the practice of the SCPA has consistently extended its scope.[143] Thus, from the competition point of view, the distinction between publicly or privately owned enterprise is irrelevant.[144]

73. Public utility is defined in the Public Utilities Act as a public company with a special legal structural form: its founder is the Republic of Slovenia or the local community. For matters related to the status of public company which are not otherwise regulated by the Public Utilities Act, the Companies Act applies. A public utility may also be established as a company with private capital holding if this is in line with the public interest reason for which the company was established. The public interest is the key element for establishing a public utility that is due to this reason different from other companies, since they perform a public utility service or monopolistic activity which is defined as a public utility service.[145]

74. When considering if a public utility is an undertaking as defined by the PRCA-1, the functional approach is being used – does such public utility performs

141. See Policy on Corporate Governance of State – Owned Enterprises, 3, available at (in Slovene): https://www.zdruzenje-ns.si/db/doc/upl/politika_upravljanja_podjetij_v_drz._lasti.pdf.
142. Policy on Corporate Governance of State-Owned Enterprises, 7–8, 12.
143. Fatur & Podobnik, *Competition Law in Western Europe and USA: Slovenia*, s. 3.2.
144. Grilc in Grilc et al., *PRCA-1 Commentary*, 59.
145. Policy on Corporate Governance of State-Owned Enterprises, 8.

economic or commercial activities. Such approach cannot be used for entity or person, which does qualify as an undertaking under the theory of functional approach but performs activities of public authorities or even works as a public authority. Entity or person works as a public authority if he performs his activities for the enforcement of public interest that presents an essential function of government operations and the activity as such is by nature and purpose connected with rules governing public powers, which are by its nature typically public.[146]

§4. Sensible Effect and *De Minimis*

75. According to Article 6/1 of the PRCA-1 which covers general prohibition of restrictive agreements in Slovenian competition law, agreements which have as their object or effect the prevention, restriction or distortion of competition on the territory of the Republic of Slovenia are prohibited and shall be null and void. This general clause thus prescribes certain material conditions that must be met in order to establish a prohibited agreement: the object of the agreement is the prevention, restriction or distortion of competition (agreements restrictive by 'object') or agreements that effect competition (agreements restrictive by 'effect').

76. Article 6/3 of the PRCA-1, however, defines legitimate restraints of competition by establishing a regime under which it is possible for agreements which otherwise restrain competition to be exempted from the basic prohibitive provision of Article 6/1 of the PRCA-1, in cases where explicitly provided positive and negative conditions are met. This is an exemption from the general provision prohibiting acts of restriction, when such acts can also result in positive consequences, particularly in the sense of economic efficiencies. This provision introduces the legal basis for utilization of some form of rule of reason type of competitive assessment to the Slovenian competition law framework. The exemption to the general prohibitive provision of Article 6/1 of the PRCA-1 will therefore apply after a thorough balancing process of the pro- and anti-competitive effects of the assessed acts of restriction. With the introduction of this provision Slovenian competition law is following the reformed EU competition law regime and eliminates the system of granting individual exemptions – the provision of Article 6/3 of the PRCA-1 therefore works independently and serves as a defence for undertakings that are accused of restrictive acts. To this end, Article 6/3 of the PRCA-1 provides that:

> The first paragraph shall be inapplicable if these agreements contribute to improving the production or distribution of goods or to promoting technical and economic progress, while allowing consumers a fair share of the resulting benefit. These agreements shall not:
>
> – impose on the undertakings concerned restrictions which are not indispensable to the attainment of these objectives; and

146. Grilc in Grilc et al., *PRCA-1 Commentary*, 60.

– afford such undertakings the possibility of eliminating the competition in respect of a substantial part of the products or services that are the subject of the agreement.

77. While under Slovenian competition law there are no guidelines or notices specific to anti-competitive practices, the 2008 enactment of the PRCA-1 introduced an explicit provision that burden of proof is carried by the undertaking when the national equivalent provision to Article 101/3 TFEU is invoked.[147]

78. If an agreement is regarded as prohibited by its object or effect, it can still be exempted from the ban following the De Minimis Rule set out in Article 7 of the PRCA-1. This article regulates restrictions of minor importance. The thresholds are 10% (horizontal agreements) and 15% (vertical agreements) of the aggregate market share of the relevant product/service market. When competition in the relevant market is restricted due to market circumstances, and in particular due to equal or similar agreements made between other undertakings, the mentioned thresholds are lowered to 5%. However, the article contains certain qualifications when the *de minimis* provision does not apply even though the thresholds were not exceeded.[148]

147. Fatur & Podobnik, *Competition Law in Western Europe and USA: Slovenia*, s. 3.6.

148. Accordingly, the *de minimis* provision will not apply to horizontal agreements which have as their object to: (i) fix prices or restrict production or sales; or (ii) share markets or sources of supply; or vertical agreements which have as their object to: (i) fix retail prices; or (ii) grant territorial protection to the participating undertakings or to third persons.

Chapter 3. Overview of Substantive Provisions

§1. Restrictive Agreements

79. The first type of restrictive practice prohibited under Slovenian competition law is the restrictive agreement. The main legislation dealing with anti-competitive practices is Article 6 (Prohibition of restrictive agreements) of the PRCA-1. Its main wording (i.e., Article 6/1 of the PRCA-1) corresponds to Article 101/1 TFEU and states:

> The following shall be prohibited and null: agreements between undertakings, decisions by associations of undertakings and concerted practices of undertakings that have as their object or effect the prevention, restriction or distortion of competition in the territory of the Republic of Slovenia.

80. Therefore, agreements concluded abroad might be subject to examination under Slovenian competition law as long as they cause or may cause effects in Slovenia (extraterritoriality principle).

81. It follows that Slovenian competition law prohibits anti-competitive agreements, decisions and concerted practices which have as their object or effect elimination, restriction or any other infringement of competition in the relevant market. Such agreements are void in their entirety or in the respective part, which might be subject to further conditions. Similar to EU competition law, the notion of 'agreement' is interpreted very broadly. It may take written or oral form and covers all forms of consensus reached by entrepreneurs with detriment to third parties. This consensus ought to be achieved on a voluntary basis and normally results in elimination of risk and in distortion or elimination of competition. Parties to the agreement coordinate their behaviour and enjoy extra profits. Those profits are earned because of the absence of effective competition. Notions of 'object' and 'effect' are likewise consistent with the practice developed by the EU Commission and the EU Courts.

82. Slovenian competition law covers horizontal as well as vertical restrictive agreements. Horizontal restrictive agreements cover anti-competitive behaviour of undertakings on the same level of production or offering services, while vertical restrictive agreements cover restrictive acts of undertakings, which operate on different levels of production or service process. The 2017 amendment of the PRCA-1 (aimed at transposing the regime from the Directive 2014/104/EU) brought along a novel definition of the term 'cartel'. Unfortunately, it is not entirely clear why the legislature decided to slightly modify the wording of the definition which was otherwise copied from the text of the directive in its entirety. As the definition from Article 3/1/20 of the PRCA-1 reads now, cartels are agreements or concerted practices between two *undertakings* (and not competitors, as per the wording of the Directive), therefore potentially including much more than only hardcore horizontal cartels. Was it an error in transposition process or did the legislator actually want to include certain vertical agreements into the definition of the 'cartel' is an issue of pure speculation as is the question of the potential impact of such a definition on the breadth of the leniency programme.

83. The concept of per se infringements is not directly applicable to the Slovenian legal system. According to provisions of the General Administrative Procedure Act (GAPA),[149] the body which is conducting the administrative procedure has to find the material truth, which basically prevents the CPA from finding certain infringements as per se illegal. Article 6/2 of the PRCA-1 does however list the same examples of infringements as Article 101/1 TFEU and states:

> In particular is prohibited to:
>
> – directly or indirectly fix purchase or selling prices or any other trading conditions;[150]
> – limit or control production, markets, technical development, or investment;[151]
> – apply dissimilar conditions to equivalent transactions with other trading parties thereby placing them at a competitive disadvantage;
> – make the conclusion of contracts subject to acceptance by the other parties of supplementary obligations which, by their nature or according to commercial usage, have no connection with the subject of such contracts;
> – share markets or sources of supply.

§2. Dominant Undertakings

84. Dominant undertaking is defined in Article 9/2 of the PRCA-1: 'an undertaking or several undertakings have a dominant position when they can, to a significant degree, act independently of competitors, clients or consumers.

85. Article 9/3 of the PRCA-1 complements this definition by providing:

---

149. Sl. *Zakon o splošnem upravnem postopku (ZUP)*, Official Gazette RS, No. 80/99, with further amendments.
150. See, for example, the CPA's decision in 3062-7/2018 CPO's decision in *GZS*, No. 306-21/2005-92 of 1 Feb. 2006, available at (in Slovene): http://www.varstvo-konkurence.si/fileadmin/varstvo-konkurence.si/pageuploads/ijz066.pdf; the CPO's decision in *Nova Ljubljanska banka, Banka Celje, Nova KBM, Abanka Vipa*, No. 306-14/2006-100 of 26 Feb. 2007, available at (in Slovene): http://www.varstvo-konkurence.si/fileadmin/varstvo-konkurence.si/pageuploads/ijz033.pdf; and the CPO's decision in *Bank Association of Slovenia*, No. 306-62/2005-59 of 15 Nov. 2006, operative part of the decision is available at (in Slovene): http://www.varstvo-konkurence.si/ostali-dokumenti/arhiv-odlocb/odlocba49/.
151. See, for example, the CPO's decision in *ASNSH*, No. 306-83/2005-18 of 19 Jan. 2006, operative part of the decision is available at (in Slovene): http://www.varstvo-konkurence.si/ostali-dokumenti/arhiv-odlocb/odlocba05/.

When deciding on the existence of a dominant position the CPA shall primarily consider market-share, financing possibilities, legal or actual entry barriers, access to suppliers or market, and existing or potential competition.

86. Moreover, a market-share threshold which determines whether an undertaking is dominant has also been defined in the legislation. Accordingly, Article 9/5 of the PRCA-1 defines the market-share threshold for dominance as follows: 'An undertaking shall be deemed to have a dominant position on the market if its market-share within the market of the Republic of Slovenia exceeds a threshold of 40 per cent.'

87. Slovenian competition law does not cover conduct through which a non-dominant firm becomes (or attempts to become) dominant (monopolization). Likewise, the legislation does not apply to conduct of non-dominant firms which are nearly as powerful as the dominant firm in the market. It covers situations of collective dominance, however. Article 9/6 of the PRCA-1 defines collective dominance as follows: 'Two or more undertakings shall be deemed to have a dominant position on the market if their aggregate market-share within the market of Republic of Slovenia exceeds a threshold of 60 per cent.'

§3. CONCENTRATIONS

88. Looking only at statistics,[152] one could easily conclude that merger control is the most important point of interest for the SCPA. While this apparently central role of merger control in Slovenian competition law is a direct consequence of the notification system requiring prompt notification of all concentrations above a certain threshold, and is therefore a bit misleading, the fact remains that the SCPA considers merger control at least as an important instrument of its competition policy as the above-described instrument directed at restrictive practices. Good examples of this approach are controversial takeover attempts in the past,[153] where the SCPA did not shy away from aggressive intervention and (sometimes too aggressive) application of a merger control system.

89. The main provisions dealing with mergers and joint ventures are Article 10 (Definition of concentration) and Article 11 (Appraisal of concentrations) of the PRCA-1. The legislation covers all types of mergers: horizontal, vertical and conglomerate. The wording of Article 11/1 of the PRCA-1 is effectively the same as the wording of Article 2/2,3 of the EU Merger Regulation and suggests the application of the SLC test.[154] The wording of Article 11/1 provides: 'Concentration

152. See Pt. I, Ch. 5, §1, I C of this monograph.
153. See, for example, the CPO's decision of 13 Dec. 2007 on initiation of proceedings against *Infond Holding, Pivovarna Laško, Pivovarna Union, Radenska, Center Naložbe, Kolonel*, available at (in Slovene): http://www.varstvo-konkurence.si/ostali-dokumenti/arhiv-sklepov/sklep15/.
154. While the previous wording of Art. 11 also suggested the application of the SLC test, the SCPA was, in accordance with Art. 13, obliged to appraise concentrations with a view to establishing whether or not there exists a threat of creating or strengthening of a dominant position, as a result

which would significantly impede effective competition in the territory of the Republic of Slovenia or in a substantial part of it, particularly as a result of the creation or strengthening of a dominant position, shall be prohibited.' Article 11/2 of the PRCA-1 corresponds to Article 2/1 of the EC Merger Regulation.

90. The definition of a concentration has constantly evolved since the introduction of Slovenian competition legislation in 1995. Accordingly, a concentration falling under the provisions of Article 10 of the PRCA-1 shall be deemed to arise where a change of control on a lasting basis results from:

- the merger of two or more previously independent undertakings or parts of undertakings; or
- the acquisition, by one or more natural persons already controlling at least one undertaking, or by one or more undertakings, whether by purchase of securities or assets, by contract or by any other means, of direct or indirect control of the whole or parts of one or more other undertakings; or
- the creation of a joint venture by two or more independent undertakings, performing on a lasting basis all the functions of an autonomous economic entity.

91. Such control of a whole undertaking or a part of shall be constituted by rights, contracts or any other means that, either separately or in combination and having regard to the considerations of facts or regulations involved, confer the possibility of exercising decisive influence on such an undertaking or part of an undertaking, in particular:

- ownership or the right to use all or part of the assets of an undertaking;
- rights or contracts that confer a decisive influence on the composition, voting or orders of the bodies of an undertaking.

92. Control is acquired by persons or undertakings that:

- are holders of rights or entitled to rights under the contracts concerned; or
- while not being holders of such rights or entitled to rights under such contracts, have the power to exercise the rights deriving from contracts.

§4. Other Prohibitions

93. There are no other prohibitions in the Slovene competition regime.

---

of which effective competition could be excluded or significantly impeded. The relationship between these two provisions was therefore a matter of interpretation. The new wording of Art. 11 now clearly suggest the application of the SLC test and is therefore aligned with the approach on the EU level.

§5. TEST OF ILLEGALITY

I. Per Se Prohibitions and Naked Restraints

94. The ambit of types of behaviour prohibited even without any tangible anti-competitive effects is narrow as such behaviour has to distinctly convey its anti-competitive nature. It could be said that these restrictive business practices are illegal per se and hence prohibited.[155] Their mere existence poses an inherent danger for competition as they are deemed the most heinous.

II. Balancing Tests

95. The well-established assessment criteria of legality – the per se rule and the rule of reason were developed at the turn of the century by American courts while interpreting relatively vague provisions of the Sherman Act.

96. The dichotomy in application of legal standards used to assess the (il)legality of restrictive behaviour can be seen as one of the general characteristics of antitrust doctrine in the field of horizontal restrictions of competition. In addition, it provides answers to questions on the scope and method of application of antitrust law.

97. The application of the per se rule appears to be a clear, one-sided test of illegality of certain types of restrictive behaviour, and its focus mainly turned to the question of the mere existence of such acts. Behaviour examined under the said standard is thence condemned without elaborate judicial analysis into the purpose or effects of the conduct in the particular case before the court.[156] The moment a type of conduct is recognized or 'characterized' as falling inside the per se rule, the only issue that demands proving is the (f)actual existence of the conduct itself.

98. Despite the unequivocal negative consequences arising from the application of such a one-sided, basic test, it is necessary to draw attention to the wide range of benefits that speak in favour of the per se rule. In the first place it is necessary to stress the high level of legal certainty and predictability that the application of the per se rule ensures as the undertakings are given prior opportunity to fine-tune their business policies and thus avoid the risk of potential legal consequences. Nor should we overlook its general preventive effect – an unambiguous, clear method of assessment clearly forewarns the potential offenders of negative consequences that are to

155. It is to be underscored that the terms *per se* and *rule of reason* are used in their American antitrust meaning as the European and consequently the Slovene competition law do not allow for such a clear distinction between the two types of illegal behaviour and also do not use the terms concerned in an equal manner.
156. Hovenkamp, *Antitrust*, 11.

follow their restrictive behaviour, thus discouraging them from entering into anti-competitive agreements. One should not, however, overlook potentially negative effects that are a typical trait of all forms of one-sided, unilateral legal standards and concepts.[157]

99. The rule of reason analysis represents the opposite side of the standard spectrum – unlike the per se rule it is primarily characterized by a multitude of factors[158] which should be evaluated with a view to reaching decision on potential illegality of certain types of behaviour. The rule of reason is a typical example of Anglo-Saxon legal tradition as it excellently illustrates the notion of procedure creating substance. It is this characteristic, however, that casts doubt on the rule of reason as the adequacy of its level of legal certainty and predictability are questioned. The broad judicial discretion, based on a wide range of assessment criteria may adversely affect mainly the predictability of the occurrence as well as potential resolution of disputes and, in addition, accounts for the tardiness and higher costs of litigation. Application of the rule of reason also lowers the level of general prevention in antitrust law, as it obscures the line between acceptable and illegal types of market behaviour.

100. The elaborate principles of rule of reason and per se complement each other in the U.S. antitrust doctrine. The 'unreasonable' restraints are analysed by per se rule – such restrictions cannot be justified by any economic or non-economic arguments – this is why they fall under the scope of the Sherman Act and are hence prohibited. On the other hand, the set of other anti-competitive restraints of trade is considered in the context of the rule of reason – an evaluation and recognition of their potential efficiencies can save them from being covered by the Sherman Act. If the court namely determines that the restraint is a 'reasonable' one, such business behaviour does not fall within the scope of activities prohibited by the Sherman Act.

101. One cannot detect a true notion of the rule of reason in the European competition law. The reason for this is to be found in the systematic of Article 101 TFEU. Its first paragraph contains a general prohibition of practices which restrict competition within the internal market, whereas the third paragraph sets out the conditions for exemptions from this prohibition. The third paragraph can therefore be used in cases where – at least as it can be inferred from the Commission Guidelines on the application of Article 81(3) TEC[159] – the offence is primarily covered by the general prohibition in the first paragraph, but meets the conditions for granting an exemption. In the case of the 'authentic', US antitrust version of the rule of reason

---

157. Cf. Ehrlich & Posner, *An Economic Analysis of Legal Rulemaking*:the inherent ambiguity of language and the limitations of human foresight and knowledge limit the practical ability of the rulemaker to catalog accurately and exhaustively the circumstances that should activate the general standard. Hence the reduction of a standard to a set of rules must in practice create both overinclusion and underinclusion.

158. Posner speaks of a '*multi-factored reasonableness*', Posner, *Antitrust Law, An Economic Perspective*.

159. Communication from the Commission – Notice – Guidelines on the application of Art. 81(3) of the Treaty (Text with EEA relevance), OJ C 101, 27 Apr. 2004, 97–118.

such behaviour would be recognized as reasonable by means of the analysis using the first paragraph of Article 101 TFEU and thus compatible with the rules on competition. Such a possibility, however, is expressly denied in the case law of the European courts.[160]

102. As the wording of Article 6 of the PRCA-1 mirrors that of Article 101 TFEU and the competition law as a whole is based on that of the EU, it is clear that the standard of illegality and its balancing tests totally resemble the described ones of the EU competition law.

III. Merger Tests

103. Please see Part I, Chapter 4, §7 of this monograph.

---

160. Cf. the CFI judgment in T-328/03 *O2 (Germany) GmbH & Co. OHG v. Commission of the European Communities*:

> Moreover, in a case such as this, where it is accepted that the agreement does not have as its object a restriction of competition, the effects of the agreement should be considered and for it to be caught by the prohibition it is necessary to find that those factors are present which show that competition has in fact been prevented or restricted or distorted to an appreciable extent. The competition in question must be understood within the actual context in which it would occur in the absence of the agreement in dispute; the interference with competition may in particular be doubted if the agreement seems really necessary for the penetration of a new area by an undertaking. Such a method of analysis, as regards in particular the taking into account of the competition situation that would exist in the absence of the agreement, does not amount to carrying out an assessment of the pro- and anti-competitive effects of the agreement and thus to applying a rule of reason, which the Community judicature has not deemed to have its place under Article 81(1) EC.

Chapter 4. Overview of Main Notions

§1. Undertaking

104. The basic definition of 'undertaking' is provided in Article 3 (Definition of terms) of the PRCA-1. The legislation covers private as well as public undertakings. According to Article 3, in connection with Article 4 of the PRCA-1, it applies to 'all subjects performing economic activities, irrespective of their legal status and ownership affiliation (undertakings)'. 'Economic activity' means 'any activity performed on the market for payment'. Accordingly, public entities and other legal entities subject to public law and performing economic activities are also subject to the PRCA-1. The same applies to natural persons, although the employees would not qualify as undertakings, since Article 4 of the PRCA-1 explicitly excludes the use of the PRCA-1 for relationships between the employees and their employers. An 'undertaking' also means an association of undertakings that is not directly engaged in an economic activity but affects or may affect the behaviour on the market of undertakings as defined above. The group and/or association of undertakings such as a trade association can qualify as one undertaking and be liable for infringement of antitrust rules, also in addition to the other undertakings, involved in anti-competitive agreements.[161] While in most cases, it is not problematic to decide whether a particular entity or person is an undertaking and might be party to the anti-competitive agreement or infringe competition law, the legal definition of an undertaking is very broad and the practice of the SCPA has consistently extended its scope.[162]

§2. Relevant Market

105. Correct delimitation of relevant markets is of crucial importance for the proper application of competition laws. It is not surprising therefore that the basic definition of 'relevant market' is provided in Article 3 (Definition of terms) of the PRCA-1, which also reflects EU competition legislation and case law. Pursuant to Article 3 of the PRCA-1, 'relevant market' means a market defined by the relevant

161. On this point see the CPO's decision of 11 May 2010 in *Ski Lift Operators* cartel case, where the CPO decided that agreements between 6 companies and 1 trade association was caught by Art. 6(1) of the PRCA-1 and Art. 81(1) TEC. The Supreme Court of RS upheld the CPO's decision in that regard. The operative part of the Decision is available at (in Slovene): http://www.varstvo-konkurence.si/ostali-dokumenti/arhiv-odlocb/odlocba183/. The judgment of the Supreme Court of RS No. G 23/2010 is available at (in Slovene): http://www.sodisce.si/znanje/sodna_praksa/vrhovno_sodisce_rs/2012032113046277/.

162. With this regard, it is interesting to note that the CPO started proceedings for failing to notify of a concentration, against the *Association of Pensioners' Societies of Slovenia*, because of their role in collecting proxies and consequently taking over the Supervisory Board of the health insurance company Vzajemna. The CPA stopped the proceedings, which means that we will not be able to see any significant case law on this issue. The Order of 14 Oct. 2010 initiating the proceedings is available at (in Slovene): http://www.varstvo-konkurence.si/ostali-dokumenti/arhiv-sklepov/sklep61/. The Order of 1 Jul. 2013 stopping the proceedings is available at (in Slovene): http://www.varstvo-konkurence.si/ostali-dokumenti/arhiv-sklepov/sklep88/.

product/service market and the relevant geographic market. This definition is further developed for 'relevant product/service market' and 'relevant geographic market'. Accordingly, a 'relevant product/service market' represents a market that, as a rule, comprises all products or services that are regarded as interchangeable or substitutable by the consumer or user given their characteristics, their prices or their intended use. In turn, 'relevant geographic market' is defined as a market that, as a rule, comprises an area in which competitors on the relevant product/service market compete in the sale or purchase of products or services, in which the conditions of competition are sufficiently homogeneous, and which can be distinguished from neighbouring areas because the competition conditions are appreciably different.

§3. Market Power/Dominant Position

106. Article 9/2 of the PRCA-1 defines a dominant position as follows: 'One or more undertakings has a dominant position, when it can behave, to an appreciable extent, independently of its competitor and customers and ultimately, of consumers.' Such an approach of the PRCA-1 follows the dominance test as introduced by the European Court of Justice (ECJ) in the famous United Brands case. The definition in Article 9/2 has an economic strength as its prime focus, applies to market power on buyers and sellers side alike an entails two essential elements: (i) capacity to restrict competition, and (ii) capacity of independent behaviour (which is economically computable market power resulting in the ability of the undertaking to increase prices above the competitive level through restrictions, resulting in collecting increased profits).[163] One can conclude that economics plays a key role in proceedings before the competition authorities.

107. Moreover, a market-share threshold which determines whether an undertaking is dominant has also been defined in the legislation. Accordingly, Article 9/5 of the PRCA-1 defines the market-share threshold for dominance as follows: 'An undertaking shall be deemed to have a dominant position on the market if its market-share within the market of the Republic of Slovenia exceeds a threshold of 40 per cent.'

108. Slovenian competition law does not cover conduct through which a non-dominant firm becomes (or attempts to become) dominant. Likewise, the legislation does not apply to conduct of non-dominant firms which are nearly as powerful as the dominant firm in the market. It covers, however, situations of collective dominance. Article 9/6 of the PRCA-1 defines collective dominance as follows:

> Two or more undertakings shall be deemed to have a dominant position on the market if their aggregate market-share within the market of Republic of Slovenia exceeds a threshold of 60 per cent.[164]

---

163. Grilc in Grilc et al., *PRCA-1 Commentary*, 143.
164. Fatur & Podobnik, *Competition Law in Western Europe and USA: Slovenia*, s. 4.2.

109. Even though the market-share thresholds create a legal presumption, such a presumption may be rebutted, since market share is an important, however, not crucial indicator of dominance. When analysing market shares, attention must be paid to its absolute and relative rate as well as its changes in a certain period of time. Market share is primarily used at the beginning of proceedings for orientation purposes and its relevance is established together with other factors.[165]

110. To this end, Article 9/3 of the PRCA-1 complements the above-cited definition in Article 9/2 of the PRCA-1 by providing: 'When deciding on the existence of a dominant position the CPA shall primarily consider market share, financing possibilities, legal or real entry barriers, access to suppliers or market, and existing and potential competition.'[166]

111. It is especially worth mentioning the barriers to entry – if they are relatively low, the importance of a substantial market share of an undertaking is substantially decreased.[167] Further the buyer (consumer) power is also one of the more prominent factors; here, one should note that the existence of buyer power includes the possibility to choose. To this end, finding of mutual influence between the buyer and the seller and buyers bargaining strength is essential. The latter is again dependant of various factors like information flow, alternative sources of supply, etc.[168] It is important to realize that the buyer power may be to consumer's benefit if the effects are transferred downstream – in cases where the buyer becomes the seller to the consumer. In order to establish this relationship and its effects on competition, a detailed analysis of the vertical relationships on the relevant market must be conducted.

112. In practical terms it should be highlighted that even if it has been established that the undertaking had a dominant position in the past, the decision-making authority is not bound by its previous finding of dominance. Consequently, in case of new proceeding, the SCPA is required to make a new assessment of dominance on the basis of new facts. In the same manner, the SCPA is also not bound by previous finding of dominance by the European Commission. However, the previous finding of dominance may serve as a basis for a damages claim.[169]

---

165. Grilc in Grilc et al., *PRCA-1 Commentary*, 144.
166. See, for example, the CPO's cases *Mobitel/WWI (Mobitel I)*, Partial Decision No. 3072-4/03-184 of 13 Jun. 2005, available at (in Slovene): http://www.varstvo-konkurence.si/fileadmin/varstvo-konkurence.si/pageuploads/ijz008.pdf, and Supplementary Decision No. 3072-4/03-206 of 20 Dec. 2005, available at (in Slovene): http://www.varstvo-konkurence.si/fileadmin/varstvo-konkurence.si/pageuploads/ijz052.pdf; and *Slopak*, Decision No. 306-125/05 of 21 Dec. 2006, available at (in Slovene): http://www.varstvo-konkurence.si/fileadmin/varstvo-konkurence.si/pageuploads/ijz056.pdf.
167. Grilc in Grilc et al., *PRCA-1 Commentary*, 146.
168. *Ibid.*, 147.
169. *Ibid.*, 148.

§4. Agreements and Concerted Practices

I. Prohibited Agreements

A. Cooperation Between Two or More Independent Undertakings

113. One of the basic identifiers of restrictive business practices regulated by Article 6 of the PRCA-1 is the existence of collaboration/cooperation between two or more economically and legally independent undertakings. Despite a seemingly clear and concise wording of the said rule (formation of a market environment where undertakings form their business decisions independently), one has to underline certain instances where the antitrust economics theory and also the European jurisprudence partially alleviates its demand for the existence of at least two independent undertakings.

B. Cooperation Between Undertakings and Consumers

114. In accordance with the recognized definition of the notion of undertaking in the field of antitrust, a consumer or a group of consumers cannot be identified as an undertaking as they lack the basic characteristic of performing on a market in the sense of supply of goods or services. Therefore, using a strict linguistic interpretation of Article 6 of the PRCA-1, cooperation between undertakings and their final consumers cannot be deemed as prohibited restrictive behaviour. Nevertheless, potentially anti-competitive consequences stemming from certain types of business collaboration between undertakings and their consumers in oligopolistic markets are not to be overlooked. Such frequently used contractual clauses are Meeting-Competition and the Most-Favoured-Customer clause. These are mainly used by undertakings to reduce the lack of information in oligopolistic markets thus creating conditions for tacit or express collusion and lessening the incentives for price-cutting. As for the MFC clause, both of its main types (retroactive and contemporaneous) may potentially lead to price-cutting incentives being lessened,[170] while their role in enabling collusive behaviour is less clear if not almost negligible. Meeting-Competition clauses, on the other hand, have great anti-competitive potential. They force their issuers to 'meet' the prices for certain goods or services in cases where such goods or services were offered to their buyers at a lower price. Encouraged by the promise of prices being met, diligent and frugal consumers are more than willing to research the relevant markets and then inform the undertaking in question of its competitors' prices. Thus, the undertaking is timely informed of its competitors' price policies and can therefore act as an efficient type

170. The incentives for price cuts are lessened because the seller abiding by the promised MFC clause cannot attract new buyers with lower process without offering the same low prices to its existing customers.

of facilitating practices.[171] In addition, such clauses enable undertakings to discriminate between better and worse informed consumers.[172] It goes without saying that the described practices cannot be interpreted restrictive agreements, although they can take the shape of concerted practices under certain conditions (oligopolistic market, long-term exclusive contracts, homogeneity of products or services, symmetry of competitors' market positions, etc.)

II. Economic Unity

115. The question of independence of two or more undertakings can be of utter importance in situations where one is to analyse potentially anti-competitive restrictive behaviour taking form of agreements between parent companies and their subsidiaries or between other types of affiliated or associated undertakings. It is to be emphasized that such agreements cannot be perceived as illegal, save in cases where the subsidiaries or other controlled companies lack actual autonomy regarding business decisions. The presumption of economic unity undoubtedly stands in cases where the parent company controls 100% of its subsidiaries' shares, while lower percentage of control raises questions of actual autonomy of business behaviour by subsidiaries and affiliated companies.[173]

III. State Intervention

116. Restrictive business practices based on acts or actions of a state are not in the ambit of the prohibition set forth by Article 6/1 of the PRCA-1. Such situations are not to be perceived as illegal especially in cases where the undertakings' behaviour has limited or no consequences for the level of competition in the market, where competition has already been previously heavily restricted or distorted because of acts of state and where undertakings cannot make their business decisions independently of the state.

117. The basic analysis criterion in such situations is, whether a detected anti-competitive effect can be linked solely to the actions of the state. If certain parameters of restrictive behaviour have been created by undertakings themselves, the act-of-state defence will not be admissible. To be more precise, state intervention must exist, it has to be unavoidable and forced upon the undertakings. State actions consisting solely of encouragement, incentives, support or confirmation of detected restrictive anti-competitive behaviour will not activate the 'act-of-state' exemption.

---

171. See also Van den Bergh & Camesasca, *European Competition Law and Economics*, 181.
172. Buccirossi, *Facilitating Practices*, 337.
173. CFI judgment in T-102/92 *Viho Europe v. Commission*.

118. To summarize, restrictive agreements between undertakings, stemming from a clear, unconditional act or measure of the state are not caught by the prohibition set forth in Article 6/1. In spite of this the SCPA will have to analyse potential effects on trade between Member States. If such an effect exists, the SCPA will not be able to implement the 'act-of-state' exemption – the agreement in question will be declared null and void as it represents a breach of Article 101 TFEU even if it is based on current national legislation. Parties to such agreements will however not be subject to neither administrative/criminal sanctions nor damages liability.[174]

IV. Meeting of Minds

119. The term 'agreement' is to be broadly interpreted. To arrive at an understanding or to conclude an agreement, it is not necessary for anything to be written down. In fact, such agreements are often not put into writing. Nothing need even be expressed – a 'nod and wink' is sufficient. An understanding must involve the meeting of two or more minds. Where the minds of the parties are at one that a proposed transaction between them proceeds on the basis of the maintenance of a particular state of affairs or the adoption of a particular course of conduct, it would seem that there would be an understanding.[175] Even actions that would not be perceived as agreements in civil (contract) law (e.g., gentlemen's agreements) can be interpreted as agreements in light of Article 6 of the PRCA-1.

V. The Agreement Restricts, Distorts Competition in the Territory of Republic of Slovenia by Object or Effect

120. The wording of Article 6/1 of the PRCA-1 prohibits only collusive behaviour with actual or potential restrictive or distortive effect on competition on the territory of Republic of Slovenia. The main condition for the activation of prohibition from Article 6/1 of the PRCA-1 is thus the existence of anti-competitive object or effect of restrictive collusive practices. In accordance with well-established jurisprudence of the Community courts and theoretic approaches Article 6/1 of the PRCA-1 thus also prohibits behaviour not yet resulting in anti-competitive consequences whether such behaviour was intended to result in distortion or restriction of competition.

121. The wording of Article 6/1 of the PRCA-1 lacks clarity as in its original form in Slovene language it might lull a non-sophisticated user into a belief that common anti-competitive intent of both (all) undertakings is necessary. The term 'object' is namely translated into 'cilj', which, in English, means 'goal', almost inevitably presupposing a common voluntary action by all the undertakings (parties to the agreement). It is to be underscored that the term 'object' refers to the inherent

174. See the ECJ judgment in C-198/01 *Consorzio Industrie Fiammiferi.*
175. *Top Performance Motors Ltd v. Ira Berk (Qld) Pty Ltd* (1975) 24 FLR 286.

anti-competitive nature of the agreement itself, not to the quality of the parties' voluntary behaviour. It is the said inherent anti-competitive nature that is the reason for the prohibition of such agreements notwithstanding the existence of anti-competitive consequences.

122. Horizontal restraints in the forms of price fixing, territorial market division, limiting the level of production are strictly prohibited. As for vertical restraints, agreements on absolute territorial exclusivity, minimum retail price maintenance schemes and agreements preventing passive sales are deemed the most dangerous and therefore prohibited as to their object.

123. However, even behaviour that is not deemed anti-competitive as to its object can result in serious anti-competitive effects. Prohibition (illegality) of such types of restrictive agreements therefore depends on the question of their effects on competition, taking into account the results of a thorough market structure analysis, the nature of the products, the market position of the parties, the market position of competitors, the market position of buyers, the existence of potential competitors and the level of entry barriers.

VI. Concerted Practices

124. Concerted practices are one of the most complex concepts in competition law. Authorities entrusted with analysing the (il)legality of market performance in the form of concerted practices are to detect, identify and establish anti-competitive behaviour from circumstantial evidence and hints. This is due to the fact that concerted practices can only be implied or imputed ex post facto using detected anti-competitive consequences in the market as the starting point for investigation and – somewhat paradoxically – also as evidence of wrongdoing. Concerted practices are 'invisible' and thus non-existent before the detection of anti-competitive consequences that have no basis in agreements or similar collusive behaviour by undertakings. This is the reason why concerted practices are extremely difficult to detect and properly identify. It is to be underscored, that the consequences in question that are to indicate anti-competitive collusive behaviour by the undertakings (usually in the form of parallel price raises or simultaneous limiting of production) can also be an outcome of absolutely legal behaviour in highly concentrated oligopolistic markets. A hasty and casual market analysis can thus result in a false conclusion that, e.g., (almost) simultaneous price changes (raises) stem from anti-competitive collusive behaviour of market players while in reality such behaviour represents rational business decisions by oligopolists.

125. It is settled economic theory that concerted practices are typical in markets conditions and structures that *ex ante* largely prevent effective competition. This – as pointed out earlier – poses a tangible threat of false negative decisions by competition authorities as concerted practices in oligopolistic markets show extreme resemblance to otherwise lawful and legitimate behaviour of interdependent rational reactions by competitors. One of the most interesting traits of oligopolistic market structures is apparent collaborative interdependent behaviour of market players which make their business decisions according to preceding actions of their competitors.[176] It is to be reiterated again that all apparent anti competitive consequences then do not necessarily stem from an otherwise invisible, intangible concerted behaviour by undertakings present in a market, nor are they necessarily anti-competitive. Reactions to competitors' preceding behaviour in the form of, e.g., not lowering the prices can thus be a perfectly normal consequence of an oligopolistic market structure – a non-conformist behaviour in the form of harsh competitive price cuts could end devastatingly unpleasant for an undertaking acting thus as its competitors could promptly punish it by lowering their prices even further, probably driving it out of the market. The mere awareness of such a prospect flattens any desire for autonomous behaviour. The described process, however, cannot be identified as a restraint of trade in the form of an agreement or concerted action, mainly due to the lack of conscious behaviour. Undertakings do follow their competitors' behaviour and adapt to it; however, these adjustments lack conscious quality – they adapt as not to be driven out of the market, not in view of upholding a cartel. The question therefore arises as to what extent, if any, parallel behaviour in an oligopolistic market is the result of a meeting of minds or whether, on the contrary, it is the result of the autonomous will of each undertaking.[177]

126. Oligopolistic markets are therefore characteristic of non-competitive equilibrium – too intensive an application of the concept of concerted practices in such conditions can be harmful and intrusive. Such market conditions (undesirable, yet not illegal) can better be improved by, e.g., removing barriers to entry for potential new competitors.[178]

§5. Restriction of Competition

I. Distortion, Restriction of Competition

127. The main goal and task of any competition policy is ensuring the highest possible level of consumer welfare. Competition law therefore should not protect market players from more efficient competitors – its basic goal is to protect competition. Primarily, competition law serves as a guarantor of consumer welfare, attaining this goal by preventing restrictive anti-competitive behaviour in the market.

128. It is to be underscored that the market condition to be attained by competition law and policy is one of efficient, effective competition, hence a condition

176. Such market conditions and behaviour can most genuinely be illustrated by the game theory.
177. Allendesalazar, *Oligopolies, Conscious Parallelism and Concertation.*
178. For a somewhat different opinion, see Grillo, *Collusion and Facilitating Practices ...* .

allowing for certain deviations from the state of perfect competition. Certain deviations, namely, can result in a higher level of consumer welfare (lower prices, higher quality of products and services, both due to efficiencies stemming from restraints of trade) or represent a natural market condition (highly concentrated structure in certain markets with network externalities).

129. It is therefore essential that the analysed alleged restraints of competition that are to be prohibited as to their effect, clearly negatively affect consumer welfare or, in other words, they have to result in certain consumer harm. By prohibiting behaviour not ensuing in consumer harm, competition policy would necessarily transform into its own opposite, resulting in a regime punishing efficient market players. In such a form, competition policy would arguably also bear all characteristics of unconstitutional conduct because of its proscriptions limiting one of the basic constitutional freedoms – free economic initiative, guaranteed by Article 74 of the Constitution of RS. Hence a procedure analysing alleged behaviour with anti-competitive effects resulting solely in findings of negative consequences for competitors cannot stand as a relevant legal basis for determining a breach of Article 6 of the PRCA-1.

II. Territory of the Republic of Slovenia

130. Territorial ambit of the PRCA-1 is limited to the market of the Republic of Slovenia – it hence prohibits only the restrictive agreements having a negative effect on effective competition in the corresponding territory. This limitation, however, does not restrict the use of the analysed provision of Article 6 of the PRCA-1 solely to behaviour by undertakings established in Slovenia – the extraterritorial quality of competition law enables its application to any behaviour negatively affecting market conditions in the territory of the Republic of Slovenia.

III. Exemptions to General Prohibition (Article 6/3 of the PRCA-1)

A. Positive Conditions

131. Restrictions that can generally be identified as anti-competitive can be exempted from the scope of Article 6 of the PRCA-1 if it meets two conditions that are cumulatively prescribed and whose wording represents an abstract legal formulation of economic efficiencies. The conditions are based on the economic teachings recognizing pro-competitive qualities of certain restrictive practices. This is particularly true in the case of vertical restraints of competition that are limited to restraining intra-brand competition.

132. The most basic form of vertical restrictions with pro-competitive consequences is undoubtedly distribution agreements. Their anti-competitive effect is usually limited only to restriction of competition between distributors of a single principal. Restrictions in the form of territorial exclusivity clauses, single-branding, full-line-purchasing obligations doubtlessly have a negative impact on competition between distributors, while they consequently weaken the position of the consumer by reducing or limiting freedom of choice.

133. On the other hand, such restriction can also result in indirect as well as direct positive consequences for consumers. The latter can be primarily defined as an improvement in the quality of sales and after-sales services by distributors, while the indirect positive effects can be seen in a potential increase in inter-brand competition as a result of the elimination of double transaction costs. The elimination of double transaction costs can also contribute to reduction of retail prices in the distribution network.

1. Improvement of Production or Distribution of Goods or Promotion of Technical and Economic Progress

134. The first condition requires the agreement to result in significant economic efficiencies that outweigh the negative effects of restrictions of competition.

135. The notion of economic efficiency is concreted in two abstract conceptual groups, the first (improving production or distribution) mainly consisting of the desire for price efficiencies, improvements in consumer information, improvements of sales and after-sales activities. The common denominators of the second group are innovative efficiencies primarily in the form of the development of new methods of production, introduction of new products or services or significant improvements to existing products or services.

136. It could be argued that the first indent includes all forms of economic efficiencies. In determining whether the analysed agreement could result in economic efficiencies the SCPA should above all assess the nature of the alleged efficiency; causal link between an agreement and the claimed efficiencies, their scope, the probability of their emergence, the timeliness of their emergence. Generally, there has to exist a direct and intense enough causal link between an agreement and alleged efficiencies, while the probability and timeliness of their occurrence must prevail over the identified negative effects of such an agreement. The SCPA enjoys s broad discretion as to which efficiencies to take into account when assessing a restrictive agreement. Typical examples of economic efficiencies can be enumerated as follows: synergies of complementary technologies, economies of scale and economies of scope, management efficiencies, distributive efficiencies, the introduction of new products or services (innovative efficiency), improvements to existing products or services.

2. Allowing Consumers a Fair Share of the Resulting Benefit

137. The other positive condition basically consists of the most revered welfare standard in competition law – consumer welfare or consumer benefit. Hence, any alleged or proven economic efficiencies stemming from a restrictive agreement exceeding the potential negative effects, are to be passed on to the consumer in their significant part. The term 'consumer' is to be broadly interpreted to cover not only the end (retail) clients but also all other legal or natural persons doing business (as clients) with the undertakings that are parties to the assessed agreement.

138. The basic test for the assessment whether the said condition has been met is an existence of a positive trade-off between the volume of transferred benefits and negative consequences that are imposed on the consumers because of a restrictive agreement. The result that still justifies an exception to the general prohibition is a neutralization of the negative consequences. The benefits have to be transferred to the extent that they reach (and neutralize) the level of adverse effects, thus placing the consumer in a 'neutral' position, i.e., the same as in the absence of the cartel. The temporal element also plays an important role in assessment of efficiencies: the time period in which the benefits will be transferred to the consumer should be as short as possible. This will quickly neutralize the negative effects of a restrictive agreement.

B. Negative Conditions

1. Imposition on the Undertakings Concerned Restrictions Which Are Not Indispensable to the Attainment of These Objectives

139. The first negative condition consists of two stages of assessment, which can, however, be defined as a unitary proportionality test. First, the parties to the restrictive agreement are to prove that the conclusion of the agreement was necessary to achieve the claimed efficiencies – essentially, the undertakings must persuade the SCPA that the efficiencies would not have occurred in the absence of the agreement. The agreement thence represents the least drastic means necessary to achieve the alleged efficiencies. The second step of the proportionality test demands from the undertakings involved to show the necessity of particular restraints of competition stemming from the agreement.

2. Affording Such Undertakings the Possibility of Eliminating Competition in Respect of a Substantial Part of the Products or Services That Are the Subject of an Agreement

140. The second negative condition set forth in the third paragraph of Article 6 of the PRCA-1 points to the fundamental policy objective, namely the prevention of restriction of competition. In the case where a restrictive agreement was to completely eliminate competition in the relevant market, neither the potential high level of economic efficiencies nor the transfer of a high proportion of the benefits to consumers will remove such an agreement from the scope of the general prohibition of Article 6/1 of the PRCA-1.

141. The potential elimination of competition must be assessed in relation to (i) the level of concentration of market structure before and after the conclusion of the agreement, (ii) the behaviour of the parties before and after the conclusion of the agreement, (iii) the nature of the products or services offered by parties to the agreement, (iv) potential competition and (v) entry barriers.

§6. Monopolization and Abuse of Dominance

I. General on Abuse of Dominant Position

142. The PRCA-1 includes provisions on anti-competitive behaviour of individual undertakings in Article 9 titled 'prohibition of abuse of the dominant position'. An appraisal of individual conduct of undertaking as an abuse is necessarily linked with the already discussed concepts of relevant market definition[179] and determination of dominance.[180] The latter is the very basic precondition for the institution of the proceedings against the undertaking.

143. Similar to EU competition law, there is no direct causality between the creation of a dominant position and its abuse under Slovenian competition law. The abuse of a dominant position as such is not defined by the PRCA-1. In Article 9/1,4 the PRCA-1 generally prohibits the abuse of a dominant position and lists several examples of abuse. Article 9/4 of the PRCA-1 list is non-exclusive and includes the following types of conduct:

- directly or indirectly imposing unfair purchase or selling prices or other unfair trading conditions;
- limiting production, markets or technical development to the prejudice of consumers;
- applying dissimilar conditions to equivalent transactions with other trading parties, thereby placing them at a competitive disadvantage;
- making the conclusion of contracts subject to acceptance by the other parties of supplementary obligations which, by their nature or according to commercial usage, have no connection with the subject of such contracts.

144. The structure of Article 9 of the PRCA-1, entailing a general clause of the prohibition, definition of a dominant position and an exemplary list of most common abusive practices, is fully in line with Article 102 TFEU.

145. The abusive practices not enlisted in Article 9/4 are prohibited under the general clause. In general, the practice may be divided into two groups:

179. See Pt. I, Ch. 4, §2 of this monograph.
180. See Pt. I, Ch. 4, §3 of this monograph.

- exploitative practices of a dominant undertaking, which aim at a direct decrease in consumers' benefit and are possible when the undertaking has significant market power; and
- exclusionary practices of a dominant undertaking, which aim at competing undertakings when competition as such exists, whereas the dominant undertaking is in the position to decrease consumers' benefit.[181]

146. As already mentioned, the definition of dominance is based on the concept of economic strength and its determination is subject of assessment of several criteria, which are evident also from the SCPA's case law. Dominance may be either single (one undertaking holding it) or collective (two or more undertakings holding it), though there are no details on the assessment of the collective dominance prescribed in the PRCA-1, except its presumption when the collective market share reaches the threshold of 60% on the relevant market. In this regard, as in other undeveloped issues in Slovenian competition law, the EU case law can represent useful assistance and help fulfil the void.

147. It should be stressed again that the dominance as such is not prohibited, but its abuse is, therefore the dominant undertaking is responsible for its negligent behaviour on the market and therefore is subject to so-called special responsibility.

148. Unlike in case of the agreements restricting competition, there are no exemptions listed in the PRCA-1 from the abuse of the dominant position. There is also no difference between exploitative practices and exclusionary practices as far as legal consequences are concerned and such division has purely theoretical value in order to better understand the various abusive behaviours.

149. As can be understood from Part I, Chapter 1 of this monograph on sources of antitrust law, there are no national legal sources with rules and principles of assessment of the individual undertaking's conduct as an abuse of the dominant position, though naturally national and EU case law and EU guidelines are followed by the SCPA.

150. It follows from the above list that exploitative as well as exclusionary abuses are proscribed by Slovenian competition law. The most frequently investigated type of abuse is price and non-price discrimination.[182] Moreover, abuse of

181. Grilc in Grilc et al., *PRCA-1 Commentary*, 151.

182. See, for example, the CPO's decisions in the following cases: *Pogrebno podjetje Maribor,* No. 3073-04/01 of 18 Aug. 2003, available at (in Slovene): http://www.varstvo-konkurence.si/fileadmin/varstvo-konkurence.si/pageuploads/ijz054.pdf; *Žale and Mojmir*, decision No. 3072-1/2004 of 28 Apr. 2005, not available online; *Mobitel/WWI*, see *Mobitel/WWI (Mobitel I)*, Partial Decision No. 3072-4/03-184 of 13 Jun. 2005, available at (in Slovene): http://www.varstvo-konkurence.si/fileadmin/varstvo-konkurence.si/pageuploads/ijz008.pdf, and supplementary decision No. 3072-4/03-206 of 20 Dec. 2005, available at (in Slovene): http://www.varstvo-konkurence.si/fileadmin/varstvo-konkurence.si/pageuploads/ijz052.pdf, *Telekom Slovenije/ABM,* Decision No. 3073-9/02 of 4 May 2004, available at (in Slovene): http://www.varstvo-konkurence.si/fileadmin/varstvo-konkurence.si/pageuploads/informacija_javnega_znacaja/ijz185.pdf.

dominance is most frequent in telecommunications and other liberalized industries.[183] We discuss these issues in detail infra in Part II, Chapter 2.

II. Justifications

151. Formally, there exist no acceptable justifications for an abuse of a dominant position under Slovenian competition law. If abuse of dominance is established, it shall be prohibited. However, an undertaking against which the procedure is initiated has the right to present facts and evidence, to express its opinions on legal issues, to reply to statements and proposals by other participants in the procedure, as well as to the facts and evidence, which the SCPA takes into consideration ex officio. Considering recent attempts by the EU Commission to introduce a more economic, effect-based approach also in this area of EU competition law, the SCPA could use this procedural framework to take certain justifications, such as efficiencies produced by the allegedly abusive practice, into account. While formally it has yet to use this possibility, the SCPA has already shown willingness to conduct a full-blown economic analysis of the effect of the allegedly abusive practice.[184] Furthermore, an undertaking against which the procedure is initiated may propose commitments/undertakings binding upon it, to eliminate the situation from which the alleged existence of abuse of dominant position derives. The SCPA decides upon such commitments/undertakings by a decision through which it also suspends the procedure until the fulfilment of commitments/undertakings or until the expiry of the deadline determined for their fulfilment.[185]

§7. CONCENTRATIONS

I. The Notion of Concentration

152. Generally, it can be stated that in terms of provisions of Articles 10 of the PRCA-1, a concentration is defined as market behaviour that brings a lasting change

183. See, for example, the following CPO's cases: *Mobitel/WWI (Mobitel I)*, Partial Decision No. 3072-4/03-184 of 13 Jun. 2005, available at (in Slovene): http://www.varstvo-konkurence.si/fileadmin/varstvo-konkurence.si/pageuploads/ijz008.pdf, and Supplementary Decision No. 3072-4/03-206 of 20 Dec. 2005, available at (in Slovene): http://www.varstvo-konkurence.si/fileadmin/varstvo-konkurence.si/pageuploads/ijz052.pdf; *Telekom Slovenije/Medinet,* Decision No. 3072-14/02 of 19 Nov. 2004, available at (in Slovene): http://www.varstvo-konkurence.si/fileadmin/varstvo-konkurence.si/pageuploads/ijz018.pdf; *Pošta Slovenije,* Decision No. 306-35/2005 of 28 May 2008, available at (in Slovene): http://www.varstvo-konkurence.si/fileadmin/varstvo-konkurence.si/pageuploads/ijz015.pdf; *Telekom Slovenije/ABM,* Decision No. 3073-9/02 of 4 May 2004, available at (in Slovene): http://www.abm.si/uvk/UVK-2004-05-04.pdf.

184. See, for example, the *Mobitel/WWI (Mobitel I)* case, Partial Decision No. 3072-4/03-184 of 13 Jun. 2005, available at (in Slovene): http://www.varstvo-konkurence.si/fileadmin/varstvo-konkurence.si/pageuploads/ijz008.pdf, and Supplementary Decision No. 3072-4/03-206 of 20 Dec. 2005, available at (in Slovene): http://www.varstvo-konkurence.si/fileadmin/varstvo-konkurence.si/pageuploads/ijz052.pdf.

185. *Ibid.*

in the structure of the participating undertakings. Such lasting change in the structure can be achieved in several ways, which are detailed in Article 10 of the PRCA-1. Typically, the concentration has been implemented by merger of two or more previously independent undertakings or by a simple change of corporate control. Change of control can occur as a result of the acquisition of control by one undertaking in another or as a change in quality of the control. The change in control has to be permanent, it is, however, to be noted that the time element is assessed in light of the market sectors in which the changes of control occur. When is the change of control permanent? It is not necessary that the change in the structure of merging undertakings lasts indefinitely or for a very long period of time. However, comparative legal analysis shows that a period of one year should not be deemed a permanent change. Assessment of permanent change of control is thus dependant on a large number of factual questions, with EU competition law lacking definitive answers on the issue.

153. It is necessary to emphasize that the time element criterion of the concept of concentration also encompasses the possibility of implementing impact brought about by structural change. Despite the fact that the definition of acquisition of control or change in its quality only demands for a possibility of exercising decisive influence, this possibility must be present at the time of assessment of concentrations. The mere fact that a transaction will enable the exercise of decisive influence in the future (i.e., potential control in the future) is not sufficient. The permanent change in control (or structure) is not sufficient, however. It is the emergence of a new, independent and economically relevant market player that is a critical feature of the structural change, and which triggers the application of the provisions of the PRCA-1 on concentrations. Concentrative conduct should therefore result in a completely autonomous market entity with separate legal personality and economic independence or in an entity without a change in legal personality but exhibiting characteristics of serious structural changes.

II. The Notion of Control

154. The basic identifier of concentrative behaviour is a change in control of an undertaking. The definition of the concept of control is especially important in cases of concentrative behaviour not bearing characteristics of mergers of two or more previously separate and independent economic units of companies or parts of companies, that is, particularly in cases where the position of control over fundamental business decisions in an undertaking is attained in other ways. It is necessary to distinguish between the performance of single or joint control. Method of control can be distinguished between ownership control on the one hand and control, which can be implemented on the basis of contracts or loan agreements.

155. Analysis of the element of change in control differs as regards the form and mode of attainment of the position enabling the option of exercising decisive influence. This assessment will be positive in nature in the case of a single control, as it will focus mainly on determining whether one of the parties has the power to determine the undertaking's business policy or has a decisive influence on the strategic decisions of the undertaking. In the case of joint control, the assessment bears a negative character as it is necessary to determine whether there are elements that facilitate a rejection of strategic business decisions due to the existence of a veto power. The analysis is therefore focused on determining whether the strategic decisions on business, commercial, industrial policy companies can be made only by agreement between the shareholders.

III. Sole or Joint Control by Majority Shareholders

156. Single decisive control over the operation of the company is primarily reserved for the majority shareholder. This represents the simplest and methodologically purest form of control over business decisions and company activity. Shareholder acquiring the share of assets sufficient to successfully vote on fundamental strategic decisions undoubtedly has direct control over the undertaking in the meaning of the second indent of Article 10/1 of the PRCA-1. In cases where two companies obtain the same number of shares in the third company (50%) and have also obtained the same percentage of voting rights, joint control over the execution of corporate governance and fundamental business decisions can be inferred. In such cases, existence of a special agreement between the shareholders is not necessary for a positive assessment of joint control.

IV. Sole or Joint Control of Minority Shareholders

157. In certain situations, control can be exercised by the minority shareholders. Independent control held by minority shareholders can be factual or legal in nature. Typically it will be possible to talk about the independent control of the legal nature in cases where a minority shareholder will have an overarching impact on the company's basic, fundamental decisions due to the voting rights, allowing him to appoint more than half of the members of the board. A situation where a minority shareholder because of statutory restrictions on voting rights of other shareholders holds a de facto majority is also possible. As previously pointed out, independent control of a minority shareholder can in addition be of a factual nature, whereby a minority shareholder obtains the possibility of exercising decisive influence due to an otherwise extremely dispersed capital structure. In such cases, a detailed analysis of the chronology of the decision-making process at previous assemblies is necessary to establish the continuity and stability of the minority shareholder's decisive influence. In the event that the minority shareholder had the ability to continuously exercise decisive influence in the previous three years due to dispersed ownership structure passive behaviour of other shareholders, it is possible to define its position as a position of single control. Only occasional possibility of exercising decisive influence by a minority shareholder will not represent the existence of control over the company.

V. Control Emanating from Agreements

158. One of the possible avenues to obtaining control or achieving a change in the quality of control are agreements facilitating the execution of decisive influence over the formation and implementation of strategic business decisions in a company. In order to assess whether the existence and effect of such contracts constitute a concentration within the meaning of Article 10 of the PRCA-1, it is necessary to analyse the individual terms of the agreement and the nature, objectives, scope and intent of the whole agreement. Fundamentally, it can be concluded that the exercise of decisive influence via agreements can be realized in two basic ways, namely by shareholder agreements and voting rights plans.

VI. Change of Control

159. Article 10/2 of the PRCA-1 defines the notion of control as 'the rights, agreements or any other means that allow exercising decisive influence in a particular undertaking'. The possibility of exercising decisive influence can therefore emanate from the ownership of the entire capital or shares, the right to use all or part of the assets of an undertaking, or from an agreement or a separate right arising from such an agreement. The possibility of exercising decisive influence (control) therefore stands as a fundamental defining element of the notion of concentration in the PRCA-1.

VII. Obtaining Control

160. There are several different modes of obtaining control in an undertaking. The fundamental and plainest manner of attaining control allowing the exercise of decisive influence is unquestionably a merger of two or more previously independent undertakings or acquisition of a previously independent undertaking by another undertaking. In such cases, the temporal element of structural change is easily noticeable, because the mere formation of a new undertaking or a change in an existing undertaking's structure undoubtedly denotes a structural change in the market. In cases of takeovers, a change in control is effortlessly established because legal or natural persons acquiring independent undertakings have previously not had a decisive impact on their business decisions. In addition to the classic manner of attaining control, the PRCA-1 covers situations where the acquisition of (or a qualitative change in) control results from purchases of assets, agreements, and all other events that represent a qualitative change in the decisive influence on the formation and implementation of business decisions. It should be stressed that in assessing the notion of concentration, Article 11 of the PRCA-1 largely disregards the question of the method of attainment of control. The issue of the manner of attainment of control is therefore secondary to the establishing of the change in control brought along by an event or practice.

VIII. SLC and the Dominance Test

161. Provisions of Article 11 of the PRCA-1 include content from Articles 11 and 13 of the repealed the PRCA of 1999 and represent a coherent regime of substantive merger control. The provision primarily consists of a prohibition of certain types of concentrations and in addition lists non-exhaustive criteria for appraisal thereof. Generally it can be concluded that the provision of Article 11 of the PRCA-1 prohibits concentrations that significantly impede effective competition within the territory of the Republic of Slovenia or a substantial part thereof, especially if the impediment results from the creation or strengthening of a dominant position. The currently valid act thus introduces a revised test of legality and establishes a regime comparable to the one set forth by the Regulation 139/2004. The new standard represents a compromise solution as it bears the characteristics of both the SLC and the dominance tests.

162. It should further be noted that the general element of assessment of legality found in Article 11 consists of a test bearing potentially negative consequences on the conditions of effective competition in the relevant market. Based on the well-established concept of significant lessening of competition (SLC) with its roots in American antitrust,[186] it has also found its role in many of the EU Member States, usually supplemented with the traditional structural test of dominance. Both tests are used to identify negative consequences on the competition brought about by large concentrations of economic power. In spite of their identical goals, the design and underlying concepts of both standards could not be more contrasting.

163. In its original form the dominance test is based on detection of the post-concentration market share. Market shares exceeding the set legal threshold and/or enabling the undertakings to behave to a large extent independently of its competitors, are deemed to create a dominant position. In cases where the results of a dominance test point at a post-concentrative dominant position, the concentration could already be deemed as incompatible with competition.

164. In contrast, the main characteristic of the SLC test is a substantive assessment of potential anti-competitive consequences. As a dynamic standard, the crux of its analysis is not a static, rigid issue of market share (structural issue), but a question of market power and its potential negative impacts on competition. This is why a more complex economic analysis, encompassing empirical evidence, assessment of potential efficiencies, etc., is the main trait of the SLC test.

---

186. Cf. s. 7 of the Clayton Act:

> No person engaged in commerce or in any activity affecting commerce shall acquire, directly or indirectly, the whole or any part of the stock or other share capital and no person subject to the jurisdiction of the Federal Trade Commission shall acquire the whole or any part of the assets of another person engaged also in commerce or in any activity affecting commerce, where in any line of commerce or in any activity affecting commerce in any section of the country, the effect of such acquisition may be substantially to lessen competition, or to tend to create a monopoly.

IX. The Relationship Between Article 11/1 and 11/2 of the PRCA-1

165. The provision of Article 11 of the PRCA-1 contains a general prohibition clause, which stands as the initial and also the final element of the appraisal of concentrations regarding their compatibility with competition rules. As already described, the current regime of appraisal of concentrations is founded on the SIEC test and (at least seemingly) no longer contains a two-step examination. The analysis of compatibility with the rules on competition is therefore deeply linked to the use of economic analysis that the concentration may have on competition. Thus, a dangerous question regarding a one- or two-step appraisal test[187] that has arisen in connection with Articles 11 and 13 of the previously valid PRCA of 1999 has now been eliminated.

X. Creation or Strengthening of Dominant Position: Significant Impediment of Effective Competition?

166. At this point it is necessary to draw attention to the difference regarding the admissibility of creation of dominance by way of internal development and growth of the company on the one hand and by means of concentration on the other. Article 9 of the PRCA-1 prohibits the abuse of dominant position, while the existence of dominance itself is not prohibited.

167. Striving for dominance is the main driving force of market rivalry. This is why the legislation permits economically efficient and innovative companies to create dominance in the market. Upon attaining such dominance, however, an undertaking is limited by the prohibition to abuse its superior position by the provisions of competition law. What then is the status of a 'test' dominance in the new regime of merger control in Slovenia?

168. The answer to this question depends on the interpretation of Article 11 of the PRCA-1. Specifically, what is the nature of the relationship between the creation or strengthening of dominant position and the significant impediment of effective competition. Could it be interpreted so as to say that any creation or strengthening of a dominant position automatically results in a significant reduction or elimination of effective competition? Such a dangerous proposition could further fuel a reasoning that the mere creation or strengthening of a dominant position post-concentration constitutes a 'per se' prohibition of concentration. An automatic proscription of any creation or strengthening of a dominant position by means of a concentration would be contrary to the constitutionally guaranteed right to free enterprise (Article 74 of the Constitution) and also inconsistent with the *ratio legis* of the PRCA-1.

187. The idea of a one-step, unitary type of appraisal test was based on the assumption that the identification of creation or strengthening of dominance was sufficient to prohibit a concentration as the existence of dominance by itself demonstrated the existence of negative effects on competition.

169. We can thence conclude that the PRCA-1 offers the dominance test merely as a methodological help. Appraisal of concentrations must therefore be based on the question whether the post-concentration market structure (having in view all other economic parameters) could result in a significant restriction of effective competition.

XI. Effective Competition

170. Effective competition can be defined as the process of market rivalry, struggle between undertakings. The expected positive consequences ensured through the processes of effective competition can be seen as resulting from special market structures caused by competition rivalry, where the fight for buyers is forcing companies to higher efficiency. In the conditions of free market access, the market structure is constantly changing as a result of competition. Effective competition can also be defined as a competitive environment not allowing any single undertaking to influence market prices. Such a definition is derived from the economic model of perfect competition. Both described definitions of effective competition have a common feature of focusing on the characteristics of the market. Successful implementation of competition policy, however, shifts the focal point of the analysis to the consequences of market structure and the behaviour of market players. In distinguishing effective from inefficient competition economic models of perfect competition and monopoly can be of assistance. The desired results of effective competition (welfare, defined by allocative and productive efficiency) are to be found between the results deriving from the extreme opposites of monopoly and pure (perfect) competition. Markets with effective competition will be characteristic of efficient production and reasonable prices in spite of their inherent imperfections or failures.

XII. SIEC Test

171. As a consequence of the merger control reform in the European Union the significant impediment to effective competition test has found its place in the PRCA-1 of 2008. As already described above, the essential positive result of the introduction of a new standard of review is the elimination of uncertainty regarding the role and function of the dominance test in the previously valid regime. The new standard is much clearer, which can undoubtedly positively impact the competition policy in the field of concentration as a whole. Due to the higher level of transparency the undertakings are in a better position to *ex ante* assess whether concentrations would be prohibited, which may have a restrictive effect on the volume of concentrative behaviour, thereby reducing the burden of SCPA, which in turn will be able to focus on other areas of competition law and policy.[188]

188. Cf. Röller & de la Mano, *The Impact of the New Substantive Test in European Merger Control.*

XIII. Appraisal of Concentrations: Procedural Steps

172. Assessment of concentrations is a complex process, which can be methodologically divided into separate stages which are to be carried out in exact succession. An exact order is necessary as the stages are mutually interdependent. The assessment procedure is hence always commenced with a definition of relevant product and geographic market, which enables a calculation of market shares of the undertakings effecting the concentration and their competitors. Relevant market definition is also a prerequisite for the implementation of the second step – the calculation of market concentration, which can serve as a preliminary indication of the potential negative consequences of the appraised concentration. The third step is the substantive appraisal of concentration, especially in the light of assessments of the potential negative consequences (unilateral, collusive and non-coordinated effects) of the concentration. The fourth step consists of identification of potential competition and assessment of the opportunities, timeliness, sustainability and sufficiency of its entry. Finally – especially in cases where preliminary results do not provide an entirely clear outcome – it is necessary to consider potential economic efficiencies resulting from the merger.

XIV. Criteria for Analysis under Article 11 of the PRCA-1

A. Potential Competition

173. Determination of the existence of potential competition in the relevant geographic and product market is an important factor in the process of appraisal of concentrations. The existence of potential competitors can prevent the post-merger undertaking from using or abusing the newly acquired market power. Potential competition therefore represents a competitive pressure that acts as an inhibitor of potential price increases and/or limitations of the production level by the undertakings concerned.

174. Potential competition can also have a preventative effect: the post-merger undertaking (or undertakings) will not increase prices because of the expected entry of potential competitors. The analysis of entry has to be extremely concise as not every type of potential competition can constitute a viable competitive constraint. Detection of potential competitors has to take into account the temporal criterion and the criteria of cost and profitability.

175. Therefore, entry has to be:

- timely: maximum two years after an implemented merger to achieving significant market importance;
- likely: if it is profitable for the entrant at pre-merger price levels and if entrant can secure such prices;
- sufficient: entry usually is sufficient if it is likely;
- without high sunk costs.

176. Evaluation of the performance and relevance of potential competition is based on the identification of potential barriers to entry and their effects. In cases where barriers to entry are high and intense, the chances of success of potential competition are very low.

B. Probability of Entry: Entry Barriers

177. Probability of entry depends on several factors. One fundamental question is surely whether it is profitable for the entrant to do business at pre-merger price levels and if the entrant can secure such prices.

178. Such a possibility may be negatively influenced by the following conditions:

- decreasing demand in the relevant product market, which will force potential competitors to share the market with the undertakings effecting the concentration;
- potential partial exclusion of the entrant through vertical integration or exclusive distribution agreements;
- predictable increase in production level and sales volumes by the undertakings effecting the concentration as a reaction to entry.

179. Likelihood of entry also depends on the existence of other barriers to entry. When high and detectable, they deter potential competitors from even entering the market.

C. Long-Term or Exclusive Contracts with Customers

180. Existence of long-term agreements between undertakings effecting a concentration and a sufficient number of clients can result in an effective foreclosure of the market. Long-term contracts will be especially dangerous in cases where they contain an exclusivity clause and provisions on prohibitively high early termination fees.

181. Generally, the main characteristics of long-term contracts that are to be examined are: the provisions related to the approval of sales benefits (e.g., regular rebates, special or super rebates for the quantity sold, promotional rebates, sale prices, shelf space purchase); period for which they are concluded; possible exclusivity; the scope of such contracts in relation to the number of clients; existence and level of early termination fees. The existence of (exclusive) long-term contracts usually creates a hostile environment for entry of potential competitors, as their pricing strategy would have to employ tactics of intense discounts in order to threaten the incumbent's position.

D. *Efficiencies*

182. A comprehensive assessment of concentration requires an analysis of potential economic efficiencies that can result from the merger. Analysis and assessment of efficiencies will be more important in cases where the appraisal procedure results in recognition of negative impacts of the concentration on effective competition. Efficiencies stemming from concentrations are manifold – the mergers can provide a way to liquidate holdings; to improve management; to allow the achievement of efficiencies; to pass through bargains; and even to prod less motivated managers to better performance.[189] Based on their production function, efficiencies can also be into the following categories: rationalization of production, which refers to cost savings from reallocating production across firms, without increasing the joint technological capabilities; economies of scale, i.e., savings in average costs associated with an increase in total output; technological progress, which may stem from the diffusion of know-how or increased incentives for R&D; purchasing economies or savings in factor prices such as intermediate goods or the cost of capital; reduction of slack (managerial and X-efficiency).[190]

183. Article 11 of the PRCA-1 defines the efficiency standard in a general manner, chiefly in terms of consideration of technical and economic development, provided that the latter confers a fair share of benefit on consumers and it does not impede competition. This definition is controversial, because it could lead to an erroneous understanding of the concept of efficiencies. The wording of the last sentence of Article 11/2 could additionally fuel this misinterpretation, as it seems to read that efficiencies can only be taken into account when the appraised concentration is deemed compatible with competition law. Such an interpretation is completely at odds with basic notions of competition law in the field of concentrations. Efficiencies should play an important role especially in cases where the concentration has negative effects on competition as they represent positive effects of concentrative behaviour, which could potentially outweigh the alleged negative, restrictive effects on competition.

1. *Europlakat/Metropolis Media*

184. The *Europlakat/Metropolis Media*[191] merger, together with the *Union/Laško*[192] merger, remains the most controversial implemented mergers in the Republic of Slovenia, to date. Europlakat and Metropolis Media were the two leading outdoor billboard-space service providers in the Slovenian market. The SCPA defined the relevant service market as the service of providing advertising space for

189. Axinn, *A Practical Approach to the New Merger Practice*.
190. Röller, Stennek & Verboven, *Efficiency Gains from Mergers*.
191. Decision No. 306-42/2006-76 of 4 Oct. 2006, available at (in Slovene): http://www.varstvo-konkurence.si/fileadmin/varstvo-konkurence.si/pageuploads/ijz064.pdf.
192. Decision No. 3071-1/02-369 of 14 Jul. 2003, available at (in Slovene): http://www.varstvo-konkurence.si/fileadmin/varstvo-konkurence.si/pageuploads/ijz014.pdf.

outdoor advertising larger than 2 m^2 and found that the market share of the combined company on the relevant market would be approximately 61%. It also found that the market shares of the other participants of the relevant markets were between 0.3% and 4%. Although these market shares are small, the SCPA concluded that the fact that there are thirty to forty-five companies competing on this market (with new entries every year and no exits) shows the dynamic nature of the market, with small rivals being able to execute competitive pressure on the combined company. It also found that buyer power of advertising agencies, the main customers on the relevant service market, served as important competitive pressure on the combined company. When it came to assessing barriers to entry in/off the relevant markets, somewhat confusingly, the SCPA found no barriers to entry on the market of providing advertising space for outdoor advertising on municipal and/or private land. It came to this conclusion, although acknowledging that most of the municipal land available for outdoor advertising is being held by the combined company and that special permits and procedures (with systemic bias towards existing holders) are required for advertising on municipal land. Furthermore, it did not conduct any serious enquiry into the acquiring of outdoor advertising space on private land. While criticizing without full access to all relevant documentation in the SCPA's file is somewhat an ungrateful task, the explanation (or lack of it) of the subject decision gives rise to several intriguing questions. Among others, it seems that the SCPA failed to provide persuasive arguments regarding fulfilment of criteria it used for the definition of relevant service market as well as regarding non-relevance of ownership of the land where outdoor advertising space is situated. Furthermore, its explanations regarding the calculation of the market share of the combined company, existing and potential competition, buyer power as well as barriers to entry seem to have some serious substantive flaws.

2. *Delo/Večer*[193]

185. The attempted takeover of newspaper and publishing company Večer, by Delo, the leading newspaper and publishing company in the Slovenian market, is the first concentration on the market of the Republic of Slovenia to be declared incompatible with the rules of competition and therefore prohibited by the SCPA. The SCPA concluded that the subject concentration would impede effective competition on the market for the publishing and issuing of daily publications with generally informative content and on the market for the selling of advertising space in daily publications in the Republic of Slovenia. In the process of appraising the concentration, the SCPA found that in the case of the concentration between Delo and Večer, this would result in significant strengthening of market power, since the market share of Delo on the market for the publishing and issuing of daily publications with generally informative content would increase from 33.43% to 58.88% with the HHI increasing from 2742 to 4443. On the market for the selling of advertising space in daily publications in the Republic of Slovenia, the combined market share

193. Decision No. 306-195/2008-57 of 23 Sep. 2009, available at (in Slovene): http://www.varstvo-konkurence.si/fileadmin/varstvo-konkurence.si/pageuploads/ijz084.pdf.

would increase to 47.80%, with the HHI increasing from 1823 to 2915. Because the market with a post-concentration index over 1800 is highly concentrated, the concentration would lead to significant strengthening of the market power of the combined entity and the removal of important competitive pressure, which the participants of the concentration were applying against each other, together with decreasing the competitive pressure towards the remaining competitors, which would in turn cause a significant impediment to competition. Such increased market power would, in accordance with the conclusions of the SCPA, significantly complicate or even prevent an entry on the market of potential competitors, because the readers of the existing newspapers on the market are very loyal, which in turn makes an entrance on the market only possible through the acquisition of an existing publisher. On the market for publishing and issuing daily publications with generally informative content, such concentration would also significantly increase the probability of coordinated anti-competitive effects. For these reasons, the SCPA ordered Delo to dispose of its majority holdings in Večer.

§8. Joint Ventures

186. In line with the merger control reform in the European Union the regime of Article 10 of the PRCA-1 also covers all forms of full-function joint ventures, their main characteristic being the formation of a joint venture, permanently operating as an autonomous economic entity. To be caught by the provision of Article 10 of the PRCA-1, the created joint venture undertaking must perform, on a lasting basis, all the functions of an autonomous economic entity thus bringing about a lasting change in the structure of the undertakings concerned.[194] To be deemed full functioning, joint ventures must satisfy a relatively wide range of criteria. The existence of a separate staff and management structure entrusted with daily operations of the joint venture is a precondition. The same requirement applies as far as the ability to gain access to sufficient financial resources and ownership of movable and immovable property. A full-function joint venture cannot be established in cases where the joint venture performs solely one specific function within the parent companies' business activities without access to the market (joint venture acting as a distributor of products or services of parent companies). In cases where the said criteria are not met, a joint venture will be analysed and assessed using Article 6 of the PRCA-1. If the SCPA determines that the conditions referred to in Article 6/3 of the PRCA-1 are not met, it shall issue an order declaring the concentration incompatible with competition rules and prohibit the concentration.

194. Commission Notice on the concept of full-function joint ventures under Council Regulation (EEC) No. 4064/89 on the control of concentrations between undertakings (98/C 66/01), replaced by Commission Consolidated Jurisdictional Notice under Council Regulation (EC) No. 139/2004 on the control of concentrations between undertakings (2008/C 95/01).

Chapter 5. Consequences of Violations and Enforcement Institutions

§1. Administrative Enforcement

I. The Antitrust Authorities

A. Formation, Composition

187. The institution principally responsible for the enforcement of competition policy in the Republic of Slovenia as of 1 January 2013 is the Public Agency of the Republic of Slovenia for the Protection of Competition (Slovenian Competition Protection Agency, CPA).[195] The CPA's seat is in Ljubljana.

188. The CPA which was established on 24 August 2012,[196] has replaced the Competition Protection Office (CPO)[197] which was established on 21 October 1994 as a public body organized within the Ministry for Economic Relations and Development (now Ministry of Economic Development and Technology).[198] The CPO had been responsible for enforcement of Slovenian antitrust and merger control rules in administrative and, since 1 January 2005, also in minor offences proceedings.[199] As of 1 May 2004 when Slovenia joined the EU, it had also been responsible for enforcement of European antitrust (i.e., Articles 101 and 102 TFEU)[200] according to Regulation 1/2003 as well as – in cases of referrals – of European merger control rules as set out in Regulation 139/2004. It was a member of European Competition Network (ECN) and International Competition Network (ICN). Its tasks are now being performed by the newly established CPA.

189. At the beginning, the CPO's powers were limited as it lacked independence being an office within the ministry. It was also severely understaffed (consisted of the Director, a couple of assistants and a secretary) and notoriously lacking professionals. These negative factors, which prevented it to be more than a passive observer, were amplified by the absence of specialized procedural rules for actions entrusted to the CPO preventing it to tackle competition law cases efficiently.[201] In

195. Sl. *Javna agencija Republike Slovenije za varstvo konkurence (AVK).*
196. Ruling of the Government of RS on the establishment of the Slovenian Competition Protection Agency, Official Gazette RS, No. 64/12.
197. Article 5 of the PRCA-1 (version prior to amendments of 2011 and 2012). English website of the CPA is available at: http://www.varstvo-konkurence.si/en/.
198. See Zabel et al., *PCA of 1993 Commentary*, 120–127.
199. Article 12 of the PRCA-1 (version prior to amendments of 2011 and 2012). Before 1 Jan. 2005, only the courts in minor offences court proceedings had jurisdiction for assessing the undertakings' practices and issuing fines. The CPO was the initiator of such proceedings. Although later the CPO (now the CPA) had jurisdiction in both proceedings, two sets of proceedings – administrative proceedings and minor offences proceedings – have to be performed.
200. The PRCA-1 – obviously by negligence of the legislator – used the pre-Lisbon Treaty denomination of the relevant articles (Arts 81 and 82 TEC instead of Arts 101 and 102 TFEU) up until the amendments of 2014.
201. Cf. Podobnik, *Framing a New Competition Law for Slovenia.*

contrast to the PCA of 1993, the competences of the CPO were broadly tailored in the PRCA of 1999. Besides the strictly prosecutorial ones, the CPO was entrusted with certain pro-active tasks, for example, with the exercise of supervision of the application of the PRCA, monitoring of and analysing the conditions on the market, submitting opinions on general issues under its competence to the Parliament and the Government, etc. The problem of the CPO's status was also directly addressed by the PRCA of 1999 which declared that the CPO was independent and autonomous in the implementation of its tasks.[202] As the CPO remained structurally and financially dependent upon the ministry, this was a mere declaratory statement with no substantive consequences.

190. Calls for greater independence of the office (echoing also from the OECD) have finally led to a reorganization of the office into an agency in 2012/13.[203] The previous status of the SCPA as the executive body in the framework of the Ministry of Economic Development and Technology has been elevated to the status of an independent and autonomous public agency established by the Republic of Slovenia.[204] The 2011 and 2012 amendments of the PRCA-1 established and regulated a novo the CPA replacing the CPO. The Government of the Republic of Slovenia is to exercise the founding rights and obligations.[205] The PRCA-1 stresses that while assessing individual cases, the CPA is not bound by guidelines or instructions of state or other bodies, while only the Government and the Parliament of RS may provide general guidelines outside individual cases' assessment.[206] The PRCA-1 also stresses that supervision over the CPA that is performed by the ministry responsible for competition in accordance with the Public Agencies Act, does not enable insight into individual cases.[207] The CPA itself determines the number of employees taking into account the available funds in accordance with its yearly financial plan.[208] Until the latest amendments of the PRCA-1 made in 2017, the CPA was to report until 30 June each year to the Government and the Parliament on its work in the preceding year.[209]

191. According to the PRCA-1, the CPA was to be launched on 1 January 2012 or, if not on that day, the next day after its registration in the court register. As the CPA was registered on 31 December 2012,[210] it was launched on 1 January 2013, while until that day the CPO was performing its tasks in accordance with the rules as set out in the PRCA-1 prior to its 2011 and 2012 amendments. The CPA has been

202. Article 13 of the PRCA-1 (version prior to amendments of 2011 and 2012).
203. See Bugarič, *Neodvisne regulativne agencije v Evropi ...* .
204. Article 5 of the PRCA-1 as amended in 2011 and 2012.
205. Article 5/1 of the PRCA-1.
206. Article 5/4 of the PRCA-1.
207. Article 12m of the PRCA-1.
208. Article 5/5 of the PRCA-1. In recent years, the number of employees of the SCPA has been additionally increased. Hopefully, this will enable it to tackle efficiently one of the most complex (professionally) and delicate (politically) fields of state policy.
209. See the deleted provision of Article 5/7 of the PRCA-1.
210. The reason for such late registration lies in the fact that the Director and the Council members were appointed only in December 2012 as previous appointments of the Commission and Council members were unsuccessful.

performing its tasks in accordance with the PRCA-1 and, subsidiariliy, the Public Agencies Act.[211] Additional provisions as to its organization and performance of its tasks are set out in the Government's Ruling on the establishment of the CPA of August 2012.[212] The CPO's work was organized within two sectors, the first dealing with economic analysis, the second with legal issues and investigations. The CPA has plausibly continued with such practice in accordance with its internal acts of organization.

192. In April 2014, the CPA was given a new competence within the field of protection of relationships in the food supply chain as the Act Amending the Agriculture Act[213] provided that the newly established Slovenian Ombudsman protecting the relationships in the food supply chain is to report to the CPA of every illegal act in the food supply chain as set out in the Agriculture Act.[214] The CPA has control over such illegal acts and assesses them in minor offences proceedings. If the undertaking in question has a dominant position as set out in the PRCA-1, the CPA is to initiate the proceedings solely on the basis of the PRCA-1, not on the basis of the Agriculture Act.[215]

193. The PRCA-1 of 2008 introduced collegial decision-making within the CPO in administrative as well as in minor offences proceedings in each individual case. The decisions of the CPO by which the proceedings were brought to an end (i.e., those establishing a breach, accepting commitments, terminating the proceedings, finding the (in)compatibility of a concentration, etc.), were issued by an ad hoc panel, comprising the director and two employees of the CPO appointed by the director.[216] The panel sit on closed sessions and issued the decisions by a majority vote. Other decisions that were to be taken as set out in the PRCA-1 (e.g., those starting the proceedings, ordering interim measures, initiating investigations, etc.) were issued by the CPO's director.[217]

194. The 2011 and 2012 amendments of the PRCA-1 introduced changes into the organizational structure and decision-making of the SCPA. According to the currently valid PRCA-1, the CPA has two bodies – a Director of the CPA and a five-member Council of the CPA.[218] Both are appointed by the Parliament on the proposal of the Government,[219] and must meet the terms for their appointment as

211. Official Gazette RS, No. 52/02, with further amendments.
212. Official Gazette RS, No. 64/12, with further amendments. The Ruling mostly reiterates what has already been set out in the PRCA-1.
213. Sl. *Zakon o spremembah in dopolnitvah Zakona o kmetijstvu (ZKme-1B)*, Official Gazette RS, No. 26/14.
214. Sl. *Zakon o kmetijstvu (ZKme-1)*, Official Gazette RS, No. 45/08, with further amendments. See Art. 61d of the Agriculture Act.
215. See Art. 172/7 of the Agriculture Act.
216. Article 13 of the PRCA-1 (versions prior to and after the amendments of 2011 and 2012).
217. *Ibid.*
218. Article 12a of the PRCA-1.
219. Articles 12b and 12h of the PRCA-1. According to the PRCA-1, the Government must choose the candidates on the basis of their expertise and professional experience in the field of competition law. The Parliament is to vote on the proposed candidates in thirty days after the Government has

set out in the PRCA-1.[220] The Director who represents and runs the CPA is one of the Council members and its president. Both the Director and Council members are appointed for five years with a possibility of re-appointment.[221]

195. According to the PRCA-1 amendment of April 2011, a five-member Commission for Protection of Competition was to be formed as a new decision-making body of the CPA next to the CPA's Director and Council.[222] Three members of the Commission would be appointed[223] of the CPA's employees (save the Director), while the other two of the experts of competition law.[224] Commission was to assess the cases in three-member ad hoc panels. The PRCA-1 amendment of July 2012, however, provided for only two bodies, i.e., the Director and the Council, which have been appointed by the Parliament in December 2012.[225]

196. Decisions in administrative proceedings by which the proceedings are brought to an end are issued by a panel consisted of all Council members,[226] while all other decisions are issued by the Director.[227] The cases are handled by the CPA's employee appointed for each individual case by the Director. The employee manages the proceedings, writes a report on the case and suggests to the panel how the decision should be drafted. The panel then elaborates on the case on a closed session called by the chairman of the panel.[228] Decisions are taken by majority of the members attending the session of the panel if majority of all members of the panel actually attends the session.[229]

197. Decisions in minor offences proceedings by which the proceedings are brought to an end are issued by an ad hoc three-member panel (a so-called minor

---

filed the proposal with the Parliament. A candidate is appointed if the majority of members of Parliament attending the voting session vote for him or her. If the candidate does not receive the required majority of parliamentary votes, the president of the Parliament informs the Government of such course of events, and the Government is to inform the President of the Parliament in fourteen days of its decision as to how it plans to proceed with the appointment. Candidates for the position of the director are proposed to the Government by the minister responsible for competition.

220. See Arts 12c and 12e for the Council members, and Arts 12h and 12j for the Director. One of the prerequisites for taking the position of the Director and a Council member is that the candidate is a Slovenian citizen. According to Art. 12c/3 of the PRCA-1, the CPA's employees may also stand as candidates for the posts of the Council members.
221. Articles 12c and 12h of the PRCA-1. The Director may be reappointed only once.
222. The Director and the Council were to be appointed by the Government.
223. By the Parliament on the Government's proposal.
224. One by the Parliament on the Government's proposal, and one by the Parliament on the proposal of the Judicial Council of the Republic of Slovenia.
225. Ruling of the Parliament of RS of 14 Dec. 2012 on the appointment of the Director of the Slovenian Competition Protection Agency, Official Gazette RS, No. 100/12, appointing as director a person unknown to the business society, competition law practitioners and academia. Rulings of the Government of RS of 14 and 20 Dec. 2012 on the appointment of the Members of the Council of the Slovenian Competition Protection Agency, Official Gazette RS, Nos 100/12 and 103/12.
226. Article 12n/1 of the PRCA-1.
227. Article 12i/3 of the PRCA-1.
228. On his or her own motion or on substantiated request of the Director.
229. If the vote is a tie, the chairman shall have a casting vote.

offences panel) consisted of Council members and the CPA's employees.[230] All other decisions are issued by the Director.[231] The panel is appointed by the CPA's Council on the Director's request.[232] As with decision-making in administrative proceedings, here, too, the CPA's employee appointed for each individual case by the Director handles the case and manages the proceedings, writes a report on the case and suggests to the panel how the decision should be drafted. The panel then elaborates on the case on a closed session called by the chairman of the panel[233] and issues the decision by majority of its members.

198. Members of the panels and the CPA's employees are not liable for damages resulting from their activity performed in accordance with the PRCA-1 unless the damage was caused intentionally or through gross negligence.[234]

B. Investigating Powers

1. Study of Sectors or Certain Types of Agreements

199. The SCPA may conduct a study of a particular sector or certain types of agreements[235] in multiple sectors when price rigidity or other circumstances indicate the possibility of impeding or distorting competition on Slovenian territory. For further details on the study of sectors or agreements, please see Part III, Chapter 1, §1, I of this monograph.

2. Request for Information

200. Prior to issuing an order on the commencement of the proceedings, the SCPA may request information[236] from any undertaking or partners, members of management or supervisory boards and employees of the undertakings. In addition to such simple request, the SCPA may also request information by issuing a special order, which must include its legal basis, purpose of the request, specification of the requested information, a reasonable deadline for provision of the information and the fine that may be imposed for providing inaccurate, incomplete or misleading information or for failure to provide information within the specified time.[237] No special legal remedy against such order is available, i.e., the parties may challenge it only within judicial protection assessing the final decision. Undertakings must

230. Articles 12č/1and 12s of the PRCA-1.
231. Article 12i/3 of the PRCA-1.
232. Article 12s of the PRCA-1.
233. *Ibid.*
234. Article 12n/2 of the PRCA-1.
235. Article 26 of the PRCA-1.
236. Articles 27 and 47 of the PRCA-1.
237. The SCPA may issue an order imposing a fine of up to EUR 50,000. The deadline for payment of the fine may not be shorter than fifteen days, and not longer than one month. In such cases, the SCPA issues an order specifying a new deadline for provision of information, and imposes further

provide the SCPA with all the requested documentation. They are, however, not obliged to admit to the infringement of competition rules.

3. Powers of Inspection

201. Both in the fields of antitrust and merger control, the powers of inspection[238] empower the authorized persons[239] to:

- enter and inspect premises, land and means of transport at the registered office of the undertaking and at other locations at which the undertaking itself or another undertaking authorized by the undertaking concerned performs the activity and business for which there is probability of an infringement of Slovenian or/and European competition rules;[240]
- examine the books, contracts, papers, business correspondence, business records and other information relating to the business of the undertaking, irrespective of the medium on which they are stored;
- take or obtain in any form copies of, forensic copies of or extracts from business books and other documentation using photocopying devices and computer equipment of the undertaking or the SCPA;[241]
- seal any business premises and business books and other documentation for the period of the inspection and to the extent necessary for the inspection;
- seize items and business books and other documentation for a period no longer than twenty working days;
- ask any representative or member of staff of the undertaking to give an oral or written explanation of facts or documents relating to the subject-matter and purpose of the inspection and record it;[242]
- examine papers disclosing the identity of persons;
- perform other actions in line with the purpose of the inspection.

---

fines to undertakings which continue to refuse to cooperate until the sum of the fines from individual orders reaches 1% of the undertaking's total turnover in the preceding business year. These orders have the quality of enforcement titles and may be challenged only in judicial proceedings reviewing the final decision.

238. Articles 28–35 of the PRCA-1.
239. I.e., the employees of the CPA or persons appointed by the CPA (specialized organizations, public institutions or individuals may perform investigations unless this would be contrary to public interest or to the interests of the parties).
240. Article 29 of the PRCA-1 sets out the rules on inspection in cases of antitrust breaches, while Art. 48 of the PRCA-1 refers to these rules in cases of merger investigations. In merger control proceedings, inspections may be performed in the undertakings taking part, as well as in those likely to have taken part in a concentration.
241. If, for technical reasons, it is not possible to make photocopies with photocopying devices or computer equipment of the undertaking or of the CPA, authorized persons may take away business books and other documentation for the time required to make photocopies.
242. When a written explanation is requested by the authorized person, the latter shall set a deadline for its submission.

202. The SCPA is also empowered to enter and inspect premises of other undertakings not under investigation, and residential premises of the members of the investigated undertaking's management or supervisory boards as well as of other staff or associates of the investigated undertaking if there are reasonable grounds to suspect that documentation relating to the subject-matter of the inspection is being kept in these premises.[243]

203. As of 10 May 2014, the SCPA requires a court order to perform inspection in the premises of the undertaking against which the SCPA initiated proceedings, while a court order for entering and inspecting other premises had to be acquired by the SCPA already prior to the 2014 amendment of the PRCA-1.

204. In accordance with Regulation 1/2003 and Regulation 139/2004, the CPA may also perform inspections for the European Commission or other competition authorities of the Member States of the EU, or may assist them in performing inspections on the territory of Slovenia.[244]

205. For further details on the SCPA's investigative and search powers, please see Part III, Chapter 1, §2, II of this monograph.

C. Adjudicating Powers

206. The SCPA is responsible for enforcement of Slovenian antitrust and merger control rules in administrative and minor offences proceedings. Further, it is responsible for enforcement of European antitrust (i.e., Articles 101 and 102 TFEU)[245] according to Regulation 1/2003 as well as – in cases of referrals – of European merger control rules as set out in Regulation 139/2004.

207. In administrative proceedings, the SCPA assesses infringements in accordance with the PRCA-1 (the GAPA applies subsidiarily),[246] while in minor offences proceedings, fines are levied in accordance with the PRCA-1 and the Minor Offences Act (MOA).[247]

208. In the field of antitrust, the SCPA may take the following decisions:[248]

---

243. Article 33 of the PRCA-1. The PRCA of 1999 regulated such inspections in much more general terms enabling a wider scope of other premises to be inspected.
244. See Art. 22 of Regulation 1/2003 and Art. 35 of the PRCA-1, and Arts 12-13 of Regulation 139/2004 and Art. 48 of the PRCA-1.
245. All up to the 2014 amendments (and even despite the fact that the PRCA-1 has been amended a couple of times after 1 Dec. 2009), the PRCA-1 – obviously by mistake – used the pre-Lisbon Treaty denomination of the relevant articles (Arts 81 and 82 TEC instead of Arts 101 and 102 TFEU).
246. Article 15/2 of the PRCA-1.
247. Official Gazette RS, No. 7/03, with further amendments (Sl. *Zakon o prekrških (ZP-1)*). See Art. 12/2 of the PRCA-1.
248. According to Art. 37 of the PRCA-1, decisions finding antitrust infringement are to be issued within two years after the proceedings have been initiated.

- finding an infringement of Articles 6 or 9 of the PRCA-1 and/or Articles 101 or 102 TFEU,[249] and requiring that it be brought to an end;[250]
- ordering interim measures;[251]
- accepting commitments.[252]

209. According to Article 25 of the PRCA-1, whenever European antitrust (i.e., Article 101 or 102 TFEU) is allegedly breached, the SCPA must treat the practices as breaches of European as well as Slovenian antitrust (the so-called uniform proceedings). If during the proceedings it is determined that there is no basis to conduct the proceedings under Articles 101 or 102 TFEU since there is no effect on trade between the Member States, the SCPA issues an order terminating the proceedings with this regard, and continues assessing the practices under Slovenian antitrust only. No legal remedy may be invoked against the order terminating the proceedings. In the famous electric cartel case, for example, the Supreme Court of RS reviewing the CPO's decision confirmed the CPO's finding of the infringement in the form of breach of Slovenian antitrust, but held that the CPO had not substantiated enough its position that European antitrust was also breached.[253]

210. After an order initiating antitrust proceedings has been issued, the undertaking may offer commitments in order to avoid that any anti-competitive situation on the market is established by the SCPA. The commitments may be offered to the SCPA within the time-limit for replying to its statement of objections. If the offered

249. Article 37 of the PRCA-1. See, for example, the following CPO's decisions: decision in *Telekom Slovenije* (*Itak Džabest*), No. 306-14/2009-239 of 13 Feb. 2012, operative part of the decision is available at (in Slovene): http://www.varstvo-konkurence.si/ostali-dokumenti/arhiv-odlocb/odlocba 228/, finding that *Telekom Slovenije d.d.* breached Art. 9 of the PRCA-1 and Art. 102 TFEU (ex Art. 82 TEC) by practicing predatory pricing; decision of 29 Dec. 2014 finding that GEN-I d.o.o. and GEN Energija d.o.o. concluded a cartel agreement fixing electricity prices 'in breach of Article 6 of the PRCA-1 and Article 81 TEC, now Article 101 TFEU' (operative part available at (in Slovene): http://www.varstvo-konkurence.si/zakonodaja-in-dokumenti/ostali-dokumenti/arhiv-odlocb/odlocba238/); in its decision of 23 Mar. 2012, the CPO found that major Slovene construction undertakings were 'in breach of Article 6 of the PRCA-1 and Article 101 TFEU' by way of sharing projects, bid rigging and exchanging information on bid prices before submitting the bids (operative part of the decision available at (in Slovene): http://www.varstvo-konkurence.si/zakonodaja-in-dokumenti/ostali-dokumenti/arhiv-odlocb/odlocba232/); in its decision of 26 Sep. 2012, the CPO found that the *Medical Chamber of Slovenia* breached Slovenian and European legislation by setting in its rules the standards for valuation and calculation of dental and medical services, and the supervision of its members in the implementation of such rules (operative part of the decision available at (in Slovene): http://www.varstvo-konkurence.si/zakonodaja-in-dokumenti/ostali-dokumenti/arhiv-odlocb/odlocba239/).

250. Sometimes, the CPO had added that in the operative part of its decisions, e.g., in its Decision of October 2006 in the case *Institute of Public Health Maribor/DDD, Dezinfekcija, dezinsekcija, deratizacija, d.o.o.*, available at (in Slovene): http://www.varstvo-konkurence.si/zakonodaja-in-dokumenti/ostali-dokumenti/arhiv-odlocb/odlocba46/.

251. Article 38 of the PRCA-1. For further details, see Pt. I, Ch. 5, §1, VI of this monograph.

252. Article 39 of the PRCA-1.

253. Judgments Nos U 5/2008, U 2/2008, U 9/2008, U 4/2008, U 6/2008 of 30 Jun. 2009, available at (in Slovene): http://www.sodisce.si/znanje/sodna_praksa/vrhovno_sodisce_rs/62881/.

commitments are acceptable for the SCPA, it issues a decision-making those commitments binding on the undertaking(s) concerned.[254] By doing that, the SCPA merely finds that there are no longer grounds for action, it does not, however, decide on the infringement. Decisions accepting commitments must be issued within two years after the SCPA has issued the order initiating the proceedings. The SCPA may, upon request or on its own initiative, reopen the proceedings where there has been a material change in any of the facts on which the decision was based, or where the undertakings acted contrary to their commitments,[255] or where the decision was based on incomplete, inaccurate or misleading information provided by the undertakings. With regard to commitments, the PRCA-1 does not differentiate between the types of anti-competitive situations in which the undertakings may propose commitments and gives the SCPA a wide discretion in deciding to accept commitments. Thus, also undertakings suspected of participating in hardcore infringements may according to the law propose commitments to the SCPA. Referring to paragraph 13 of the preamble to Regulation 1/2003 stating that commitment decisions are not appropriate in cases where the Commission intends to impose a fine, the commentators opine that in cases of hardcore cartels the SCPA may not accept commitments[256] what accords to the purpose and spirit of the system of commitments. Commitment decisions have been issued by the CPO and the CPA both in the application of Articles 102 TFEU and/or 9 of the PRCA-1[257] as well as in the application of Articles 101 TFEU and/or 6 of the PRCA-1.[258]

---

254. The decision may be adopted for a specified period.
255. Fines of up to 10% of the total turnover of the undertaking in the previous business year may be imposed on undertakings that have acted contrary to their commitments.
256. Grilc in Grilc et al., *PRCA-1 Commentary*, 398; Grilc, *Zaveze* … , 1444.
257. See the CPO's decision No. 3072-4/03-184 of 13 Jun. 2005 (available at (in Slovene): http://www.varstvo-konkurence.si/fileadmin/varstvo-konkurence.si/pageuploads/ijz008.pdf) accepting commitments by Mobitel for the period until 1 May 2009 regarding its alleged abuse of its dominant position on the retail market of public mobile services. See also the CPO's decision No. 306-35/2005-98 of 28 May 2008 (available at (in Slovene): http://www.varstvo-konkurence.si/fileadmin/varstvo-konkurence.si/pageuploads/ijz015.pdf) accepting five years' term commitments by *Pošta Slovenije* who was supposed to breach Arts 9 of the PRCA-1 and 82 TEC by, *inter alia*, discriminating agents ordering dissemination of unsolicited mail *vis-à-vis* its direct customers, inserting in its contracts non-compete clauses or clauses on exclusive dealing. See also the CPO's decision No. 306-178/2007-189 of 26 Jun. 2009 in the *Mercator* case where the CPO found that Mercator has probably breached Arts 82 TEC and 9 of the PRCA-1 by, *inter alia*, including in its supply agreements unfair rebates. Commitments were accepted for the period between 26 Jun. 2009 to 1 Jul. 2014 (available at (in Slovene): http://www.varstvo-konkurence.si/fileadmin/varstvo-konkurence.si/pageuploads/ijz073.pdf).
258. See, for example, the CPO's decision No. 306-113/2008-54 of 20 Aug. 2010 in the *Samsung Electronics Austria* case where the CPO had initiated proceedings against Samsung Electronics Austria and eight of its Slovene service centres which had tacitly agreed to dismiss all warranty requests by the customers of independent Samsung distributers in the Slovenian market. The CPO found that such agreement is likely in breach of Art. 101 TFEU and afterwards accepted commitments by *Samsung Electronics Austria* (for the period of three years as of the date the undertakings involved had received the decision) to guarantee appropriate repair services to Samsung products within its European warranty scheme (available at (in Slovene): http://www.varstvo-konkurence.si/fileadmin/varstvo-konkurence.si/pageuploads/ijz095.pdf). See also the CPO's decision of 7 May 2009 accepting commitments by *Spar Slovenija, Engrotuš* and *Poslovni sistem Mercator* to terminate the practices of jointly assessing the requests by their suppliers for higher prices of the goods supplied, and of refusing to deal with the suppliers had they offered their goods to other merchants – the CPO

211. The SCPA must terminate the proceedings by issuing an order:[259]

- if it does not find an infringement;
- if special circumstances of the case show that proceedings would not be reasonable;
- if the European Commission initiates antitrust proceedings or takes a decision in the same case.[260]

While it may terminate the proceedings if a national competition authority in another Member State has initiated proceedings under Article 101 or 102 TFEU, or has already taken a decision in the same case.[261]

212. In the ambit of merger control, the SCPA may, in principle, act as follows:[262]

- where it concludes that the concentration notified does not fall within the scope of merger control rules, it records that finding by means of a decision;[263]
- where it finds that the concentration notified, although falling within the scope of merger control rules, does not raise serious doubts as to its compatibility with the rules of competition, it decide not to oppose it and declares that it is compatible with the rules of competition;[264] the SCPA may attach to its decision conditions and obligations intended to ensure that the undertakings concerned comply with the commitments they have entered into vis-à-vis the SCPA with a view to rendering the concentration compatible with the rules of competition;[265]
- where it finds that the concentration notified falls within the scope of merger control rules and raises serious doubts as to its compatibility with the rules of competition, it decides to initiate proceedings, which are to be closed by means of a decision on the compatibility or on the incompatibility of the concentration.[266]

---

found that both Art. 6 of the PRCA-1 and Art. 81 TEC were probably breached and accepted commitments for the period up until 1 Jun. 2014 (available at (in Slovene): http://www.varstvo-konkurence.si/fileadmin/varstvo-konkurence.si/pageuploads/ijz072.pdf).

259. Article 40 of the PRCA-1.
260. No legal remedy against such order terminating the proceedings is available. These rules reflect the ECN framework as set out in Regulation 1/2003 and in the Commission Notice on cooperation within the Network of Competition Authorities (2004/C 101/3).
261. No legal remedy against such order terminating the proceedings is available.
262. According to Art. 46/6 of the PRCA-1, the SCPA must act within twenty-five working days after a complete notification has been lodged with the SCPA.
263. Article 46/2 of PRCA-1.
264. Article 46/3 of PRCA-1. Such decision is deemed to cover restrictions directly related and necessary to the implementation of the concentration.
265. Article 51 of PRCA-1.
266. According to Arts 50–51 of the PRCA-1, the SCPA is to issue the decision in sixty or seventy-five working days after it has initiated the proceedings. Such decision is deemed to cover restrictions directly related and necessary to the implementation of the concentration.

The Annual Report of the CPA for 2018[267]shows that in 2018 the CPA issued forty-three decisions in administrative proceedings where the proceedings were brought to an end. One of these cases assessed restrictive practices, one abuse of a dominant position, while forty-one were merger cases. In one restrictive practices assessment proceedings the CPA issued an order terminating the proceedings. Two minor-offences decisions were issued against a legal person and its responsible natural person (one in a restrictive practices case, and one in a merger case).

213. The PRCA of 1993 set out an unusual judicial review mechanism by filing an action in civil proceedings. Such three-stage judicial review proceedings (i.e., civil proceedings before the competent Court of First Instance, appeal proceedings before the competent high court and extraordinary remedies proceedings before the Supreme Court of RS) were replaced by administrative review proceedings before the Administrative Court of RS as set out in the PRCA of 1999. Jurisdiction to assess the CPO's decisions was vested with the Administrative Court of RS until 2008 when the new PRCA-1 entered into force.

214. According to Article 55 of the PRCA-1 in force between 2008 and 2013, the SCPA's decisions could be challenged before the Supreme Court of RS (acting as the first and the last instance of judicial review). The SCPA's orders could also be challenged before the Supreme Court of RS,[268] unless such review was explicitly excluded. The following two types of orders against which there was no separate legal remedy available, could nevertheless be challenged within judicial review of the SCPA's decisions: an order requesting an undertaking to provide SCPA with information,[269] and an order on inspection.[270]

215. In August 2013, the jurisdiction to assess the SCPA's decisions was transferred back to the Administrative Court of RS while the Supreme Court of RS has been re-vested with jurisdiction in administrative judicial review proceedings as the second instance in the administrative dispute proceedings.

216. For details as to judicial review of the SCPA's administrative decisions and orders, see Part III, Chapter 4 of this monograph.

217. In minor offences proceedings before the SCPA, fines are levied to legal persons (as well as to sole entrepreneurs and individuals performing a professional activity) as well as to natural persons in charge of the legal persons and sole entrepreneurs. Minor offences proceedings are initiated as follow-on proceedings after the SCPA has closed administrative infringement proceedings, or as stand-alone

267. Available at (in Slovene): http://www.varstvo-konkurence.si/fileadmin/varstvo-konkurence.si/pageuploads/letna_porocila/Letno_porocilo_AVK_2018.pdf.
268. Only those orders, however, that may be appealed in accordance with the GAPA. Art. 55/4 of the PRCA-1.
269. Regulated in Art. 27 of the PRCA-1.
270. Regulated in Art. 28 of the PRCA-1.

proceedings establishing, first, the infringement, and then levying fines.[271] Such double-tier system of administrative and minor offences proceedings before the SCPA followed by different judicial review proceedings has been often criticized as irrational and inefficient.[272] The proceedings are initiated ex officio or on request by a state attorney, state authorities, local community authorities or holders of public authority.[273] The SCPA informs in writing the legal person/sole entrepreneur/individual performing a professional activity, and persons in charge of a legal person/sole entrepreneur of the charges and of the privilege against self-incrimination. Other caveats of criminal proceedings apply as well. The addressees of the SCPA's writing may respond in a short period of five days. The SCPA then issues a decision levying fines.[274] Investigations in minor offences proceedings are usually not performed. According to the general rules of minor offences proceedings, any gains from the infringement must be reclaimed from the offender.[275]

218. In accordance with the MOA-1, all orders imposing fines may be reviewed by the Local Court in Ljubljana.[276] Appeals against such judgments are also available. They are lodged with the High Court in Ljubljana in eight days after the judgment of the Local Court in Ljubljana is served with the appellant (be it the undertaking or the SCPA).[277]

---

271. See, for example, the CPO's decision No. 306-20/2006-4 of 3 Mar. 2006 finding, first, that the Chamber of Commerce and Industry of Slovenia infringed Art. 5 of the PRCA of 1999 by fixing prices and rebates for books (the CPO refers also to its administrative decision finding this infringement No. 306-21/2005-92 of 1 Feb. 2006, available at (in Slovene): http://www.varstvo-konkurence.si/zakonodaja-in-dokumenti/ostali-dokumenti/arhiv-odlocb/odlocba07/), and thereby committed a minor offence in accordance with Art. 52/1 of the PRCA, and imposing a fine of SIT 10 million (EUR 41,729) on the Chamber, as well as a fine of SIT 1 million (EUR 4,173) upon the Secretary-General of the Chamber's Print and Media Association being the person in charge of the anti-competitive practices (available at (in Slovene): http://www.varstvo-konkurence.si/fileadmin/varstvo-konkurence.si/pageuploads/ijz009.pdf). The same fines were imposed by the CPO in its Decision No. 306-89/2005-32 of 20 Feb. 2006, where the CPO found the *Association of Tourist Agencies of Slovenia* in breach of Art. 5 of the PRCA of 1999 by issuing a decision on fixing the agencies' initial fees they could charge their customers. The Association as well as its president were found guilty of committing a minor offence and were fined (see (in Slovene): http://www.varstvo-konkurence.si/fileadmin/varstvo-konkurence.si/pageuploads/ijz013.pdf). See also the minor offences Decision No. 306-100/2006-24 of 9 Nov. 2006 in the cartel case *Public Health Maribor/DDD, Dezinfekcija, dezinsekcija, deratizacija, d.o.o.*, available at (in Slovene): http://www.varstvo-konkurence.si/fileadmin/varstvo-konkurence.si/pageuploads/ijz003.pdf.
272. See, for example, Zajc, *Removing Obstacles: The Competition Law Regime of Slovenia*, 186–187.
273. Article 50/1 of the MOA-1.
274. According to Art. 75 of the PRCA-1 (and Art. 42 of the MOA-1 specifically for minor offences proceedings in the ambit of competition law cases), the statute of limitations is five years after the offence has been committed, i.e., the proceedings may not be initiated after five years have lapsed after the offence has been committed, while the proceedings may not be continued after ten years have lapsed after the offence has been committed. In cases of ongoing offences, the date when the offence was terminated is set as the date of committing the offence which is important in cases where the undertakings have continuously been in breach of competition law.
275. Article 190 of the MOA-1.
276. Article 214/5 of the MOA-1, setting specific jurisdiction for competition law minor offences court review proceedings. Minor offences orders outside competition law are namely reviewed by local courts throughout Slovenia, not only in Ljubljana.
277. Article 151 of the MOA-1.

D. Other Institutional Tasks

219. In addition to the general jurisdiction in administrative and minor offences proceedings, the CPA is authorized to monitor and analyse the conditions on the market to the extent necessary for the development of effective competition, and submit its opinions on general issues under its competence to the National Assembly of the Republic of Slovenia and to the Government of the Republic of Slovenia.[278] These tasks were performed also by the CPO. Article 121 of the PRCA-1 states anew as of 2012 that the SCPA cooperates in drafting of the competition policy as well as in bilateral relations and international organizations. The director of the CPA has to report on the cooperation within the EU (i.e., within the ECN) to the CPA's Council and to the relevant ministry.

220. Further, according to the PRCA-1, the SCPA has legal standing to file a nullity claim in cases of breaches of Article 6/1 of the PRCA-1 prohibiting restrictive agreements, and Article 44/3 of the PRCA-1 setting out the standstill obligation during the assessment of concentrations by the SCPA. As the PRCA-1 itself states that restrictive agreements are null (the SCPA usually declares that in operative parts of its decisions), nullity is a direct feature of such practices. Unless the authority was, for example, to allege nullity of a decision taken on a shareholders' meeting organized in breach of the standstill clause, it is unclear why the SCPA would have interest in filing nullity actions with the courts. According to the information available to the author, to date no such actions have been filed.

221. As of April 2014, the CPA is vested with new competences within the field of unfair trading practices in the food supply chain. The amendment to the Agriculture Act provided that the newly established Slovenian Ombudsman protecting the relationships in the food supply chain[279] is to report to the CPA of every practice in the food supply chain which is prohibited by Article 61f of the Agriculture Act.[280] According to Article 172 of the Agriculture Act, the CPA has control over such illegal acts and assesses them in minor offences proceedings. It is also stated that if the undertaking in question has a dominant position as set out in the PRCA-1, the CPA is to initiate the proceedings solely on the basis of the PRCA-1, not on the basis of the Agriculture Act.[281] Setting up the office of the new ombudsman is most plausibly a reaction to the European Commission's Communication of 2014 on unfair trading practices in the business-to-business food supply chain[282] and to a strong lobby of Slovenian farmers and other producers of food, supported by the Chamber

278. Article 12 of the PRCA-1 (versions prior to and after the amendments of 2011 and 2012).
279. See the ombudsman's webpage (in Slovene only): http://www.varuhverigehrane.si/. See also the webpage of the Ministry of Agriculture, Forestry and Food (in Slovene only): http://www.mkgp.gov.si/si/o_ministrstvu/varuh_odnosov_v_verigi_preskrbe_s_hrano/.
280. Article 61d/2 of the Agriculture Act.
281. Article 172 of the Agriculture Act.
282. Communication from the Commission to the European Parliament, the Council, the European Economic and Social Committee and the Committee of the Regions, Tackling unfair trading practices in the business-to-business food supply chain (COM(2014) 472 final, 15 Jul. 2014), available at: http://ec.europa.eu/internal_market/retail/docs/140715-communication_en.pdf.

of Agriculture and Forestry of Slovenia (CAFS).[283] As was the case with CAFS, the first ombudsman, too, had somewhat discriminatively (in terms of the TFEU and the basic principles of the functioning of the internal market of the EU) emphasized the quality of Slovenian food and other Slovenian products and set as one of his goals – although he is to protect (only) the food supply chain from unfair trading practices –to convince the consumers that Slovenian food is safe and that it should be on the consumers' plates.[284]

II. Government Direct Enforcement Activities

222. As clarified supra in §1, I A of this Chapter, the CPO had been (at least by law) independent and autonomous in the implementation of its tasks already before it was transformed into an agency in 2012. The SCPA's independence from the Government has now been additionally stressed and has hopefully been intact also in practice.

223. Under Slovenian law, Slovenian Government is not entitled to enforce directly the antitrust rules as opposed to the SCPA. Enforcement of Slovenian and European antitrust in the Republic of Slovenia is vested with the SCPA only.[285]

III. Other Administrative Agencies Applying Antitrust Rules

224. Strictly speaking, enforcement of Slovenian and European antitrust in the Republic of Slovenia is vested with the SCPA only. However, other Slovenian agencies also pay due regard to basic notions and concepts of competition law and policy in their assessment under specific sector regulation.

IV. Administrative Fines

A. Categorization of Fines

225. Infringements of the PRCA-1 are characterized as minor offences. Prior to enactment of the PRCA-1 of 2008, the fines were relatively low and were fixed in absolute amounts[286] what attributed to a low deterrent effect of the incrimination of

283. See http://www.kgzs.si/gv/eu-in-svet/english.aspx.
284. See, e.g., http://www.rtvslo.si/slovenija/varuh-prehranske-verige-verjamem-v-kmetijstvo-in-priloznosti-slovenskega-podezelja/359344. See also Hojnik & Vlahek, *Promocija slovenskih živilskih proizvodov in enotni trg EU*.
285. See also the following paragraph.
286. Articles 52–55 of the PRCA of 1999 and their amendments of 2004 and 2007.

anti-competitive behaviour, taking into consideration in particular that criminal proceedings have in practice almost never been initiated, let alone have led to imprisonment of persons in charge of the infringements.[287]

226. Between 14 July 1999 (entry into force of the PRCA) and 1 May 2004 (entry into force of the PRCA amendment of 2004), the fines for legal persons breaching antitrust were ranged between SIT 10 and SIT 30 million (EUR 41,729.31–EUR 125,187.94), while their responsible persons could be fined with SIT 1–SIT 1.5 million (EUR 4,172,931–EUR 6,259.40). Entrepreneurs could be fined from SIT 3 to SIT 15 million (EUR 12,518.79–EUR 62,593.97). In cases of non-notified concentrations, legal persons could be fined from SIT 3 to SIT 10 million (EUR 12,518.79–EUR 41,729.31), its responsible persons from SIT 300,000 to SIT 500,000 (EUR 1,251.88–EUR 2,086.47) and entrepreneurs from SIT 1 to SIT 5 million (EUR 4,172,931–EUR 20,864,66). The limitation period for the offence was two years after the offence had been committed.

227. In 2004, the PRCA was amended for the first time. The fines for legal persons were amended to SIT 30–SIT 90 million (EUR 125,187.94–EUR 375,563.81) and for their responsible persons to SIT 1–SIT 3 million (EUR 4,172.93–EUR 12,518.79). The fines for entrepreneurs were amended to SIT 10–SIT 50 million (EUR 41,729.31–EUR 208,646.56), for entrepreneurs' responsible persons to SIT 0.5–SIT 1.5 million (EUR 2,086.47–EUR 6,259.40). For non-notification of concentrations the legal persons were fined SIT 6–SIT 20 million (EUR 25,037.59 – EUR 83,458.62), their responsible persons SIT 0.6–SIT 1 million (EUR 2,503.76–EUR 4,172.93), entrepreneurs SIT 2–SIT 10 million (EUR 8,345.86–EUR 41,729.31), and entrepreneurs' responsible persons SIT 0.2–SIT 0.6 million (EUR 834.59–EUR 2,503.76).

228. In 2007, the PRCA (including its provisions on fines) was amended for the second time. The fines were put in line with the introduction of the euro in Slovenia in 2007. The fines were set to EUR 125,000–EUR 375,000 for a legal person and to EUR 4,100–EUR 12,500 for its responsible person. The fines for an entrepreneur were set to EUR 41,700–EUR 208,600 and to EUR 2,000–EUR 6,200 for entrepreneur's responsible person. For non-notification of concentrations legal persons were fined EUR 25,000–EUR 83,400, their responsible persons EUR 2,500–EUR 4,100, entrepreneurs EUR 8,300–EUR 41,700, and their responsible persons EUR 800–EUR 2,500. The limitation period for the offence was amended from two to three years after the offence had been committed.

229. With the adoption of the presently valid PRCA-1, the legislator (being inspired by the rules set out in Regulation 1/2003) made important alterations regarding the fines imposed for illegal anti-competitive behaviour: fixed-amount fines were replaced by turnover-based fines. At least to some extent, the deterrent effect of the fines has thereby been intensified. Imposition of periodic penalty payments has to date, though, not been available.

287. See Pt. I, Ch. 5, §3 of this monograph.

230. As of 2008, fines of up to 10% of the total turnover of the undertaking concerned in the previous business year may be imposed on a legal person (including affiliated companies)/sole entrepreneur/individual performing a professional activity that has breached merger control rules[288] or Slovenian and/or European antitrust,[289] or has acted in contravention of an enforceable decision issued by the SCPA pursuant to Articles 37–39 of the PRCA-1. Fines ranging from EUR 5,000 to EUR 10,000 can also be imposed on the responsible person.[290] In case of aggravating circumstances,[291] the fines for the responsible persons can be elevated to range from EUR 15,000 to EUR 30,000.[292]

231. As there is no exact method defining the calculation of the level of fines, general rules of the MOA-1 apply. According to Article 26 of the MOA-1, the level of the fine depends on the gravity of the offence and on the offender's negligence or intent. The following circumstances of the case are in particular to be taken into account when determining the fine: the level of the offender's liability for the offence, the offender's incentives for committing the offence, the level of threat to or of breach of the insured interest, the circumstances in which the offence was committed, former lifestyle of the offender, his or her personal circumstances, his or her conduct after committing the offence, in particular whether he or she has recompensated the damage. In setting the fine to a legal entity or an entrepreneur, its economic strength and any formerly set fines are to be taken into account. In mitigating circumstances, fines below the set threshold may be imposed, while in cases set out by the law the fines may also be remitted. In mitigating circumstances lessening the gravity of the offence or in cases where the offender has fulfilled his or her obligations he or has breached by the offence or has recompensated the loss caused by the offence, only a warning may be issued to the offender.[293] Pecuniary benefits obtained by the offender by committing the offence are to be taken from the offender.[294] The rule of the MOA-1 that the offender is to pay only half of the fine

288. I.e., in cases they have (i) failed to notify the SCPA of a concentration, or failed to do so within the time limit set out in Art. 43 of the PRCA-1; (ii) implemented a concentration in breach of Art. 44 of the PRCA-1; (iii) failed to comply with the remedies or obligations imposed by the SCPA in its decision on compatibility of the concentration with competition rules, and (iv) implemented a concentration declared incompatible with competition rules or have not complied with any measure ordered pursuant to Art. 53 of the PRCA-1, aimed at dissolving consequences of concentration.
289. I.e., Arts 6 or 9 of the PRCA-1 or Arts 101 or 102 TFEU.
290. In the CPO's *Chamber of Commerce and Industry of Slovenia* case, for example, the Secretary-General of the Chamber's Print and Media Association was fined (Decision No. 306-20/2006-4 of 3 Mar. 2006, available at (in Slovene): http://www.varstvo-konkurence.si/fileadmin/varstvo-konkurence.si/pageuploads/ijz009.pdf). In the *Association of Tourist Agencies of Slovenia* case, the association's president was fined (Decision No. 306-89/2005-32 of 20 Feb. 2006, available at (in Slovene): http://www.varstvo-konkurence.si/fileadmin/varstvo-konkurence.si/pageuploads/ijz013.pdf.
291. I.e., if the nature of the minor offence is particularly serious due to the amount of damage inflicted, or due to the amount of the illegally acquired pecuniary benefit, or due to the offender's intent or intended unlawful gain.
292. Articles 73–74 of the PRCA-1.
293. Article 21 of the MOA-1.
294. Article 28 of the MOA-1.

if it pays it in eight days after the decision levying the fine is final, and if it declines the right to request review of the decision, does not apply to the fines imposed for breaches of competition law.[295]

232. Obstruction of investigation or refusal to provide information to the SCPA may be fined as long as the sum of individual fines imposed for each individual breach reaches 1% of the undertaking's total turnover in the preceding business year.[296]

233. The PRCA-1 sets out a five-year limitation period running from the date of the infringement[297] that can be terminated in accordance with the MOA-1 (but may in any case not be longer than ten years).[298] The PRCA of 1999 set a two-year (as of 2007, three) and a four-year (as of 2007, six) limitation period respectively. In quite a few cases, the CPO was unable to impose fines although it had established the infringement as the limitation periods had already lapsed.

234. In accordance with the MOA-1, the SCPA's orders imposing fines are reviewed as priority by the Local Court in Ljubljana.[299] Appeal and other remedies against the court's decision are also available.

235. Before the currently valid PRCA-1 entered into force in 2008 amending the rules on the amount of the fines to be imposed by the CPO, the fines were low if imposed at all due to the lapse of the limitation period set for minor offences. For example, in the Chamber of Commerce and Industry of Slovenia case finding the Chamber in breach of Article 5 of the PRCA of 1999 by fixing prices and rebates for books, and thereby in committing a minor offence in accordance with Article 52/1 of the PRCA, the CPO imposed in 2006 a fine of SIT 10 million (EUR 41.729) on the Chamber, as well as a fine of SIT 1 million (EUR 4.173) upon the Secretary-General of the Chamber's Print and Media Association being the person in charge of the anti-competitive practices.[300] The same amounts of fines were imposed by the CPO in 2006 on the Association of Tourist Agencies found in breach of Article 5 of the PRCA of 1999 by issuing a decision on fixing the agencies' initial fees they could charge their customers, and to its president.[301] Also in 2006, the same amount of fines were imposed to Public Health Maribor and DDD, Dezinfekcija, dezinsekcija, deratizacija, d.o.o. and their responsible persons,[302] as well as to Slovenian

295. Article 56a/2 of the MOA-1.
296. Articles 27 and 31 of the PRCA-1.
297. Article 75 of the PRCA-1.
298. Article 75 of the PRCA-1 in conjunction with Art. 42 of the MOA-1.
299. Articles 214/5 and 60/3 of the MOA-1.
300. The CPO's minor offences Decision No. 3/2006;306-20/2006-4 of 3 Mar. 2006 is available at (in Slovene): http://www.varstvo-konkurence.si/fileadmin/varstvo-konkurence.si/pageuploads/ijz009.pdf. Costs of the minor offences proceedings (a lump-sum amount) were also paid by the undertaking and the responsible person concerned.
301. Decision No. 306-89/2005-32 of 20 Feb. 2006, available at (in Slovene): http://www.varstvo-konkurence.si/fileadmin/varstvo-konkurence.si/pageuploads/ijz013.pdf.
302. Decision No. 4/2006;306-100/2006-24 of 9 Nov. 2006, available at (in Slovene): http://www.varstvo-konkurence.si/fileadmin/varstvo-konkurence.si/pageuploads/ijz003.pdf.

Natural Spas Association and its responsible person.[303] In 2007, the CPO imposed a fine of EUR 125,187.78 on Slopak d.o.o.[304] for abusing its dominant position, and a fine of EUR 4,172.93 on the person responsible.[305]

236. In recent years (as of 2008 when the rules on setting the fines were changed with the PRCA-1), the imposition of fines by the SCPA has somewhat intensified but has still not reached the level of the fines imposed in other Member States. Statistics show that between 2006 and 2015, fines in the total amount of only EUR 1.2 million were paid to the state budget by the breaching persons (approx. EUR 50,000 in 2007, EUR 125,000 in 2010, EUR 645,500 in 2011, EUR 405,960 in 2015), while additional EUR 1.1 million was obtained in 2013 and 2014 by those fined for obstructing the SCPA's investigation (*Pro Plus* and *Geoplin*).[306] Some of the highest fines imposed by the SCPA for antitrust breaches (later reviewed by the courts) were, for example, EUR 500,000 in the *Luka Koper* case in 2010,[307] EUR 300,000 in 2013 in the *SODO* case[308] and EUR 230,000 in 2013 in the *Medical Chamber of Slovenia* case.[309] However, in July 2014, a somewhat seminal decision as to the amount of fines was issued by the CPA imposing a fine of approx. EUR 4.9 million to Produkcija Plus d.o.o. – Pro Plus (i.e., approx. 9.7% of Pro Plus's total turnover in the previous business year) for its long-lasting abuse on the market for TV advertising via exclusivity clauses and conditional loyalty rebates, and an additional fine of approx. EUR 20,000 to the company's general manager. The CPA issued a decision on the abuse in April 2013, the decision was upheld by the Supreme Court in December 2013, and finally, in July 2014, the CPA issued a decision setting fines. Pro Plus initiated court proceedings to review the CPO's decision setting the fines.

303. Decision No. 2/2006;306-124/2005-8 of 28 Feb. 2006, available at (in Slovene): http://www.varstvo-konkurence.si/fileadmin/varstvo-konkurence.si/pageuploads/ijz003.pdf.

304. The CPO's minor offence Decision No. 1/2007; 306-136/2006-13 of 28 Mar. 2007 available at (in Slovene): http://www.varstvo-konkurence.si/fileadmin/varstvo-konkurence.si/pageuploads/ijz002.pdf.

305. On the motion of the undertaking and its responsible person, the fines could be paid in three and four instalments.

306. See http://www.finance.si/8822240/Zakaj-v-Sloveniji-zaradi-kartelov-skoraj-nih%C4%8De-ne-pla%C4%8Da-globe?metered=yes&sid=429294657.

307. The competent local court has supposedly upheld the fine to the amount of nearly EUR 400,000 for Luka Koper and approx. EUR 13,000 for its general manager; http://www.delo.si/gospodarstvo/za-luko-koper-500-000-evrov-globe.html; http://www.dnevnik.si/kronika/luki-koper-kazen-zaradi-monopolnega-polozaja-pri-vleki-ladij; http://www.finance.si/8822240/Zakaj-v-Sloveniji-zaradi-kartelov-skoraj-nih%C4%8De-ne-pla%C4%8Da-globe?metered=yes&sid=429294657.

308. CPO's decision of 9 Aug. 2012 is available at (in Slovene): http://www.varstvo-konkurence.si/fileadmin/varstvo-konkurence.si/pageuploads/informacija_javnega_znacaja/Odlocba_306-5-2011-22_-_preciscena.pdf, while the CPO's minor offences decision in this case is not available online. Data on the amount of the fine was obtained in media (interview with the CPA's director in Delo): http://www.delo.si/zgodbe/sobotnapriloga/andrej-krasek-avk-zdi-se-mi-da-bi-imeli-mir-ce-ne-bi-delali-nic.html.

309. The CPO's substantive Decision No. 306-32/2010-33 of 26 Sep. 2012 is available at (in Slovene): http://www.varstvo-konkurence.si/fileadmin/varstvo-konkurence.si/pageuploads/informacija_javnega_znacaja/ijz154.pdf, while the CPO's minor offences decision in this case is not available online. Data on the amount of the fine was obtained in media (interview with the CPA's director in Delo): http://www.delo.si/zgodbe/sobotnapriloga/andrej-krasek-avk-zdi-se-mi-da-bi-imeli-mir-ce-ne-bi-delali-nic.html.

In November 2014, the Local Court in Ljubljana amended the CPA's decision and terminated the minor offence proceedings against Pro Plus thereby annulling the fine as in the opinion of the judge the undertaking did not breach antitrust (although the CPO had already found the breach and its decision on the breach itself – that was issued in separate CPO proceedings, i.e., separate to the later CPA minor offences proceedings – had already become final and was upheld by the Supreme Court of RS).[310] A similar two-tier proceedings with possible contradictory results have taken place in the so-called skiing cartel case where the minor offences judge of the Local Court in Ljubljana decided in April 2015 to appoint an expert in order to assess whether the breach took place or not (so as to be able to review the CPA's decision on the fine) although the CPA already found the breach in 2010 and its decision was partially upheld by the Supreme Court of RS in December 2013 and January and February 2014.[311] It is evident from these cases that such two-tier system, i.e., where the SCPA sets the fines in minor offences proceedings separate to administrative proceedings assessing the breach, and where separate review proceedings taking place at different courts are set out, is inefficient, lengthy and can lead to contradictory results in the same case. Various stakeholders, including the CPA, have been urging the competent ministries to initiate the amendment of the system but have so far unfortunately remained unsuccessful.[312]

237. Slovenian undertakings have already been fined also by the European Commission. On 9 July 2014, for example, the European Commission issued a decision finding the infringement of European antitrust and setting fines in the total amount of EUR 427.7 million for French pharmaceutical company Servier and five generic companies, including Slovenian pharmaceutical company Krka d.d., for curbing entry of cheaper versions of cardiovascular medicine.[313] Krka was fined with EUR 10 million for participating in the cartel.[314] Krka attacked in September 2014 the Commission's decision by filing a nullity action with the General Court in Luxembourg.[315] The General Court in December 2012 issued a judgment in favour

---

310. See, for example, http://www.rtvslo.si/gospodarstvo/postopek-proti-pro-plusu-ustavljen-milijonska-globa-nicna/350598.
311. For further details of the case, see Pt. III, Ch. 4, §1 of this monograph. See also http://www.finance.si/8822240/Zakaj-v-Sloveniji-zaradi-kartelov-skoraj-nih%C4%8De-ne-pla%C4%8Da-globe?metered=yes&sid=429294657.
312. http://www.finance.si/8822240/Zakaj-v-Sloveniji-zaradi-kartelov-skoraj-nih%C4%8De-ne-pla%C4%8Da-globe?metered=yes&sid=429294657.
313. Decision C(2014) 4955 final of 9 Jul. 2014 in case AT.39612 – Perindopril (Servier).
314. http://europa.eu/rapid/press-release_IP-14-799_en.htm.
315. Case T-684/14 *Krka v. Commission*, Judgment of 12 Dec. 2018. As ensues from Krka's application, it relied on six pleas in law. It alleged that: (i) the Commission failed to properly analyse the legal, factual and economic context of Krka's situation; (ii) the Commission wrongly concluded that Krka and Servier were actual or potential competitors under Art. 101 TFEU; (iii) the Commission's wrong conclusion that the patent settlement concluded between Krka and Servier restricted competition by object under Art. 101(1) TFEU rests on erroneous factual and legal analysis as well as on a wrongful application of the established principles on restrictions by object; (iv) the Commission violated Krka's right of defence by inconsistently examining the Assignment and Licence Agreement and erred in concluding that the Assignment and Licence Agreement amounts to a

of Krka.[316] The case is currently pending in appeal proceedings before the Court of Justice[317]

B. Leniency Programme

238. National leniency programme has been implemented in Slovenia by the PRCA-1 of 2008 in order to align the competition regime regarding fines with that of the European Union. It was, however, launched in practice only in January 2010. As the initial programme as set out in the PRCA-1 of 2008 did not follow completely the ECN Model Leniency Programme (e.g., it did not offer the prospect of reduction of fines to cooperating persons), the PRCA-1 has been amended in 2009 setting out detailed rules of the programme, and providing a legal basis for the adoption of the Decree on the procedure for granting immunity from fines and reduction of fines in cartel cases.[318]

239. Leniency programme as currently regulated in Article 76 of the PRCA-1, provides for immunity from fines as well as for reduction of fines to potential whistleblowers. Its characteristics are similar to those of the Commission Notice on Immunity from fines and reduction of fines in cartel cases[319] whereby the regime set out in the PRCA-1 itself regulates solely the more fundamental issues, while the Decree on the procedure for granting immunity from fines and reduction of fines in cartel cases contains the rules of procedure. As regards the basic qualifications for granting immunity from fines, the PRCA-1 enumerates the following conditions that are to be met by the offender:

- the offender must be the first to provide evidence, which in the SCPA's view, will enable it to carry out inspections in administrative or minor offences proceedings with regard to the alleged cartel; or
- the offender must be the first to provide evidence, which in the SCPA's view, will enable it to find an infringement in administrative and minor offences proceedings; and
- must fully and completely disclose its participation in the alleged cartel;
- must cooperate with the SCPA throughout the procedure;

restriction of competition by object under Art. 101(1) TFEU; (v) the Commission erred in concluding that the agreements concluded between Krka and Servier restricted competition by effect under Art. 101(1) TFEU; and (vi) the Commission failed to accurately assess the arguments raised by Krka under Art. 101(3) TFEU.

316. http://curia.europa.eu/juris/document/document.jsf;jsessionid=7D3199BD353DB32B7F64AB8A75B338D8?text=&docid=208853&pageIndex=0&doclang=EN&mode=lst&dir=&occ=first&part=1&cid=3716773.

317. C-151/19 P *Commission v. Krka*, appeal lodged in April 2019..

318. Sl. *Uredba o postopku odpustitve in znižanja globe storilcem, ki so udeleženi v kartelih*, Official Gazette RS, No.112/09, with further amendments.

319. OJ C 298, 8 Dec. 2006, 17–22.

– must end its involvement in the alleged cartel immediately following its application, except if that would, in the SCPA's view, in any way jeopardize the inspections;
– must not have coerced others to join the cartel or to remain in it.

240. As leniency regime caters also for the reduction of fines, Article 76 of the PRCA-1 sets forth the following conditions that are to be met by offenders wishing to qualify for such reductions:

– they must provide evidence of their involvement in the alleged cartel which represents significant added value with respect to the evidence already in possession of the SCPA;
– must cooperate with the SCPA throughout the procedure; and
– must end their involvement in the alleged cartel immediately following its application, except if that would, in the SCPA's view in any way jeopardize the inspections.

241. The reduction of fines is graded according to the time of fulfilment of the conditions by the offenders who wish to participate in the programme: the first offender to provide significant added value will be granted a reduction of 30%–50%, the second one to provide significant added value a reduction of 20%–30%, while all subsequent ones that provide significant added value will be granted a reduction of up to 20%.

242. Inspired by the European Commission's Leniency Notice, the SCPA's Decree provides the offenders wishing to be granted immunity from fines with the possibility of presenting the information and evidence to the SCPA in hypothetical terms, as well as of receiving from the SCPA the acknowledgement of receipt of their application for immunity from fines guaranteeing that the SCPA will assess the applications in relation to the same alleged cartel in order as it receives them.

243. In contrast to the leniency programme of the European Commission, the SCPA's programme is available to legal persons/sole entrepreneurs/individuals performing a professional activity, as well as to natural persons. According to the SCPA's Decree, an application lodged by a legal person/sole entrepreneur/individual performing a professional activity is deemed to encompass application by the person in charge of such undertaking, while vice versa applies only if the application of the person in charge states explicitly that it applies also to the legal person/sole entrepreneur/individual performing a professional activity.

244. Although the SCPA's leniency programme is not flawless, it is modern and balances well the interests of the undertakings on the one hand, and of the SCPA on the other. However, it has to our knowledge thus far been rarely applied by the CPA (and never by its predecessor the CPO).[320] Such statistics could be attributed to the

320. Referring to Slovene media, the authors are aware of only one (and all in all first) leniency case. In the bus services providers cartel one of eleven members that had agreed on bidding in the public

inefficient detection and prosecution of cartels by the SCPA. As long as the undertakings will most likely stay unpunished, they have no incentive to come forward with the information. Until competition culture and public enforcement of antitrust in Slovenia is fostered, the SCPA's leniency programme will remain unattractive.

245. One of additional hurdles for a successful leniency programme in the first years of its application could stem also from the fear of potential leniency applicants that their leniency statements could assist the victims of the infringements in claiming damages from them. In cases of application of Articles 101 or 102 TFEU, the CJEU's interpretation in Pfleiderer[321] and Donau Chemie[322] was of some, albeit vague assistance to the undertakings in determining the plausibility that access to leniency statements will be granted by the national court. After the implementation deadline of the new Directive 2014/104/EU of the European Parliament and of the Council of 26 November 2014 on certain rules governing actions for damages under national law for infringements of the competition law provisions of the Member States and of the European Union[323] expired, and in particular once the Member States implemented the directive appropriately, the questions of access to leniency statements have been regulated in national legislation enabling the undertakings to decide with more certainty as to future development of their case to apply for leniency or not. Disclosure of evidence included in the file of a competition authority is regulated in Articles 6 and 7 of the directive (Chapter II Disclosure of evidence, Articles 5–8). It is to be underscored that Article 6/6 states that Member States shall ensure that, for the purpose of actions for damages, national courts cannot at any time order a party or a third party to disclose leniency statements and settlement submissions. A claimant may, however, present a justified request that a national court access the documents contained in such evidence for the sole purpose of ensuring that their contents fulfil the definitions of 'leniency statement' or 'settlement submission'. In that assessment, national courts may request assistance from the competent competition authority, the authors of the concerned documents may also have the possibility to be heard, but in any case, the court shall not provide access to those documents to the other parties or third parties. As of 20 May 2017, the amended PRCA-1 sets out the rules on non-disclosure of leniency statements and settlement submissions mirroring the rules set out in the directive.[324]

---

tender of the Ministry for Transport in 2010 was supposedly a whistle-blower and qualified for immunity from or for reduction of the fine (http://168.63.31.19/posel/novice/krasek-prizaneselpomembnemu-akterju-avtobusnega-kartela). Doubts as to the appropriateness of the SCPA's decision to grant leniency in this case were present in the media as the SCPA had collected all relevant information as to the infringement and had issued the statement of objections already prior to receiving information from the whistle-blower who was also supposed to have had a leading role in the cartel. The CPA's decision finding an infringement was issued on 30 Sep. 2013 (operative part of the decision is available at (in Slovene): http://www.varstvo-konkurence.si/zakonodaja-in-dokumenti/ostali-dokumenti/arhiv-odlocb/odlocba271/).

321. C-360/09, Judgment of 14 Jun. 2011.

322. C-536/11, Judgment of 6 Jun. 2013.

323. OJ L 349, 5 Dec. 2014, 1–19. The text of the directive (also in English) is available at: http://eur-lex.europa.eu/legal-content/EN/TXT/?uri=uriserv:OJ.L_.2014.349.01.0001.01.ENG.

324. Articles 62a, 62č, 62d and 62f of the PRCA-1.

246. As to the cases of Slovenian antitrust infringements, there was no direct regulation of access to leniency documents for the purposes of civil law enforcement until the directive was implemented and the legislator decided – as was anticipated[325] – to apply its rules also to infringements of Slovenian antitrust. The Decree on the procedure for granting immunity from fines and reduction of fines in cartel cases stated only that leniency applications are deemed business secrets,[326] Public Information Access Act and its provisions on exceptions to grant access[327] as well as general provisions of the Civil Procedure Act (CPrA)[328] were applied[329].

V. Administrative Injunctions and Other Restrictive Orders

247. Where the SCPA determines that there is an infringement of Slovenian or European antitrust, it may impose on them any behavioural or structural remedies adequate to restore the competitive process. It may require the undertakings or associations of undertakings concerned to bring the infringement to an end,[330] and prohibit them to perform anti-competitive processes in the future.[331] Positive remedies which will most commonly be used in cases of abuses of dominant position may also be imposed on the undertakings. According to the PRCA-1, the SCPA may, inter alia, order an undertaking to divest its assets, to divide the undertaking, to divest its shares in other undertakings, to transfer industrial property rights and other rights, to conclude licencing or other contracts, or to grant access to infrastructure.[332] The PRCA-1 does not regulate in detail the prerequisites for ordering the remedies, however, the rules as set out in Article 7 of Regulation 1/2003 providing guidance to the European Commission when deciding for the appropriate type of a remedy might as well be taken into consideration by the SCPA.

248. In October 2012, for example, the CPO issued a decision finding that the Medical Chamber of Slovenia breached Slovenian and (as of 1 May 2004) European antitrust by setting in the period of 1995–2012 in its rules the standards for valuation and calculation of dental and medical services and the supervision of its

325. See Vlahek, *Nova Direktiva 2014/104 ...* ; Vlahek, *Challenges of Private Enforcement of Antitrust in Slovenia.*
326. Article 6 of the Decree.
327. Article 6 of the Act.
328. Articles 227–229 and 231–234 of the CPrA.
329. In its Judgment No. I Cpg 708/2013 of 21 Nov. 2013 in *T2 v Telekom Slovenije*, the High Court of Ljubljana stated that the PRCA-1 provisions on access to the SCPA file apply only to the SCPA administrative proceedings, not to private enforcement proceedings. See Pt. I, Ch. 5, §2, II B 2 of this monograph.
330. Articles 37/1,4 and 53 of the PRCA-1.
331. In its Decision No. 306-132/2006-69 of 28 Nov. 2008 in *Slovenian Ship and Freight Agents Association*, the CPO explicitly prohibited the members of the Association every future contracting and cooperation in taking decisions regarding the prices of their services (available at (in Slovene): http://www.varstvo-konkurence.si/fileadmin/varstvo-konkurence.si/pageuploads/informacija_javnega_znacaja/Odlocba_306-132-2006-69_-_preciscena.pdf).
332. Article 37/2,3 of the PRCA-1.

members in the implementation of such rules.[333] The following remedies were imposed by the CPO: the chamber must inform its members in thirty days after it has received the CPO's decision, of the fact that its rules are prohibited and null and no more in force; within six months after it has received the CPO's decision, the chamber must amend its rules in those parts which are in breach of antitrust; and finally, it must inform the CPO in eight days after the set periods of thirty days and six months for implementing these measures have lapsed, of the measures taken, and serve the CPO with adequate proof of the measures taken.

249. Similarly, in April 2011, the CPO imposed obligations on the Society of Composers, Authors and Publishers for Copyright Protection in Slovenia (SAZAS) which was found to breach Slovenian and European antitrust by obliging its members in the period of 2004–2009 to invest in its funds, and by sharing the collected funds in the period of 2006–2009 among its members on the basis of non-transparent, biased and retroactive rules which were adopted only by a limited group of SAZAS members, granting thereby certain members a better position on the market. The CPO issued seven positive behavioural remedies and prescribed detailed rules for their implementation.[334]

250. Finding in 2006 that the economic interest grouping The Bank Association of Slovenia breached Slovenian antitrust by taking a decision obliging the banks to certain anti-competitive practices that would enable launching on the market of a new service called BanKredit, the CPO ordered it to inform its members of the nullity of the association's decision; to request in writing its members to facilitate the establishment of such contractual relationships with their business partners (i.e., traders and others) which allow them to grant instalment sales, loans using standing orders or other appropriate payment instruments (the decision prescribes in detail further steps for implementing these measures appropriately, e.g., that consumers and the banks' business partners may arrange all payment details in the premises of the partners); to inform in writing its members that the statements regarding the new regime that had been sent in signature to the members, are irrelevant; to inform its members that contracts on standing orders that were still in force may be fully performed; to inform the Association of Trade in writing of the operative part of the CPO's decision. The CPO granted the association eight days to perform the ordered remedies, and another eight days to inform the CPO of the substance and proof of the measures taken.[335]

---

333. CPO's decision No. 306-32/2010-33 of 26 Sep. 2012, available at (in Slovene): http://www.varstvo-konkurence.si/fileadmin/varstvo-konkurence.si/pageuploads/informacija_javnega_znacaja/ijz154.pdf.
334. Decision No. 306-35/2009-108 of 8 Apr. 2011, available at (in Slovene): http://www.varstvo-konkurence.si/fileadmin/varstvo-konkurence.si/pageuploads/informacija_javnega_znacaja/202_306-35-2009_sazas.pdf.
335. Decision No. 306-62/2005-59 of 15 Nov. 2006, operative part of the decision is available at (in Slovene): http://www.varstvo-konkurence.si/zakonodaja-in-dokumenti/ostali-dokumenti/arhiv-odlocb/odlocba49/.

251. Remedies may be imposed also within the merger control regime, where the SCPA may order appropriate measures to ensure that the undertakings concerned dissolve the concentration, in particular through the dissolution of the merger or the disposal of all the shares or assets acquired, so as to restore the situation prevailing prior to the implementation of the concentration.[336]

252. Fines of up to 10% of the total turnover of the undertaking in the previous business year may be imposed on the legal persons/sole entrepreneurs/individuals performing a commercial activity that have breached the decisions ordering such remedies.[337] Responsible natural persons may also be fined.[338]

VI. Interim Measures

253. One of the novel concepts introduced to Slovene competition law by the PRCA-1 of 2008, is the regime of interim measures.[339] The SCPA, acting on its own initiative may by decision, on the basis of a prima facie finding of infringement of Slovenian or European antitrust, order interim measures in cases of urgency due to the risk of serious and irreparable damage to effective competition. A decision ordering interim measures applies for a specified period of time and may be renewed in so far this is necessary and appropriate. Fines of up to 10% of the total turnover of the undertaking in the previous business year may be imposed on the legal persons/sole entrepreneurs/individuals performing a commercial activity that have breached the decision ordering interim measures.[340] Responsible natural persons may also be fined.[341]

254. It is to be underscored that the PRCA-1 deviates from the regime set forth by Regulation 1/2003 as it does not provide for a party against which interim measures are ordered to be heard before the order for interim measures is issued. It was interpreted by the SCPA that the interim measures regime observes the adversarial principle, as the respective party has a right to challenge the order for interim measures ex post facto before the competent court within three days of its service on the party.[342] Such interpretation falls short of the constitutional safeguards stemming from Article 22 of the Constitution of RS and the jurisprudence of the Constitutional Court of RS. Such position is further substantiated by the decision of the Supreme Court of RS, which has stated in 2010 in clear and unequivocal terms that

336. Article 53 of the PRCA-1.
337. Article 73/1 of the PRCA-1.
338. Article 73/2,3 of the PRCA-1.
339. Article 38 of the PRCA-1.
340. Article 73/1 of the PRCA-1.
341. Article 73/2,3 of the PRCA-1.
342. The court is to assess the SCPA's order without delay and in any case within fifteen days after the action has been filed with the court.

an invasive measure such as ordering interim measures cannot be issued in a non-adversarial procedure.[343] According to the Supreme Court of RS, the adversarial nature of the proceedings will manifest in particular in the right to be heard and to make statements, less in the right to access to file which may be reserved to later stages of the proceedings.

§2. Civil Enforcement

I. Competent Civil Courts

255. Jurisdiction in first instance civil and commercial cases is divided between local and district courts on the basis of various criteria.[344] In general, local courts have jurisdiction in those cases where the disputed value does not exceed EUR 20,000, whereas district courts hear the cases where the disputed value exceeds EUR 20,000.[345] However, in certain matters, jurisdiction is divided regardless of the disputed value. For example, district courts have exclusive jurisdiction in commercial cases (save in those concerning easements and real encumbrances, lease or tenancy relations, and disturbance of possession where local courts always hear the cases), in bankruptcy proceedings, as well as in matters concerning 'protection of competition'.[346]

256. There are no specialized civil or commercial courts in Slovenia, only specialized divisions for civil and commercial cases are organized within larger district courts, high courts as well as the Supreme Court of RS.[347] First instance cases before local and (mostly also before) district courts are held before a single judge which is currently also the case in cases of private enforcement of competition, while prior to the 2008 CPrA amendment, these were handled by a panel of judges, not by a single judge. It would possibly be reasonable to reintroduce such rule in order to guarantee the quality of the decision-making in antitrust cases. A step in this direction was made by the introduction of Article 486a in the CPrA's Chapter on commercial disputes in September 2017. According to this article, a judge having jurisdiction to assess a first instance case may exceptionally ask the president of the respective high court to transfer the case to a three-member judicial panel if the case raises complex legal or factual questions. As with other disputes, high courts having (inter alia) supervisory jurisdiction over local and district courts, hear the cases in panels of three judges, while the Supreme Court as the third instance court (assessing cases in extraordinary remedy proceedings) hears the cases in panels of

343. Decision No. G 8/2010 of 20 Apr. 2010 (in Slovene: http://www.sodisce.si/vsrs/odlocitve/2010040815244809/).
344. This chapter is based on and cited from Vlahek, *Challenges of Private Enforcement of Antitrust in Slovenia.*
345. Articles 30 and 32 of the CPrA.
346. *Ibid.*
347. Galič, *Civil Procedure, Slovenia*, 183.

three or five judges.[348] In contrast to some other legal areas,[349] there is also no specialized court in Slovenia assessing competition law issues. We would petition for such regulation coupled with a demand for guaranteeing that only judges proficient in competition law are appointed to assess competition law cases. This is in particular important in the initial stage of handling antitrust damages and other antitrust related civil and commercial cases before Slovenian courts when private enforcement of antitrust is only evolving. The problem with introducing a specialized civil court for competition matters is, however, the fact that there are simply not that many competition law related cases pending before the Slovenian courts. In addition, more and more competition law related damages actions will be follow-on actions not requiring the assessment of antitrust breaches although specialized knowledge of competition law by civil law judges will still be required also in cases of follow-on actions. Specialization of judges is, however, urgent within the judicial assessment of the CPA's decisions, i.e., on the Administrative Court of RS. A specialized competition court that would assess both the CPA's decisions and damages actions would be the optimal solution but is probably not realistic due to the structure of the judicial system in Slovenia.

257. According to Article 481 of the CPrA, specific provisions on commercial disputes set out in Articles 480–497 of the CPrA apply to cases where both parties are registered commercial companies or institutes, co-operatives, local communities or the state, irrespective of whether a dispute between them results from pursuing their commercial activity.[350] According to Articles 482 and 483 of the CPrA, certain types of disputes,[351] including disputes concerning the 'protection of competition' are always deemed commercial regardless of a party's status.

258. As in competition law cases usually two commercial entities will be in dispute (e.g., one telecommunications operator will be claiming damages from another operator having dominant position on the relevant market arguing that the defendant had breached Article 102 TFEU or/and Article 9 of the PRCA-1), a district court will have jurisdiction and procedural provisions of commercial disputes will apply. The disputed value in such cases will also most plausibly exceed EUR 20,000 triggering the jurisdiction of district courts. Even regardless of the disputed value and of the type of dispute (be it civil or commercial) such cases would surely be

---

348. In some cases within the jurisdiction of the high courts, a sole judge issues decisions, while in some cases within jurisdiction of the Supreme Court, a panel of seven judges issues decisions. For further details, see the relevant provisions of the CPrA and the Courts Act (Sl. *Zakon o sodiščih (ZS)*, Official Gazette RS, No. 19/94, with further amendments). See also Galič, *Civil Procedure, Slovenia*, 183.
349. Such as intellectual property where only the District Court in Ljubljana has jurisdiction at first instance.
350. Litigations between one of these persons and a natural person who is a registered proprietor of a business (the so-called sole trader), as well as litigations between two sole traders are, however, deemed commercial only if the dispute has arisen within their commercial activity.
351. Disputes between partners, partners and commercial companies, commercial companies and their management, disputes arising out of contracts on concession, disputes relating to bankruptcy, patents, trademarks, disputes concerning the protection of competition, etc. See also Galič, *Civil Procedure, Slovenia*, 183.

characterized as matters concerning 'protection of competition,' thus automatically switching jurisdiction to district courts in accordance with Article 32 of the CPrA, as well as activating specific provisions regulating commercial disputes set out in Articles 480–497 of the CPrA. Thus, also in small claims actions (i.e., those where the disputed value does not exceed EUR 2,000[352]) in non-commercial disputes (e.g., in damages actions between a consumer and his or her operator who had abused its dominant position), district courts applying procedural rules in commercial matters would have jurisdiction. Due to the complexity of competition law-related issues (even in cases of follow-on private actions) and the need to apply competition law and other legal rules relevant within the sphere of enforcement of competition law consistently, giving jurisdiction to district courts in all cases of antitrust private enforcement is reasonable.

259. The CPrA provides for a set of specific provisions applicable to disputes concerning 'protection of competition'. According to Article 444 of the CPrA, disputes within 'protection of competition' can never be characterized as small claims disputes.[353] Further, Article 483 of the CPrA states that in disputes concerning the 'protection of competition', special rules of the CPrA governing commercial disputes (i.e., Articles 480–497 of the CPrA) apply. Article 485 of the CPrA, for example, states that in commercial litigation concerning the determination of (non-)existence of a contract, or the performance of contractual obligation or cancellation of a contract, or the right to damages sustained due to breach of contractual obligations, the territorial jurisdiction is vested, in addition to the court of general jurisdiction,[354] also to the court on the territory of which the defendant should have rendered the performance stipulated by the contract. Moreover, Article 487 of the CPrA states that in cases of urgency, the court may fix the hearing immediately after the preliminary examination of the statement of claims, and it may do so by way of telephone, telegraph or other means of telecommunications. Additionally, Article 488 of the CPrA provides that when after receiving the defence plea the court establishes that the facts are not disputed between the parties, and that no other obstacle hinders the court to render the award, it may do so without fixing a hearing (unless a party requests it). According to Article 490 of the CPrA, the second instance court may in some circumstances inform the party that lodged the appeal that it intends to

352. In commercial disputes, this limit is EUR 4,000. Art. 495 of the CPrA.
353. Articles 442–458 of the CPrA regulating small claims disputes therefore do not apply to such cases.
354. In disputes against legal persons, the general territorial jurisdiction is vested in the court on the territory where the legal person has its registered office (according to Art. 48 of the CPrA, in the event of doubt, the registered office is deemed to be the place where the management of the legal person is located). In some cases, however, rules on special territorial jurisdiction apply (Arts 49–65 of the CPrA). For example, if the same action is brought against several persons who are under territorial jurisdiction of several courts, the territorial jurisdiction shall be vested in the court of territorial jurisdiction over one of the co-defendants (Arts 35–38 of the CPrA). Further, the territorial jurisdiction to decide upon tort liability is vested, in addition to the court of general territorial jurisdiction, also in the court on the territory of which the tort has been committed, as well as in the court on the territory of which the damage has occurred.

dismiss the appeal and ask it if it wishes to proceed with the appeal.[355] In commercial cases, the CPrA's provisions on the staying of the proceedings do not apply.[356] Further, according to Article 494 of the CPrA, the parties to a commercial litigation may not produce oral statements on the record outside the hearing, the court may also limit the scope of the written submissions as well as the oral presentation on the hearing, etc. Apart from the substance covered in these special provisions of the CPrA regulating commercial disputes,[357] general provisions of the CPrA are to be applied.[358]

260. In Slovenian competition law cases, competitors are in practice those filing actions while consumers have to date to the author's knowledge not yet instituted any proceedings. Class actions within competition law have not been possible in Slovenia until 21 April 2018[359] when the Collective Actions Act (CAA)[360] started to apply. Before the enactment of the CAA, collective redress was limited to injunctive and declaratory relief. The Consumer Protection Act,[361] for example, regulated declaratory and condemnatory (obliging to omission) representative actions filed by organizations for the protection of consumers. These types of actions were not particularly relevant for collective private enforcement of competition law.[362] Slovenian consumers have, however, taken part in at least two group competition law related out-of-court activities aiming at forcing the (alleged) infringers to refund the overcharges paid on the basis of their restrictive practices (the so-called electricity cartel) and to refund the sums paid by the customers of a telecommunications undertaking as a consequence of tying/bundling of two telecommunications services.[363] The CAA that regulates both compensatory and injunctive collective actions and settlements, applies also to cases of Slovenian/European antitrust infringements.[364]

355. If the party decides to withdraw the appeal, a part of its court fee is reimbursed.
356. Article 492 of the CPrA.
357. As of 2008, Art. 34 of the CPrA (providing that such cases are always assessed by a panel of judges, never by a single judge to whom the cases are otherwise assigned at local court as well as in the majority of district courts proceedings) and Art. 367 of the CPrA (listing the cases of 'protection of competition' among the cases where revision by the Supreme Court of RS is always allowed – as before 2008 revision was always possible in cases of 'protection of competition', Art. 490 of the CPrA was irrelevant with this regard) which were also 'protection of competition' specific, are no longer in force.
358. For more details on Slovenian civil procedure, see Galič, *Civil Procedure, Slovenia.*
359. For further details on legal standing in general and in antitrust private enforcement cases under Slovenian law before the enactment of the Collective Actions Act of 2017, see Vlahek, *Challenges of Private Enforcement of Antitrust in Slovenia.*
360. Sl. *Zakon o kolektivnih tožbah (ZKolT)*, Official Gazette of RS, No. 55/17. For further details on the CAA, see Galič & Vlahek, *Challenges in Drafting and Application...*; and Galič & Vlahek, *Zakon o kolektivnih tožbah.*
361. Sl. *Zakon o varstvu potrošnikov (ZVPot)*, Official Gazette RS, No. 20/98, with further amendments.
362. See Vlahek, *Challenges of Private Enforcement of Antitrust in Slovenia*; Galič, *Skupinske tožbe na področju potrošniškega prava.*
363. For further details, see Vlahek, *Challenges of Private Enforcement of Antitrust in Slovenia.*
364. See Art. 2 of the CAA defining the scope of the act. The CAA provides for collective settlements and collective actions in the following areas: consumer law, labour law, financial instruments market law, antitrust, environmental accidents, and (only in the form of injunctive relief) within anti-discrimination law. Galič & Vlahek, *Challenges in Drafting and Application ... .*

According to the CAA, a collective action may not be filed before the competition authority has decided on the antitrust infringement (had administrative infringement proceedings already been initiated).[365] If, however, the competition authority has initiated infringement proceedings after the collective action was filed, the court stays the collective proceedings until the administrative/judicial proceedings assessing the antitrust infringement are finalized.[366]

261. In 2018, approximately 838,000 cases were filed with Slovenian courts while further 175,000 cases were transferred as unsolved from 2017. Of all of these cases more than 853,000 cases were solved in 2018. The district courts solved 5,885 cases pending as commercial disputes. The high courts solved 2.054 of commercial cases, while the Supreme Court solved 340 commercial cases.[367] The estimated time for solving a case in a commercial matter was 4.7 months at the Supreme Court, 4.5 months at the high courts, and 11.1 months at the district courts.[368] There is unfortunately no detailed official statistics available that would enable to detect only competition law related cases, or the length of their assessment. A general overview of the time frames of handling damages and other private enforcement of antitrust cases, can, however, be detected from the analysis of case law referred to in Part I, Chapter 5, §2, II B 2 of this monograph.

II. Sanctions

A. *Nullity*

262. Questions of nullity are covered in Articles 86–93 of the Code of Obligations (CO).[369] The basic principle, enshrined in Article 86/1 of the CO, reads as follows: A contract that contravenes the constitution, mandatory rules or moral principles shall be null and void if the purpose of the contravened rule does not assign any other sanction or if the law does not prescribe otherwise for the case in question. Violations of Articles 6 and 9 of the PRCA-1 and of Articles 101/1 and 102 TFEU undoubtedly represent a contravention to compulsory regulations. It is, however, to be noted that when deliberating on such cases, Slovenian courts will not need applying Article 86/1 of the CO as the consequence of nullity for agreements that represent restraining business practices stems directly from the wording of Article 6/1 of the PRCA-1 (Agreements …, decisions … and concerted practices … are prohibited and null) as well as of Article 101/2 TFEU (Any agreements or decisions prohibited pursuant to this article shall be automatically void.). After finding an infringement of European and/or Slovenian antitrust, the CPO has

365. Article 9 of the CAA. Galič & Vlahek, *Challenges in Drafting and Application …* .
366. *Ibid.*
367. See http://www.sodisce.si/mma_bin.php?static_id=2019053010295563.
368. *Ibid.*
369. Sl. *Obligacijski zakonik (OZ)*, Official Gazette RS, No. 83/01, with further amendments.

often (though not in its recent decisions) declared in the operative parts of its decisions (i.e., in ordering (dispositive) parts) that an agreement of undertakings or a decision of associations of undertakings is prohibited and null.[370]

263. According to Article 92 of the CO, the proceedings for nullity may be instituted ex officio or at the request of any person with vested interest in the declaration of nullity.[371] According to Article 93 of the CO, the right to invoke nullity does not expire. The decision on nullity has a declaratory character and erga omnes effects. In addition, Article 90 of the CO stipulates that a null and void contract shall not become valid if the prohibition or other cause of nullity later ceases.

264. Consequences of nullity are covered by Article 87/1 of the CO. If a contract is null and void, each contracting party must return everything to the other party what was received on the basis of such contract; otherwise, adequate monetary equivalent must be provided. In addition, Article 87/2 of the CO states that when a contract is null and void because it contravenes fundamental moral principles, the court may refuse to grant restitutionary relief to the party tainted by turpitude.

B. *Damages*

1. Regulation of Damages Actions for Breaches of European and/or Slovenian Antitrust

265. The PCA of 1993 as well as the PRCA of 1999 did not provide for any competition law specific instruments to alleviate private enforcement of competition law in Slovenia. They merely stated that anyone sustaining a loss as a consequence of competition law infringement could seek damages in accordance with the general rules of obligations.[372]

266. The PRCA-1 of 2008 has broadened its traditional administrative scope by including a new Article 62 regulating some of the core aspects of damages claims

370. See, for example, the CPO's decision in *The Bank Association of Slovenia*, No. 306-62/2005-59 of 15 Nov. 2006, operative part of the decision is available at (in Slovene): http://www.varstvo-konkurence.si/zakonodaja-in-dokumenti/ostali-dokumenti/arhiv-odlocb/odlocba49/; and in the *Institute of Public Health Maribor/DDD, Dezinfekcija, dezinsekcija, deratizacija, d.o.o.* case, Decision No. 306-100/2006-24 of 9 Nov. 2006, available at (in Slovene): http://www.varstvo-konkurence.si/fileadmin/varstvo-konkurence.si/pageuploads/ijz003.pdf. finding that the agreement on bid rigging on tenders issued by the *Public Economic Institute for Commodity Reserves* concluded between the *Institute of Public Health Maribor* and a commercial company *DDD, Dezinfekcija, dezinsekcija, deratizacija, d.o.o.* was prohibited and null.

371. Accordingly, Art. 181 of the CPrA states that any party with legal interest may bring an action at any time for the purpose of determining the existence or nonexistence of a legal relationship. See Galič, *Civil Procedure, Slovenia*, 89–90.

372. Article 27 of PCA of 1993, and Art. 44 of the PRCA of 1999. Until 1 Jan. 2002 when the CO came into force, rules on damages applicable in Slovenia were set out in the Yugoslav Law of Obligations of 1978.

within private enforcement of antitrust. When drafting the PRCA-1 of 2008, the Slovenian legislator had been inspired by the CJEU's case law as well as by the European Commission's activities aiming at fostering private enforcement of antitrust in the Member States. Although at that time no binding secondary legislation of the EU existed regulating antitrust damages actions, the drafters of the PRCA-1 had already modelled the Slovenian regime upon the planned future European regulation of antitrust damages claims enshrined, inter alia, in the European Commission's White Paper of April 2008 on damages actions for breach of EU antitrust rules.[373] Article 62/1 of the PRCA-1 stated that anyone who intentionally or negligently breached Articles 6 or 9 of the PRCA-1 or Articles 101 or 102 TFEU, is liable for damages resulting from such breach. Article 62/2 of the PRCA-1 provided for a binding effect of a final SCPA's or European Commission's decision finding a breach of Slovenian or European antitrust, whereby such obligation did not prevent Slovenian courts to apply Article 267 TFEU regulating preliminary ruling proceedings. Article 62/3 of the PRCA-1 stated that during the administrative proceedings before the SCPA or the European Commission, the limitation is suspended up until the finality of the proceedings. Article 62/4 obliged Slovenian courts to inform the SCPA of every action requesting damages for breaches of Slovenian or European antitrust.

267. Apart from case law of the CJEU (Courage and Crehan of 2001,[374] Manfredi of 2006,[375] City Motors of 2007,[376] X BV of 2009,[377] Pfleiderer of 2011[378] and Donau Chemie of 2013,[379] Otis of 2012,[380] Kone of 2013[381]) setting out some basic principles of private enforcement of European antitrust, and some general and more or less declarative statements on the importance of private enforcement within the

373. White paper on damages actions for breach of the EC antitrust rules, COM(2008) 165 final.

374. C-453/99 *Courage Ltd v. Bernard Crehan and Bernard Crehan v. Courage Ltd and Others*. In its ruling, the CJEU (ECJ at the time) confirmed undoubtedly for the first time that damages may be claimed for breaches of European antitrust, and explained that parties to anti-competitive agreements, too, may under specific circumstances claim damages.

375. *Vincenzo Manfredi v. Lloyd Adriatico Assicurazioni SpA (C-295/04), Antonio Cannito v. Fondiaria Sai SpA (C-296/04) and Nicolò Tricarico (C-297/04) and Pasqualina Murgolo (C-298/04) v. Assitalia SpA*. In its ruling, the CJEU (ECJ at that time) interpreted the *status quo* of European regulation of antitrust damages claims and set out the prerequisites for regulation of relevant issues by the Member States.

376. C-421/05 *City Motors Groep NV v. Citroën Belux NV* where the CJEU (ECJ at that time) confirmed its findings in *Courage and Crehan* and *Manfredi*.

377. C-429/07 *Inspecteur van de Belastingdienst v. X BV* where the CJEU (ECJ at the time) interpreted the European Commission's amicus curiae cooperation with national courts as laid down in Art. 15/3 of Regulation 1/2003.

378. C-360/09 *Pfleiderer AG v. Bundeskartellamt* where the CJEU has interpreted how the national courts are to tackle with the issue of access of private enforcement plaintiffs to leniency documentation.

379. C-536/11 *Bundeswettbewerbsbehörde v. Donau Chemie AG and others* where the CJEU had based its decision on its reasoning in *Pfleiderer*.

380. C-199/11 *Europese Gemeenschap v. Otis NV and others* where the CJEU has ruled on the question whether the European Commission may represent the EU in private damages actions against the undertakings which were found in breach of EU competition law established by the Commission.

381. C-557/12 *Kone AG, Otis GmbH, Schindler Aufzüge und Fahrtreppen GmbH, Schindler Liegenschaftsverwaltung GmbH, ThyssenKrupp Aufzüge GmbH v. Ö BB-Infrastruktur AG*, where the

EU entailed, for example, in Regulation 1/2003,[382] no detailed and systematic legislation on antitrust damages actions has been adopted within the EU until 2014. A Directive on rules governing damages actions for infringements of European antitrust was drafted by the European Commission in 2009. It was, however, faced with strong opposition (in particular due to its provisions on collective redress) and sup posedly therefore withdrawn from the debate. A new Directive on certain rules governing actions for damages under national law for infringements of the competition law provisions of the Member States and of the European Union was drafted by the Commission in June 2013[383] and was forwarded to the European Parliament and the Council in adoption. The new Directive 2014/104 was adopted on 26 November 2014.[384] It entered into force on 25 December 2014. Its implementation deadline was set to 27 December 2016. Slovenia implemented it in 2017 by adopting the law amending the existent PRCA-1.[385] The amendments entered into force on 20 May 2017. Article 22 of the directive sets out important rules as to temporal application of national legislation implementing the directive. These were implemented by Article 13 of the 2017 PRCA-1 amendment stating that Articles 62a, 62c-62f and 62l/4 of the PRCA-1 apply in damages proceedings starting after 26 December 2014 where the courts have not yet issued a first instance decision bringing the proceedings to an end. These provisions also apply in damages proceedings where an action was filed after 26 December 2014 and where the decision ending the proceedings was annulled. They do not, however, apply in damages proceedings where the action was filed before 26 December 2014 and the first instance decision was annulled after this date. If the first instance decision ending the proceedings was issued before 26 December 2014, these provisions do not apply and the proceedings take place in accordance with the rules existent prior to the 2017 PRCA-1 amendments.

268. The directive addresses the following issues:[386]

- full compensation principle (Chapter I, Articles 1/1 and 3);
- disclosure of evidence (Chapter II, Articles 5–8);
- effect of NCAs' decisions in private lawsuits (Chapter III, Article 9);

CJEU has stated that national legislation excluding liability of members of a cartel for the so-called umbrella effects in the form of higher prices set by cartelists' competitors, is not in line with EU law.

382. See, for example, para. 7 of the Preamble.
383. Proposal for a Directive of the European Parliament and of the Council on certain rules governing actions for damages under national law for infringements of the competition law provisions of the Member States and of the European Union (Text with EEA relevance), COM(2013) 404 final, available at (in English): http://eur-lex.europa.eu/LexUriServ/LexUriServ.do?uri=COM:2013:0404:FIN:EN:PDF.
384. Directive 2014/104/EU of the European Parliament and of the Council of 26 Nov. 2014 on certain rules governing actions for damages under national law for infringements of the competition law provisions of the Member States and of the European Union (Text with EEA relevance), OJ L 349, 5 Dec. 2014, 1–19; available at (also in English): http://eur-lex.europa.eu/legal-content/EN/TXT/PDF/?uri=CELEX:32014L0104&from=EN.
385. *ZPOmK-1G*, Official Gazette RS, No. 23/17.
386. For further analysis of the directive and its implementation in Slovenia, see Vlahek, *Nova Direktiva 2014/104 ...* ; Vlahek, *Challenges of Private Enforcement of Antitrust in Slovenia.*

- limitation periods (Chapter III, Article 10);
- joint and several liability of infringers (Chapter III, Article 11);
- passing-on (Chapter IV, Articles 12–16);
- quantification of harm and rebuttable presumption that cartels cause harm (Chapter V, Article 17);
- consensual dispute resolution (Chapter VI, Articles 18–19).

269. With regard to the rest of the rules which are still governed by national law, Article 4 of the directive requires the Member States to respect the principles of effectiveness and equivalence. Until the new directive was implemented into Slovenian law, the existing provisions of national law complemented the existent European regime as regards damages actions in cases of breaches of Articles 101 or 102 TFEU. With regard to breaches of Slovenian antitrust, only Slovenian law applied (although the concepts of EU law are of importance to purely national cases as well, since Slovenian competition law is to a great extent transcribed from European competition law). With respect to all those issues of antitrust damages actions that were not covered by EU law and/or by Article 62 of the PRCA-1, general provisions of the CO on damages applied.[387]

a. Full Compensation Principle

270. Under Slovenian law, full compensation of the real value of pecuniary loss suffered is guaranteed to the victims.[388] The actual loss, loss of profit as well as interest may be claimed.[389] Within private enforcement of competition law, only single damages may be awarded.[390] These principles accorded fully to the European regime as valid prior to the new directive, as well as to the current regime as set out in Article 3 of the new directive.[391] The latter states that the Member States shall ensure that any natural or legal person who has suffered harm caused by an infringement of competition law is able to claim and to obtain full compensation for that harm. Full compensation shall place a person who has suffered harm in the position in which that person would have been had the infringement of competition law not been committed and shall thus cover the right to compensation for actual

387. For further details, see Jadek Pensa in Juhart et al., *CO Commentary*, 665–683, 795–819; Plavšak in Juhart et al., *CO Commentary*, 683–742; Ahtik & Vlahek, *Določanje odškodnin v primeru kršitev antitrusta*.
388. See Plavšak in Juhart et al., *CO Commentary*, 755–760, 942–990; Jadek Pensa in Juhart et al., *CO Commentary* 919–921. Non-pecuniary damages may also be claimed under the CO, but within competition cases that is unlikely.
389. See Plavšak in Juhart et al., *CO Commentary*, 755–760; a detailed analysis of these notions useful for the parties is provided by Možina in Schulze (ed.), *Common European Sales Law*, 635–678; see also Ahtik & Vlahek, *Določanje odškodnin v primeru kršitev antitrusta*.
390. Slovenian tort law is based on the principle of full compensation and single damages. Only in exceptional cases, damages exceeding single damages may be awarded. According to the Copyright and Related Rights Act, for example, treble damages may be awarded if the act was breached intentionally or in gross negligence.
391. See Vlahek in Grilc et al., *PRCA-1 Commentary*, 495–500; Ahtik & Vlahek, *Določanje odškodnin v primeru kršitev antitrusta*.

loss and for loss of profit, plus the payment of interest. Full compensation under the directive shall not lead to overcompensation, whether by means of punitive, multiple or other types of damages.

271. The 2017 PRCA-1 amendment drafted Article 62 anew stating that anyone who suffered harm due to a competition law infringement has the right to damages under the general rules of the law of obligations unless the PRCA-1 states otherwise. It adds that the infringer who caused the harm is to compensate the victim default interest from the moment the harm was sustained to the moment of their payment irrespective of the moment the victim filed the damages action.

b. Disclosure of Evidence

272. Articles 5–8 of the new directive set out detailed rules on disclosure of evidence in private antitrust lawsuits. Article 5 lays down the rules on disclosure of evidence by the defendant and by third parties.[392] It requires the Member States to ensure that in proceedings relating to an action for damages, upon request of a claimant who has presented a reasoned justification containing reasonably available facts and evidence sufficient to support the plausibility of its claim for damages, national courts are able to order the defendant or a third party to disclose relevant evidence which lies in their control, subject to the conditions set out in the directive. Member States must also ensure that national courts are able, upon request of the defendant, to order the claimant or a third party to disclose relevant evidence.[393] The courts must have the power to order the disclosure of specified items of evidence or relevant categories of evidence circumscribed as precisely and as narrowly as possible on the basis of reasonably available facts in the reasoned justification. The courts must limit the disclosure of evidence to that which is proportionate. In determining proportionality, the courts must consider the legitimate interests of all parties and third parties concerned, in particular: the extent to which the claim or defence is supported by available facts and evidence justifying the request to disclose evidence; the scope and cost of disclosure, especially for any third parties concerned, including preventing non-specific searches for information which is unlikely to be of relevance for the parties in the procedure; and whether the evidence the disclosure of which is sought contains confidential information, especially concerning any third parties, and what arrangements are in place for protecting such confidential information. Further, the Member States had to ensure that national courts have the power to order the disclosure of evidence containing confidential information where they consider it relevant to the action for damages, and that when ordering the disclosure of such information, national courts have at their disposal effective measures to protect such information. The interest of undertakings to avoid actions for damages following an infringement of competition law shall not constitute an interest that warrants protection. When ordering the disclosure of evidence, the

392. Without prejudice to Art. 5/4,7 and to Art. 6, Art. 5 does not prevent the Member States from maintaining or introducing rules which would lead to wider disclosure of evidence.

393. According to Art. 5/1, this paragraph is without prejudice to the rights and obligations of national courts under Regulation (EC) No. 1206/2001.

courts must give full effect to applicable legal professional privilege under EU law or national law. Those from whom disclosure is sought must be provided with an opportunity to be heard before a national court orders disclosure. According to Galič, the leading Slovenian Professor of civil procedure, Article 5 adopts a middle-way solution between the full scale US style discovery, and the strict traditional civil law discovery regime.[394]

273. Articles 6 and 7 of the directive set out additional rules for disclosure of evidence contained in the NCA's file trying to eliminate a possible hurdle for a successful leniency programme (and thus for a successful public enforcement of antitrust) stemming from the fear of potential leniency applicants that their leniency statements could assist the victims of the infringements in claiming damages from them.[395] Before the adoption of the directive, the CJEU's interpretation in Pfleiderer[396] and Donau Chemie[397] was of some, albeit vague assistance to the undertakings in determining the plausibility that access to leniency statements would be granted by the national court. The new directive regulates the questions of access to leniency statements more unambiguously and enables the undertakings to decide with more certainty as to future development of their case to apply for leniency or not. Article 6 of the directive[398] states that when assessing, in accordance with Article 5/3 of the directive, the proportionality of an order to disclose information, national courts must, in addition to what is required by Article 5/3, consider: whether the request has been formulated specifically with regard to the nature, subject matter or contents of documents submitted to a competition authority or held in the file thereof, rather than by a non-specific application concerning documents submitted to a competition authority; whether the party requesting disclosure is doing so in relation to an action for damages before a national court; and –in relation to Article 6/5, 10, or upon request of a competition authority pursuant to Article 6/11 – the need to safeguard the effectiveness of the public enforcement of competition law. According to Article 6/5, national courts may order the disclosure of the following categories of evidence only after a competition authority, by adopting a decision or otherwise, has closed its proceedings: information that was prepared by a natural or legal person specifically for the proceedings of a competition authority; information that the competition authority has drawn up and sent to the parties in the course of its proceedings; and settlement submissions that have been withdrawn. According to Article 6/6 of the directive, the national courts may not at any time order a party or a third party to disclose leniency statements and settlement submissions. A claimant may, however, present a reasoned request that a national court access such evidence for the sole purpose of ensuring that their contents correspond to the definitions of 'leniency statement' or 'settlement submission' as set

394. Galič, *Disclosure of Documents in Private Antitrust Enforcement Litigation.*
395. For details as to leniency programme in Slovenia, see Podobnik, *Program prizanesljivosti* ... .
396. C-360/09 *Pfleiderer AG v. Bundeskartellamt.*
397. C-536/11 *Bundeswettbewerbsbehörde v. Donau Chemie AG and others.*
398. Article 6 is without prejudice to the rules and practices on public access to documents under Regulation (EC) No. 1049/2001, and to the rules and practices under EU or national law on the protection of internal documents of competition authorities and of correspondence between competition authorities.

out in Article 2 of the directive. In that assessment, national courts may request assistance only from the competent competition authority. The authors of the evidence in question may also have the possibility to be heard, but the court must in no case permit other parties or third parties access to that evidence. If only parts of the evidence are covered by such request, the remaining parts thereof shall, depending on the category under which they fall, be released in accordance with the relevant rules of Article 6. The disclosure of evidence in the file of a competition authority that does not fall into any of the categories listed in Article 6 may be ordered in actions for damages at any time, without prejudice to Article 6. Member States shall ensure that national courts request the disclosure from a competition authority of evidence included in its file only where no party or third party is reasonably able to provide that evidence. To the extent that a competition authority is willing to state its views on the proportionality of disclosure requests, it may, acting on its own initiative, submit observations to the national court before which a disclosure order is sought.

274. Article 8 of the directive requires the Member States to empower the courts to effectively impose penalties on parties, third parties and their legal representatives in case they breach their duties as to disclosure of evidence.

275. Galič stated with regard to the new European regime of disclosure in antitrust damages cases that: '[t]he creation of EU-wide litigation disclosure mechanism in the Antitrust Damages Directive will [...] inevitably have to have general impacts for civil procedure law in Slovenia[...]'[399] and that '[i]n Slovenia, a transposition of the Directive's litigation disclosure mechanism will require a fundamental change in the very key procedural principles.'[400] After making an in-depth analysis of Slovenian rules on disclosure, he concludes that:

> it is true that the transposition of the litigation disclosure mechanism of the Antitrust Damages Directive will undermine the existing principles of Slovenian civil procedure. This however goes on the account of the fact that with regard to disclosure of evidence, the Slovenian law is outdated and is partially based on erroneous premises. Therefore the required transposition of the Directive's requirements should therefore be perceived as a positive step. This step will however will be successful only if a general reassessment of the disclosure of evidence in Slovenian civil procedure law will follow.[401]

276. This signalled the need for very deliberate legislative steps that were to be taken within the project of implementation of the new directive that should (and eventually did) serve also for reforming relevant aspects of Slovenian law outside the sphere of private enforcement of antitrust.[402] In Slovenia, there was no direct regulation of access to SCPA's leniency documents for the purposes of civil law

399. Galič, *Disclosure of Documents in Private Antitrust Enforcement Litigation.*
400. *Ibid.*
401. *Ibid.*
402. Namely, the general rules of the CPrA on disclosure were also amended.

enforcement until the 2017 PRCA-1 amendment.[403] The Decree on the procedure for granting immunity from fines and reduction of fines in cartel cases stated only that leniency applications are deemed business secrets,[404] Public Information Access Act[405] and its provisions on exceptions to grant access,[406] as well as general provisions of the CPrA[407] were thus the relevant legal basis.[408] Once the directive was implemented, the PRCA-1 contains detailed rules on disclosure in Articles 62a, 62č, 62d, 62e and 62f. The implementation of the rules of the damages directive on disclosure of evidence into Slovenian law served also as a forum for the debate on the amendment of the general rules on disclosure set out in the CPrA.

c. Effect of NCAs' Decisions

277. Inspired by Article 16 of Regulation 1/2003, Article 62/2 of the PRCA-1 in force already before the 2017 PRCA-1 enactment alleviated the plaintiff's position regarding the burden of proving that antitrust (be it European or Slovenian) had been breached as it provided that (without prejudice to the rights and obligations under Article 267 TFEU) the national courts assessing damages claims are bound by final decisions issued by the SCPA and the European Commission finding the infringement. Thus, in such cases, the plaintiffs needed to only prove that they had sustained loss, that the defendant was at fault, and that there was a causal relationship between the infringement and the loss sustained. It is important to note that, at least with regard to cases of European antitrust breaches, Article 62/2 of the PRCA-1 was to be read in conjunction with Article 16/1 of Regulation 1/2003 which sets out additional rules to be observed by the courts that have at the time not been copied in the PRCA-1.[409] It must also be underscored that already prior to inserting Article 62/2 into the PRCA-1, Slovenian courts were in principle bound by final administrative acts, such as the SCPA's final decision. This was stressed also by the High Court in Ljubljana in its recent judgment of 21 November 2013 in the *Blitz v. Kolosej* case.[410]

278. The new directive provided for a novel set of rules regulating the effect of Member States' NCAs' decisions. Article 9/1 of the directive requires the Member States to ensure that an infringement of competition law found by a final decision of a national competition authority or by a review court is deemed to be irrefutably established for the purposes of an action for damages brought before their national

403. See Vlahek & Podobnik, *Slovenia*, 285–287.
404. Article 6 of the Decree.
405. Sl. *Zakon o dostopu do nformacij javnega značaja (ZDIJZ)*, Official Gazette RS, No. 24/03, with further amendments.
406. Article 6 of the Act.
407. Articles 227–229 and 231–234 of the CPrA.
408. In its Judgment No. I Cpg 708/2013 of 21 Nov. 2013 in *T2 v. Telekom Slovenije*, the High Court of Ljubljana stated that the PRCA-1 provisions on access to the SCPA file apply only to the CPO administrative proceedings, not to private enforcement proceedings.
409. For further details, see Vlahek in Grilc, *PRCA -1 Commentary*, 504–510.
410. For further details on the case, see Pt. I, Ch. 5, §2, II B 2 of this monograph.

courts under Article 101 or 102 TFEU or under national competition law. According to Article 9/2, they must also ensure that where a final decision is taken in another Member State, that final decision may, in accordance with national law, be presented before their national courts as at least prima facie evidence that an infringement of competition law has occurred and, as appropriate, may be assessed along with any other evidence adduced by the parties. Article 9/3 adds, however, that the rules of Article 9/1,2 are without prejudice to the rights and obligations of national courts under Article 267 TFEU, i.e., to stay the national judicial proceedings and ask the Court of Justice for a preliminary ruling.

279. The rules set out in Article 9/1,3 of the directive were laid down in Article 62/2 of the PRCA-1 by Slovenian legislator already in 2008, while the rule set out in Article 9/2 of the new directive had to be implemented accordingly by the 2017 PRCA-1 amendment.[411] The rules on the effect of the NCAs' decisions are now laid down in Article 62g of the PRCA-1.

280. In Slovenia, the plaintiffs have initially been filing damages actions mostly as stand-alone actions. The CPO was often inefficient in the assessment of the cases and when it finally issued the decisions, the undertakings have instituted lengthy court review proceedings. In order to avoid any time allowed under the statute of limitations from running out, the parties have decided to file lawsuits alleging all elements of tort liability. Should the SCPA issue a final and binding decision in the meanwhile finding the infringement, the courts would be bound by such decision, otherwise they would have to assess the alleged infringement as well. The civil law judges are presumably mostly reluctant to cope with the assessment of the alleged anti-competitive practices and tend to stall the stand-alone damages proceedings and await the SCPA's decision to become final and binding. It is important to note that in some cases in which private lawsuits are pending, the CPO terminated administrative proceedings according to Article 40 of the PRCA-1, as it had not found that an infringement had taken place. In such decisions, the CPO did not find that there was no infringement; it merely found that it had not found the infringement leaving the courts with the full assessment of the undertakings' practices. However, as the SCPA itself was unable to find an infringement, the courts would plausibly decide in favour of the defendants.

d. Limitation

281. Another antitrust-specific provision of the PRCA-1 existent already prior to the 2017 PRCA-1 amendment was Article 62/3 reflecting the CJEU's reasoning in Manfredi as well as the European Commission's ideas entailed in its White Paper as regards the effect of the initiation of administrative infringement proceedings on the limitation period for damages claims. This article provided that the limitation

411. See Vlahek & Podobnik, *Slovenia*, 287–289.

period (for damages claims only)[412] is suspended while public enforcement of competition rules by the SCPA or the Commission (and review courts) is still ongoing. Article 62/3 of the PRCA-1 which entered into force on 26 April 2008, posed uncertainties as to its temporal application as prior to its entry into force, suspension of limitation during the public enforcement proceedings was not set out. In cases where the limitation period started to run (but had not yet lapsed) already prior to entry into force of Article 62/3 of the PRCA-1, it was disputed in business practice whether Article 62/3 enabling suspension of limitation could be activated in such cases or not.[413]

282. Article 10 of the new directive set out detailed rules on when the limitation period begins to run, the duration of the limitation period and the circumstances under which the period is interrupted or suspended.[414] It states that limitation periods shall not begin to run before the infringement of competition law has ceased and the claimant knows, or can reasonably be expected to know: of the behaviour and the fact that it constitutes an infringement of competition law; of the fact that the infringement of competition law caused harm to it; and the identity of the infringer. It requires the Member States to ensure that the limitation periods for bringing actions for damages are at least five years, and that a limitation period is suspended or, depending on national law, interrupted, if a competition authority takes action for the purpose of the investigation or its proceedings in respect of an infringement of competition law to which the action for damages relates. The suspension shall end at the earliest one year after the infringement decision has become final or after the proceedings are otherwise terminated.

283. The provisions of Article 62/3 of the PRCA-1 had to be amended in order to implement it accordingly. Until then, CJEU's case law, Article 62/3 of the PRCA-1 and general national rules on the statute of limitations as set out in the CO applied.[415]

The CO is the basic law regulating limitation and (cogent) limitation periods for bringing a claim.[416] Once the statute of limitation runs out the right to claim performance ceases (but the debtor may still perform his or her obligation voluntarily, the creditor's right itself does therefore not cease).[417] Limitation applies only if the other party in proceedings refers to it, the courts must therefore not take account of

---

412. As in cases of overcharges, for example, the claim based on unjustified enrichment will most possibly be filed, it is not clear whether rules of Art. 62 dealing explicitly with damages claims could be applied. This should be addressed by the legislator as well.

413. For further details, see Vlahek, *Challenges of Private Enforcement of Antitrust in Slovenia*; Vlahek & Podobnik, *Slovenia*, 276.

414. For further details on the regime set out in the directive, see Vlahek & Podobnik, *Provisions of the damages directive ...* .

415. For details on limitation under Slovenian law, see Pt. I, Ch. 5, §2, II B 1 (iv) of this monograph.

416. Articles 335–370 CO.

417. Under Slovenian law, there is a distinction between limitation and so-called preclusion, the latter denoting situations in which a right itself ceases to exist (Art. 345 of the CO). According to the predominant view of the courts and legal theory, the courts must take account of preclusion *ex officio*.

limitation ex officio.[418] General limitation period is five years, while with regard to claims arising from commercial contracts, limitation period is three years.[419] Limitation period for damages claims[420] is three years as of when the victim became aware of the damage and the person causing damage, and the claim must be brought within five years as of when the damage had actually occurred. If the damage is caused by contractual breach, the limitation period is that as set out for contractual claims. Unless the law provides otherwise, the limitation period starts to run the first day after the creditor had the right to claim the performance, or after the debtor had breached his or her duty not to act.[421] The CO sets out also detailed rules on the suspension and the interruption of limitation.[422] One of the basic rules is that limitation is not interrupted by merely addressing a claim to the debtor. In order to interrupt limitation, the creditor must file an action with the courts or other competent institution.

284. Limitation in competition damages actions is now regulated in Article 62j of the PRCA-1 and the CO applies only with regard to those issues not covered by the specific provisions of Article 62j of the PRCA-1. The PRCA-1 now sets out a short subjective five-year limitation period as well as a long stop period of ten years. Both periods cannot start before the infringement has ceased and can be suspended during the administrative proceedings before the NCA and up to a year after the finality of the NCA's decision.[423]

e. Joint and Several Liability of Infringers

285. Article 11 of the new directive stipulated *a novo* joint and several liability of infringers. Article 11/1 states that undertakings which have infringed competition law through joint behaviour are jointly and severally liable for the harm caused by the infringement of competition law, with the effect that each of those undertakings is bound to compensate for the harm in full, and the injured party has the right to require full compensation from any of them until he has been fully compensated. Article 11/2,3 states that by way of derogation from this rule, the Member States shall ensure that, without prejudice to the right of full compensation, where the infringer is a small- or medium-sized enterprise (SME) as defined in the relevant EU law, the infringer is liable only to its own direct and indirect purchasers where: its market share in the relevant market was below 5% at any time during the infringement of competition law; and the application of the normal rules of joint and several liability would irretrievably jeopardize its economic viability and cause its assets to lose all their value. This derogation does not apply where: the SME has

418. Article 335 of the CO. Once the limitation period runs out, the debtor may, however, renounce the limitation (Arts 340–341 of the CO).
419. Article 349 of the CO.
420. Article 352 of the CO. Specific provisions for damages caused by criminal acts and corruption are set out in Arts 353 and 354 of the CO.
421. Article 336 of the CO.
422. Articles 358–370 of the CO.
423. For further details on this limitation regime and its implementation, see Vlahek & Lutman, *Uredítev zastaranja* ... ; and Vlahek & Podobnik, *Provisions of the damages directive* ... .

led the infringement of competition law or has coerced other undertakings to participate therein; or it has previously been found to have infringed competition law. Article 11/4 states that by way of derogation from Article 11/1, the Member States shall ensure that an immunity recipient is jointly and severally liable: to its direct or indirect purchasers or providers; and to other injured parties only where full compensation cannot be obtained from the other undertakings that were involved in the same infringement of competition law, whereby any limitation period applicable to such cases has to be reasonable and sufficient to allow injured parties to bring such actions. Further, Article 11/5 requires the Member States to ensure that an infringer may recover a contribution from any other infringer, the amount of which shall be determined in the light of their relative responsibility for the harm caused by the infringement of competition law. The amount of contribution of an infringer which has been granted immunity from fines under a leniency programme must not exceed the amount of the harm it caused to its own direct or indirect purchasers or providers. Finally, Article 11/6 requires the Member States to ensure that, to the extent the infringement of competition law caused harm to injured parties other than the direct or indirect purchasers or providers of the infringers, the amount of any contribution from an immunity recipient to other infringers must be determined in the light of its relative responsibility for that harm.

286. Already prior to the implementation of the directive into the PRCA-1, the general rule on joint and several liability for damages was set out in Article 186 of the CO.[424] It corresponded to the basic rule set out in Article 11/1 of the new directive, while the rules set out in Article 11/2,3,4,5,6, had to be implemented into the PRCA-1 accordingly. They are now laid down in Articles 62h and 62i of the PRCA-1.[425]

f. Passing-On

287. Article 12 of the directive sets out the rules on passing-on of overcharges and the right to full compensation. To ensure the full effectiveness of the right to full compensation, the Member States must ensure that compensation of harm can be claimed by anyone who suffered it, irrespective of whether they are direct or indirect purchasers from an infringer, and that compensation of harm exceeding that caused by the infringement of competition law to the claimant, as well as the absence of liability of the infringer, are avoided. To that end, the must lay down procedural rules appropriate to ensure that compensation for actual loss at any level of the supply chain does not exceed the overcharge harm suffered at that level. The directive adds that its chapter on the passing-on shall be without prejudice to the right of an injured party to claim and obtain compensation for loss of profits due to a full or partial passing-on of the overcharge. Further, the Member States must ensure that the rules of the chapter on the passing-on apply accordingly where the

424. Vlahek & Podobnik, *Slovenia*, 297–280.
425. For further details, see Vlahek *Nova Direktiva 2014/104 …* , 195–196; and Vlahek, *Novosti …*, 576–580.

infringement of competition law relates to a supply to the infringer. The courts must have the power to estimate, in accordance with national procedures, the share of any overcharge that was passed on.

288. Article 13 of the directive regulates the passing-on defence. It requires the Member States to ensure that the defendant in an action for damages can invoke as a defence against a claim for damages the fact that the claimant passed on the whole or part of the overcharge resulting from the infringement of competition law. The burden of proving that the overcharge was passed on shall be on the defendant, who may reasonably require disclosure from the claimant or from third parties.

289. Article 14 lays down the rules on indirect purchasers. Where in an action for damages the existence of a claim for damages or the amount of compensation to be awarded depends on whether, or to what degree, an overcharge was passed on to the claimant, taking into account the commercial practice that price increases are passed on down the supply chain, the burden of proving the existence and scope of such a passing-on shall rest with the claimant, who may reasonably require disclosure from the defendant or from third parties. The indirect purchaser shall be deemed to have proven that a passing-on to that indirect purchaser occurred where that indirect purchaser has shown that: the defendant has committed an infringement of competition law; the infringement of competition law has resulted in an overcharge for the direct purchaser of the defendant; and the indirect purchaser has purchased the goods or services that were the object of the infringement of competition law, or has purchased goods or services derived from or containing them. This shall not, however, apply where the defendant can demonstrate credibly to the satisfaction of the court that the overcharge was not, or was not entirely, passed on to the indirect purchaser.

290. Article 15 of the directive regulates actions for damages by claimants from different levels in the supply chain. To avoid actions for damages by claimants from different levels in the supply chain leading to a multiple liability or to an absence of liability of the infringer, the Member States must ensure that in assessing whether the burden of proof resulting from the application of Articles 13 and 14 of the directive is satisfied, national courts seized of an action for damages are able, by means available under EU or national law, to take due account of any of the following: actions for damages that are related to the same infringement of competition law, but that are brought by claimants from other levels in the supply chain, judgments resulting from such actions for damages; relevant information in the public domain resulting from the public enforcement of competition law.[426]

291. Article 16 of the directive requires the European Commission to issue guidelines for national courts on how to estimate the share of the overcharge which

426. This Article shall be without prejudice to the rights and obligations of national courts under Article 30 of Regulation (EU) No. 1215/2012.

was passed on to the indirect purchaser. These guidelines were published in August 2019 in the form of the Commission's communication.[427]

292. Rules on passing-on of overcharges as set out in Chapter IV of the new directive had to be implemented into the PRCA-1. Although Slovenian general legislation already accorded to the basic rule that compensation of harm can be claimed by anyone who suffered it, irrespective of whether they are direct or indirect purchasers, that the defendant may invoke the passing-on defence, etc., detailed substantive as well as procedural rules regarding passing-on of overcharges had to be inserted into the PRCA-1 in order to implement the directive accordingly in the antitrust-specific legislation.[428] They are laid down in Articles 62l and 62m of the PRCA-1. Commission guidelines for national courts on how to estimate the share of the overcharge which was passed on to the indirect purchaser will undoubtedly be of additional assistance to Slovenian courts.

g. Quantification of Harm

293. Until the adoption of the new directive, quantification of harm was addressed only by EU soft-law, i.e., Commission *Communication on quantifying harm in actions for damages based on breaches of Article 101 or 102 of the TFEU* of 2013.[429] It is now regulated in Article 17 of the new directive that requires the Member States to ensure that neither the burden nor the standard of proof required for the quantification of harm renders the exercise of the right to damages practically impossible or excessively difficult. The national courts must be empowered, in accordance with national procedures, to estimate the amount of harm if it is established that a claimant suffered harm but it is practically impossible or excessively difficult precisely to quantify the harm suffered on the basis of the evidence available. The directive also states that it shall be presumed that cartel infringements cause harm and that the infringer shall have the right to rebut that presumption. The Member States were also required to ensure that, in proceedings relating to an action for damages, a national competition authority may, upon request of a national court, assist that national court with respect to the determination of the quantum of damages where that national competition authority considers such assistance to be appropriate.

294. Under the general rules of Slovenian civil procedure, the burden of proof rests upon the party who raises an issue (more precisely, who is obliged to raise an

427. Communication from the Commission, Guidelines for national courts on how to estimate the share of overcharge which was passed on to the indirect purchaser (2019/C 267/07), C 267/4, 9 Aug. 2019.

428. See Vlahek & Podobnik, *Slovenia*, 282–283.

429. Communication from the Commission on quantifying harm in actions for damages based on breaches of Art. 101 or 102 of the Treaty on the Functioning of the European Union, (2013/C 167/07), C(2013) 3440, available at (in English): http://eur-lex.europa.eu/LexUriServ/LexUriServ.do?uri=OJ:C:2013:167:0019:0021:EN:PDF. Other documents on which the communication is based, are available at (in English): http://ec.europa.eu/competition/antitrust/actionsdamages/documents.html.

issue).[430] There are also some explicit rules concerning shifting of the burden of proof,[431] but do not apply with regard to harm and its quantum. In Slovenia, the standard of proof (describing the amount and quality of evidence required to discharge a burden of proof) is very high.[432] Pursuant to Article 215 of the CPrA, the judge should decide according to the rules on the burden of proof (the burden rests upon the party who raises an issue) if he or she cannot reliably establish the (non-)existence of the disputed fact. The judge must be (practically) convinced (persuaded) about the existence of a certain fact, if not, the judge should find against the party whom a burden of proof for this fact rests upon (thus, even if the court finds it more probable – but still not with a degree beyond a doubt of a reasonable person – that this fact actually exists).[433] Article 216/1 of the CPrA provides that when the liability of a party is established, and only the quantum remains in dispute, a court may, in exceptional circumstances, use judicial discretion to establish the missing facts.[434] The court may act in such manner if unreasonable difficulties would ensue the determination of these facts through means of evidence; for example, the cost of evidence would be entirely disproportionate to the value of the claim.[435] It is important to note that in such cases, judicial discretion is applied to establish the facts (e.g., the amount of damages) and not to interpret the law (e.g., the notion of 'just satisfaction').[436] These rules had to be redrafted within antitrust private enforcement in order to implement Article 17/1 of the new directive into Slovenian legislation.[437] The novel Article 62k lays down the rules on the judicial discretion in determining the amount of the damages. Slovenian courts have already started tackling with quantification of damages in antitrust cases. One of the seminal judgments as regards the burden of proof and the method of quantification of damages in antitrust cases was the judgment of the High Court in Ljubljana in the *ABM v. Telekom Slovenije* case.[438] In applying Article 216/1 of the CPrA, the High Court stressed that in antitrust damages cases it is focal that the parties[439] reveal to the court and prove all relevant facts on their business activities. Unless they do so, the court is faced with the so-called cognitive crisis. The method of quantification

---

430. Galič, *Civil Procedure, Slovenia*, 174.
431. *Ibid.*
432. *Ibid*, 175.
433. *Ibid.* As further pointed out by Galič, in the doctrine as well as in case law, the harshness of the high standard of proof (combined with a very limited scope of pre-trial production of evidence and a very limited access to evidence in the possession of the opponent) is sometimes rectified by shifting a burden of proof. Some authors also try to relax the standard of proof and propose a solution that a standard of proof in a civil case should not, as Art. 215 of the CPrA could imply, be practically identical as the one in criminal cases (i.e., beyond reasonable doubt), and opt for a clearly overwhelming degree of probability to be sufficient in a civil case. Galič, *Civil Procedure, Slovenia*, 175.
434. Galič, *Civil Procedure, Slovenia*, 176.
435. *Ibid.*, 176–177.
436. *Ibid.*, 177.
437. See Vlahek & Podobnik, *Slovenia*, 280–282.
438. No. I Cpg 125/2013 of 28 May 2013, available at (in Slovene): http://www.sodisce.si/znanje/sodna_praksa/visja_sodisca/2012032113061939/.
439. Even the defendant if certain facts favouring the claimant who cannot prove the damage are within the defendant's 'cognitive sphere' and thus for him to rely to and prove.

applied by the High Court (using, inter alia, the infringer's profit as the claimant's profit in the but-for scenario) was later confirmed by the Supreme Court of RS.[440]

295. Article 17/2 as well as Article 17/3 of the new directive also had to be implemented anew in the Slovenian legal system. They are now mirrored in Article 62k of the PRCA-1 stating that it is presumed that cartels cause harm unless the infringer proves otherwise. The same article also regulates the courts' cooperation with the NCAs regarding the determination of the damages amount.

h. Consensual Dispute Resolution

296. Articles 18 and 19 of the new directive address the issue of potential consensual resolution of competition law damages cases and its effects on damages actions and the setting of fines.[441]

297. Article 18 sets out the rules on suspensive and other effects of consensual dispute resolution. Article 18/1 requires the Member States to ensure that the limitation period for bringing an action for damages is suspended for the duration of any consensual dispute resolution process. The suspension shall apply only with regard to those parties that are or that were involved or represented in the consensual dispute resolution. Article 18/2 states that without prejudice to provisions of national law in matters of arbitration, the Member States must ensure that national courts seized of an action for damages may suspend their proceedings for up to two years where the parties thereto are involved in consensual dispute resolution concerning the claim covered by that action for damages. Article 18/3 adds that a competition authority may consider compensation paid as a result of a consensual settlement and prior to its decision imposing a fine to be a mitigating factor.

298. Article 19 of the directive regulates the effect of consensual settlements on subsequent actions for damages. It requires the Member States to ensure that, following a consensual settlement, the claim of the settling injured party is reduced by the settling co-infringer's share of the harm that the infringement of competition law inflicted upon the injured party. Any remaining claim of the settling injured party shall be exercised only against non-settling co-infringers. Non-settling co-infringers shall not be permitted to recover contribution for the remaining claim from the settling co-infringer. The Member States shall ensure that where the non-settling co-infringers cannot pay the damages that correspond to the remaining claim of the settling injured party, the settling injured party may exercise the remaining claim against the settling co-infringer. Such derogation may be expressly excluded under the terms of the consensual settlement. When determining the amount of contribution that a co-infringer may recover from any other co-infringer in accordance with their relative responsibility for the harm caused by the infringement of competition

440. No. III Ips 98/2013 of 23 May 2014, available at (in Slovene): http://www.sodisce.si/znanje/sodna_praksa/search.php?q=III%20Ips%201/2008&database%5BSOVS%5D=SOVS&_submit=i%EF%BF%BD%C3%A8i&order=date&direction=desc&page=0&id=2012032113067865.
441. See Vlahek & Podobnik, *Slovenia*, 290–293.

law, national courts shall take due account of any damages paid pursuant to a prior consensual settlement involving the relevant co-infringer.

299. Under Slovenian law, limitation period is interrupted (Sl. pretrgano; it starts running anew), its run is not merely suspended (Sl. zadržano; it does not run during the suspension) by filing a lawsuit or by performing any other act against the debtor before the court or other competent authority in order to determine, secure or collect a claim.[442] Limitation period can therefore not be interrupted by any activity oriented to enforcing the claim, but only by activities initiated before a competent authority.[443] According to theory and court practice, filing a request for arbitration or statement of claim in arbitration proceedings equals filing a claim with the court.[444] Such conclusion can be derived from both Article 365 of the CO as well as Article 38 of the Arbitration Act[445] stating that as regards the parties, arbitration award has the effect of a final and binding court judgment. It is not clear whether Article 18/1 of the new directive (and the corresponding Article 62n of the PRCA-1) requiring suspension of limitation during any consensual dispute resolution process (including arbitration as ensues from paragraph 48 of the Preamble to the directive) is to be applied also to arbitration.

300. A specific provision on limitation periods is set out in Article 17 of the Mediation in Civil and Commercial Matters Act[446] stating that limitation periods are suspended (not interrupted as in the case of court or arbitration proceedings or other proceedings before the competent authority as set out in Article 365 of the CO) during mediation proceedings (whereby mediation proceedings are defined in Article 3 as proceedings in which the parties voluntarily and with assistance of a neutral third person (mediator) attempt to reach an amicable settlement of their dispute arising out of or in connection to a contractual or other legal relationship, irrespective of how such proceedings are named or referred to (mediation, conciliation, dispute intervention, or similar). Such regulation corresponds to the aim of Article 18/1 of the new directive, but specific provisions were nevertheless inserted into the PRCA-1 (Article 62n) in order to regulate antitrust-specific issues at one place.

301. Article 18/2 of the new directive states that, without prejudice to provisions of national law in matters of arbitration, Member States shall ensure that national courts seized of an action for damages may suspend (for a maximum of two

---

442. Articles 365 and 369 of the CO.
443. Judgment of the Supreme Court of RS No. III Ips 91/2004 of 31 Jan. 2006, available (in Slovene) at: http://www.sodisce.si/znanje/sodna_praksa/vrhovno_sodisce_rs/31766/.
444. Damjan, *Učinek mediacije na tek rokov*, 40. Confirmed, *inter alia*, by the following judgments: Judgment of High Court in Celje No. VSC Cp 1488/2001 of 30 May 2002; Judgment of the Supreme Court of RS No. III Ips 91/2004 of 31 Jan. 2006, available (in Slovene) at: http://www.sodisce.si/znanje/sodna_praksa/.
445. Sl. *Zakon o arbitraži (ZArbit)*, Official Gazette RS, No. 45/08.
446. Sl. *Zakon o mediaciji v civilnih in gospodarskih zadevah (ZMCGZ)*, Official Gazette RS, No. 56/08. See also the newly enacted Law on Out-of-Court Consumer Dispute Resolution (Sl. *Zakon o izvensodnem reševanju potrošniških sporov (ZIsRPS)*, Official Gazette RS, No. 81/15) that entered into force on 14. Nov. 2015.

years) proceedings where the parties to those proceedings are involved in consensual dispute resolution concerning the claim covered by that action for damages. Article 305b of the CPrA states that if both parties agree to try to resolve their dispute through a scheme of ADR (out-of-court or court-annexed),[447] the court suspends the litigation (for maximum of three months). Article 15 of the Act on Alternative Dispute Resolution in Judicial Matters,[448] similarly, states that in cases where the parties agree that they will try to solve the dispute by means of judicial alternative dispute resolution regulated in that act, the court may suspend the court proceedings (Sl. prekinitev postopka) for a maximum time of three months, and refer the parties to such dispute resolution. Further, Article 19 of the Act on Alternative Dispute Resolution in Judicial Matters authorizes the court to suspend its proceedings for a maximum time of three months if it decides (on its own initiative according to the circumstances of each case) to refer the parties to mediation organized within the court. In addition, Article 209 of the CPrA enables the parties to agree that the court proceedings are stayed (Sl. mirovanje postopka) until any of the parties moves for the continuation thereof, whereby such a motion cannot be made until three months have lapsed since the day when the proceedings were stayed. If none of the parties has moved for the continuation of the proceedings within four months from the day when they were stayed, the action is deemed to be withdrawn.[449] The new rules of Article 18/2 of the directive differ to some extent from the rules already laid down in Slovenian legislation, and thus had to be implemented anew into Slovenian legislation. They are laid down in Article 62n of the PRCA-1.

302. Article 18/3 of the new directive states that a competition authority may consider that compensation paid as a result of a consensual settlement and prior to its decision imposing a fine to be a mitigating factor in the setting thereof. As has been mentioned in Part I, Chapter 5, §1, IV A of this monograph, the minor offences legislation (the MOA-1 which applies subsidiarily to the PRCA-1) states which circumstances of the case are in particular to be taken into account by the authority as mitigating factor. The offender's conduct after committing the offence, in particular whether he or she has recompensated the damage, is listed among them. Slovenian legislation therefore already paid due regard to the fact that the offender has repaid damages to the victims of the infringement. A specific rule for competition law infringements was also inserted in the new Article 62o of the PRCA-1.

303. Article 19 of the new directive had to be addressed by the Slovenian legislator in order to implement the directive appropriately. The relevant provisions are now laid down in Article 62o of the PRCA-1.

447. Galič, *Civil Procedure, Slovenia*, 159. Galič explains that the CPrA acknowledges to a limited extent also the forms of out-of-court ADR – irrespective of the fact whether these are performed independently from the court or whether they concern the programmes of ADR established as court-annexed. Galič, *Civil Procedure, Slovenia*, 114.

448. Sl. *Zakon o alternativnem reševanju sodnih sporov (ZARSS)*, Official Gazette RS, No. 97/09, with further amendments.

449. Galič, *Civil Procedure, Slovenia*, 160.

i. Relevant Issues Not Covered in the New Directive

304. All issues that are not covered in the directive are to be resolved under national legislation that has to respect the principles of effectiveness and equivalence as set out in Article 4 of the new directive (and in the relevant case law of the CJEU).

305. One of the issues that might be relevant in antitrust private enforcement is, for example, the infringer's fault which is not addressed by the directive, thereby offering various interpretations (e.g., that it is for the Member States to regulate this question; that fault is not a relevant element in antitrust damages liability; that the infringer is irrefutably deemed liable for damages caused by the infringement, etc.).[450]

306. The previous Article 62/1 of the PRCA-1 (i.e., the one before the 2017 PRCA-1 amendment) established explicitly tort liability for infringements of Slovenian or European antitrust: Anyone intentionally or negligently breaching Article 6 or 9 of the PRCA-1 or Article 101 or 102 TFEU, is liable for the damage sustained by that. The redrafted provisions of the PRCA-1 are silent on the issue of fault. If the general rules of tort liability based on fault apply, then the plaintiff will have to show that the following elements have been met, i.e., that the defendant has breached European and/or Slovenian antitrust, that the plaintiff has sustained a loss, and that there is a causal link between the breach and the loss sustained, while the defendant's fault, i.e., that it committed a wrongful act intentionally or negligently, will be presumed according to Article 131 of the CO. It must be stressed that Slovenian legislation adopts the concept of fault liability with shifted burden of proof concerning fault. The alleging party need not prove that the defendant acted wrongfully. On the contrary, the alleged wrongdoer has to prove the absence of his or her fault, otherwise the fault is presumed.[451] Other elements of liability as well as exculpatory reasons are, in general, to be proven by the alleging party (the PRCA-1, however, sets out a different rule regarding the causal link in cases of cartel infringements).

2. Damages Actions for Breaches of Antitrust Before Slovenian Courts

307. In the past fifteen years, antitrust damages actions and other forms of relief have been intensified in Slovenia. Court proceedings have almost exclusively been initiated by competitors of undertakings that have allegedly abused their dominant position on the relevant markets. Damages actions are concerned mainly with the

450. For further details, see Vlahek, *Novosti* ..., 570–571.

451. Article 131/1 of the CO states that any person that inflicts damage on another shall be obliged to reimburse it, unless it proves that the damage was incurred without any culpability. That only *culpa levis* is presumed cannot be derived from CO, but was explained on the joined session of the highest courts of the former Yugoslavia in 1980. In cases outside *culpa levis,* fault is presumed only if a statute expressly states so or if that can be undoubtedly derived from the purpose of a given provision. See *Jadek Pensa* in *Juhart et al.: CO Commentary*, 796 and 801. Despite this, Slovenian courts and the rest of the theory apply the rule of Art. 131 of the CO in all cases and do not differentiate cases according to the types of fault. See, e.g., Galič, *Civil Procedure, Slovenia*, 174.

abuses of dominant position in the telecommunications sector.[452] At least one lawsuit, however, refers to the abuse in the postal services sector,[453] one in the cinematographic sector,[454] and one in the maritime transport sector.[455] Telekom Slovenije d.d. being a leading national telecommunications service operator, is by far the most targeted undertaking with other telecommunications operators filing damages actions against it claiming it had abused its dominant position by predatory pricing, margin squeeze, tying, etc. These are the most notorious cases: *T2 v. Telekom Slovenije*,[456] *Sinfonika v. Telekom Slovenije*,[457] *Akton v. Telekom Slovenije*,[458] *Tušmobil v. Telekom Slovenije*,[459] *ABM v. Telekom Slovenije*,[460] *S5 vleka*

452. *WWI v. Mobitel*; *Si.mobil v. Telekom Slovenije* and *Tušmobil v. Telekom S=lovenije*; *T2 v. Telekom Slovenije*; *Sinfonika v. Telekom Slovenije; ABM v. Telekom Slovenije; Quantum v. Telekom Slovenije*; *Akton v. Telekom Slovenije*; *Amis v. Telekom Slovenije*; For detailed analysis of these cases, see Vlahek, *Challenges of Private Enforcement of Antitrust in Slovenia.*
453. *Euromedia MB v. Pošta Slovenije*. For detailed analysis of the case, see Vlahek, *Challenges of Private Enforcement of Antitrust in Slovenia.*
454. *Blitz v. Kolosej*. For detailed analysis of the case, see Vlahek, *Challenges of Private Enforcement of Antitrust in Slovenia.*
455. *S5 vleka ladij v. Luka Koper*. For detailed analysis of the case, see Vlahek, *Challenges of Private Enforcement of Antitrust in Slovenia.*
456. In 2007, T2 d.o.o. (one of Slovenian Internet service providers) filed a lawsuit with the District Court in Ljubljana against Telekom Slovenije d.d. claiming that it had abused its dominant position by discriminating between T2 and its downstream market competitor SiOL d.o.o. It sought pecuniary and non-pecuniary damages in the amount of approx. EUR 204 million (approx. EUR 130 million, plus approx. EUR 74 million of interest plus other charges). The judge rejected the claim. The High Court in Ljubljana rejected T2's appeal and upheld the first instance court judgment in November 2013. In Jan. 2014, the plaintiff filed an extraordinary remedy of revision to the Supreme Court of RS. Vlahek, *Challenges of Private Enforcement of Antitrust in Slovenia.*
457. This is one of the rare cases where a final and binding decision has already been issued. Sinfonika d.d., an electronic telecommunications undertaking alleged that Telekom Slovenije abused its dominant position by introducing a central office exchange service (Centrex) with predatory prices, high switching costs, etc. The claim was approx. EUR 354,000 plus interest and was rejected by the District Court in Ljubljana in 2010 stating that while the grounds for liability for damages (the abuse of dominant position) were provided, the plaintiff failed to provide evidence it had suffered damage. The decision was upheld by the High Court in Ljubljana in 2011. Vlahek, *Challenges of Private Enforcement of Antitrust in Slovenia.*
458. Akton filed a lawsuit for EUR 1.5 million (later increased to approx. EUR 2.6 million) alleging Telekom Slovenije's abuse by charging prices for termination of calls in Slovenia that were higher than those set by the PECA. Akton requested Telekom Slovenije to repay it the sums charged above the set prices. The District Court in Ljubljana fully rejected the claim in November 2014. *Vlahek: Challenges of Private Enforcement of Antitrust in Slovenia.*
459. In February 2015, the District Court in Ljubljana awarded Tušmobil d.o.o. damages in the amount of approx. EUR 1.7 million (plus interest), while the action was dismissed with regard to the rest of the claim. Tušmobil (Tuš Telekom d.o.o. at the time) filed the lawsuit in 2007 requesting over EUR 21 million for the damage caused by Telekom Slovenije d.d. abusing its dominant position by favouring its wholly owned subsidiary SiOL d.o.o., and by violating provisions of sectoral legislation. Vlahek, *Challenges of Private Enforcement of Antitrust in Slovenia.*
460. Administrative infringement proceedings against Telekom Slovenije started already in September 1999 on request by ABM d.o.o. who claimed, inter alia, that Telekom Slovenije abused its dominant position by refusing to include the ABM's CDs for Internet access in its 'ISDN 3000' packages without just cause giving preference to the CDs offered by SiOL d.o.o. being a subsidiary of Telekom Slovenije. After lengthy administrative and court review proceedings, the abusive practice of Telekom Slovenije was finally confirmed in 2007 by the Administrative Court of RS and in 2008 by the Supreme Court of RS. Already in 2002, ABM d.o.o. filed damages action seeking EUR

ladij v. Luka Koper,[461] *WWI v. Mobitel,*[462] *Si.mobil v. Telekom Slovenije,*[463] *Amis v. Telekom Slovenije,*[464] *(Quantum v. Telekom Slovenije,*[465] *Akton v. Telekom Slovenije,*[466] *Akton v. Telekom Slovenije,*[467] *Amis v. Telekom Slovenije,*[468] *Blitz v. Kolosej,*[469] *Euromedia MB v. Pošta Slovenije.*[470]

4.2 million for a loss sustained due to abusive behaviour of Telekom Slovenije. In March 2012, the District Court in Ljubljana awarded ABM damages in the amount of EUR 2.3 million plus interest. High Court in Ljubljana lowered the amount of damages to approx. EUR 62,000, while the Supreme Court of RS ordered Telekom Slovenije to pay ABM over EUR 9.4 million plus interest. Vlahek, *Challenges of Private Enforcement of Antitrust in Slovenia.*

461. In 2010, S5 vleka ladij d.o.o. filed a claim for EUR 2 million with the District Court of Koper that issued an interlocutory judgment finding that the plaintiff's claim is well-founded regarding the period in which the infringement took place, while it dismissed the claim as regards the rest of the period claimed by the plaintiff as relevant for awarding damages. In February 2013, the High Court of Koper upheld the plaintiff's appeal finding that the 1st instance court incorrectly refused to take into account the period after the infringement ended solely on the ground that during that period the infringement ceased to exist. The High Court referred the case back to the first instance court. Vlahek, *Challenges of Private Enforcement of Antitrust in Slovenia.*
462. In May 2005, Western Wireless Int. d.o.o. (WWI) requested damages in the amount of SIT 48.8 billion (EUR 203.9 million) for the loss of its business due to Mobitel d.d.'s anti-competitive behaviour, while Mobitel sued WWI for SIT 106 million (EUR 442,330) requesting payment of the services it had rendered to WWI. The parties concluded an out-of-court settlement in April 2006. Vlahek, *Challenges of Private Enforcement of Antitrust in Slovenia.*
463. Si.mobil d.d. and Telekom Slovenije d.d. settled in December 2014 with regard to Si.mobil's stand-alone damages claim of EUR 286,392 million against Mobitel (merged by acquisition with Telekom Slovenije in June 2011) for its alleged abuse of dominant position on the retail market of mobile telecommunications services by using predatory pricing within its mobile subscription package *Itak Džabest.* For detailed analysis of the case, see Vlahek, *Challenges of Private Enforcement of Antitrust in Slovenia.*
464. Telekom Slovenije and Amis d.o.o. settled for SIT 343,565,000 (EUR 1.43 million) before the CPO's decision finding Telekom Slovenije's abuse became final and before Amis had filed damages actions against Telekom Slovenije. For detailed analysis of the case, see Vlahek, *Challenges of Private Enforcement of Antitrust in Slovenia.*
465. On 15 Jul. 2014, Telekom Slovenije d.d. received a lawsuit from the District Court of Ljubljana lodged by Quantum d.o.o. claiming damages in the amount of EUR 450,000 due to the abuse of dominant position by Telekom Slovenije. The plaintiff alleges that during 1994 and 1998, Telekom Slovenije did not enable it to charge calls to Internet hubs through user access via the 9xxx call number range according to the local tariff rate, due to which Quantum allegedly incurred damages. For detailed analysis of the case, see *Vlahek: Challenges of Private Enforcement of Antitrust in Slovenia.*
466. Two antitrust related lawsuits were filed against Telekom Slovenije by Akton d.o.o. In 2010, Akton filed a lawsuit alleging abuse of a dominant position by Mobitel d.d. (now Telekom Slovenije d.d.) with regard to performing its services of transferring international mobile voice calls on number blocks +386 43 and +386 49 to international switchboard, and requested damages in the amount of nearly EUR 7 million. For detailed analysis of the case, see Vlahek: *Challenges of Private Enforcement of Antitrust in Slovenia.*
467. Another lawsuit was filed by Akton against Telekom Slovenije for EUR 1.5 million (later increased to approx. EUR 2.6 million) and was fully rejected in November 2014. For detailed analysis of the case, see *Vlahek: Challenges of Private Enforcement of Antitrust in Slovenia.*
468. In May 2008, Telekom Slovenije received a lawsuit from Amis d.o.o. for the payment of damages in the amount of nearly EUR 57 million arising out of the alleged abuse of its dominant position in the inter-operator broadband access market, in the unbundled local loop and sub-loop access market, and in the fibre-optics connections to collocations spaces market. For detailed analysis of the case, see Vlahek, *Challenges of Private Enforcement of Antitrust in Slovenia.*
469. Blitz Film & Video Distribution d.o.o. initiated court proceedings with the District Court in Ljubljana already in 2008 (after the CPO had issued the infringement decision but before the decision

C. Interim Measures

308. There are no specific provisions on interim measures in the field of private competition enforcement proceedings (Article 38 of the PRCA-1 applies only to interim measures issued by the SCPA), therefore general rules on interim measures (in the form of provisional orders), regulated in Articles 266–279 of the Enforcement and Securing of Civil Claims Act (ESCCA)[471] apply.

309. Provisional orders may be issued before or after judicial proceedings are instituted and up until the enforcement takes place.[472] Where judicial proceedings have not yet been initiated, the provisional order is issued by the local court that would have had jurisdiction in enforcement proceedings.[473] Where protective measures are requested within civil or any other judicial proceedings, they will be granted by the court before which the proceedings have been brought.[474] Provisional orders may, however, not be issued where preliminary measures regulated in Articles 256–265 of the ESCCA may be ordered for attaining the same goal.[475]

310. The court will issue a provisional order securing a pecuniary claim where the creditor demonstrates (i) the probability that the claim exists or that it will arise vis-à-vis the debtor, and (ii) that there is a probable risk that the debtor's assets will be transferred, hidden or otherwise disposed of, making it impossible or rather difficult to enforce the claim; the creditor does, however, need not show the risk if he or she demonstrates that by the measure requested the debtor would sustain only insignificant loss. It is presumed that the risk exists if the claim is to be enforced abroad (save within the EU).[476]

---

had become final) claiming approx. EUR 940,000 of damages sustained by Kolosej kinematografi d.o.o.'s infringement. In April 2012, the District Court issued an interlocutory judgment finding (only) that with regard to a part of films the plaintiff's claim is substantiated as regards the issue of liability (in part, it rejected the claim as unsubstantiated), but it did not decide on the amount of damages. Both parties appealed to the High Court in Ljubljana. In November 2013, the High Court upheld the appeals, quashed the judgment and remitted the case for a retrial providing the first instance court with substantial guidance as to proper procedural and substantive handling of the case. For detailed analysis of the case, see Vlahek, *Challenges of Private Enforcement of Antitrust in Slovenia.*

470. Being one of the providers of unsolicited mail distribution, Euromedia MB d.o.o. filed a claim with the District Court in Ljubljana against Pošta Slovenije d.d. requesting approx. EUR 8 million of loss of profit. For detailed analysis of the case, see Vlahek, *Challenges of Private Enforcement of Antitrust in Slovenia.*

471. Sl. *Zakon o izvršbi in zavarovanju (ZIZ)*, Official Gazette RS, No. 51/98, with further amendments.

472. Article 267 of the ESCCA.

473. That is dependent on the object to be safeguarded. See Arts 77, 100, 152, 162, 163.a, 164, 166, etc., of the ESCCA.

474. Article 266 of the ESCCA.

475. Article 269 of the ESCCA.

476. Article 270 of the ESCCA.

311. To secure a pecuniary claim, the court may order any type of provisional order it deems appropriate for attaining the desired security, in particular:[477] (i) prohibiting the debtor from disposing of his or her movable property,[478] as well as seizing such property; (ii) prohibiting the debtor from transferring or encumbering his real estate or his rights in rem, and recording such prohibition in the land register; (iii) prohibiting the debtor's debtors from paying debts to the debtor and from handing over property to him or her, as well as prohibiting the debtor from receiving property, recovering debts or disposing of them; (iv) instructing the organization dealing with payment transactions to refuse payments from the debtor's account in the amount for which the provisional order has been issued. It must be stressed that by ordering such measures, the subject of security is not automatically pledged. A creditor who acquires a provisional order, does not enjoy priority in case of the debtor's bankruptcy or priority over another creditor who acquires an attachment of the same property in the framework of enforcement proceedings.[479]

312. The court will issue protective measures securing a non-pecuniary claim where the creditor demonstrates with probability:[480] (i) that the claim exists or that it will arise vis-à-vis the debtor, and (ii) that one of the following prerequisites are met: that there is a risk that enforcement of the claim will be impossible or rather difficult;[481] or that the measure is necessary to prevent that force is used or hardly recoverable damage is sustained; or that in case the measure turns out to be unfounded, the debtor will not suffer any consequences worse than those that would have arisen for the creditor had the measure not been issued.

313. The following interim measures may, inter alia, be issued in order to secure non-pecuniary claims:[482] (i) prohibiting the debtor from disposing of movable property to which the claim refers, as well as seizing such property; (ii) prohibiting the debtor from transferring or encumbering his real estate or his rights in rem to which the claim refers, and recording such prohibition in the land register; (iii) prohibiting the debtor from doing anything that might cause damage to creditor, as well as prohibiting him or her from making any changes in the property to which the claim refers; (iv) prohibiting the debtor's debtor from handing over to the debtor the property to which the claim refers.

314. Upon request by the creditor and by observing the circumstances of the case, the court may, if necessary, issue more than one protective measure.[483] The

477. Article 271 of the ESCCA.
478. Such prohibition is recorded in the Register of non-possessory liens and seized movable property administered by the Agency of the Republic of Slovenia for Public Legal Records and Related Services (AJPES).
479. Galič, *Civil Procedure, Slovenia*, 122.
480. Article 272 of the ESCCA.
481. As with pecuniary claims, the creditor does not need to show the risk if he or she demonstrates that by the measure requested the debtor would sustain only insignificant loss. It is presumed that the risk exists if the claim is to be enforced abroad (save within the EU).
482. Article 273 of the ESCCA.
483. Article 276 of the ESCCA.

creditor may declare that instead of a protective measure he or she is willing to accept that the debtor deposits a monetary sum as security. The court may also allow such security on the request of the debtor. In these cases, the court suspends the proceedings and annuls the acts that had already been performed.[484]

315. The court may also issue a provisional order where the creditor has not demonstrated the probability of the claim and the risk if, within a prescribed period, the creditor deposits a monetary sum as security for any loss the debtor might incur because the order had been issued and enforced. On the other hand, although the creditor has demonstrated the probability of existence of the claim as well as the risk, the court may nevertheless request the creditor to deposit a monetary sum before ordering measures if the debtor requests so and the court deems it appropriate in view of the circumstances of the case.[485]

316. When issuing a provisional order, the court must determine the duration of the measure. It may prolong it upon request by the creditor.[486] If the order is issued before any proceedings are initiated, the court provides the creditor with instructions of what type of proceedings to initiate in order to justify the measure. Same goes for the cases where the measure is issued for securing a claim that has not yet arisen. The court also sets a deadline to institute proceedings and to produce evidence thereof, and informs the creditor that it will terminate the proceedings and annul the acts already performed if he or she fails to do so. The same consequence arises when: (i) the court, acting upon request of the debtor, finds the measure is no longer necessary; (ii) the debtor deposits the amount of the claim (plus interest and costs) with the court; (iii) the debtor demonstrates that the claim has already been paid or sufficiently secured at the time the provisional order had been issued; (iv) it is established that the claim has not arisen or has ceased to exist.[487] The debtor has a right to demand from the creditor damages sustained by the measure that was unfounded or not justified by the creditor.[488]

317. Provisional orders may be issued without a hearing and without having heard the other party who may file an objection against the order within fifteen days. The objection does not, however, prevent the enforcement of the measure.[489]

484. Article 274 of the ESCCA.
485. Article 275 of the ESCCA.
486. Article 276 of the ESCCA.
487. Article 278 of the ESCCA.
488. Article 279 of the ESCCA.
489. Galič, *Civil Procedure, Slovenia*, 123.

§3. Criminal Enforcement

I. Criminal Sanctions for Antitrust Violations

A. *Criminal Liability of Individuals*

318. The currently valid Criminal Code (CrC-1) of 2008 in force as of 1 November 2008[490] incriminates 'unlawful restriction of competition' as one of the crimes against economy. Article 225 of the CrC-1, as in force today, provides:[491]

1. Whoever, in pursuing an economic activity contrary to regulations governing the protection of competition, violates the prohibition of restrictive agreements between undertakings, abuses the dominant position of one or more undertakings, or creates a prohibited concentration of undertakings and thus prevents or significantly impedes or distorts competition in the Republic of Slovenia, or on the European Union market, or its significant part, or significantly influences trade between Member States, which results in a large pecuniary benefit for such undertaking or undertakings, or a large pecuniary damage for another undertaking, shall be sentenced to imprisonment for not less than six months, and not more than five years.
2. A perpetrator of the criminal act of breaching the prohibition of restrictive agreements set out in the preceding paragraph, who has disclosed the act before it has been detected or before he or she knew it had been detected, and who has cooperated in its investigation and remedying of its consequences, and has not forced others to take part or to further cooperate in the restriction of competition, may have his or her punishment remitted.

319. Although Article 225 of the CrC-1 of 2008 has been amended in May 2012 (its title has been changed from the nebulous 'creation of monopoly position' to 'unlawful restriction of competition', and its second paragraph, introducing a form of leniency, inserted),[492] the provisions are still poorly drafted. For example, they refer only to restrictive agreements and abuses of dominant position, while they ignore other unlawful restrictive practices, i.e., decisions of associations and concerted practices. However, the Code incriminates somewhat ambiguously the 'creation of prohibited concentrations'.[493] Further, the effect on trade is set out as an

---

490. Sl. *Kazenski zakonik (KZ-1)*, Official Gazette RS, No. 55/08, with further amendments. The Penal Code of 2008 has been to date amended five times, i.e., in 2009, 2011, 2015, 2016, and 2017.

491. The provisions are translated exactly as they are formed in the Slovene language so as to show the poor quality of the text.

492. Act Amending the Criminal Code (Sl. *Zakon o spremembah in dopolnitvah Kazenskega zakonika (KZ-1B)*), Official Gazette RS, No. 91/11. Cf. Grilc & Bajec, *225. člen*, 733, 734.

493. It is not clear what exactly is incriminated: the mere omission of notification of a concentration to the authorities, or the implementation of concentration that has been notified to and found incompatible by the authorities (the word 'prohibited' speaks for the latter). In any case, it would be reasonable that only the unlawful activity (in the form of abuse of dominant position) being the outcome of the concentration is incriminated, not the concentration itself. Cf. Grilc & Bajec, *225. člen*, 733, who stress (referring also to comparative regulation) that only the most serious, and not all competition law breaches should be incriminated.

alternative outcome of restrictive behaviour to prevention, restriction or distortion of competition in RS or EU, which is not in line with the core definitions of antitrust. It is obvious that no competition law expert took part in their drafting. The same market activity (completely illogically entitled as 'creation of monopoly position') was regulated already in the previous CrC of 1994 in force as of 1 January 1995.[494] The only substantive difference between Article 231 of the CrC of 1994, and Article 225 of the CrC-1 of 2008, is the level of the imprisonment sanction, as before 2008, the perpetrator could be imprisoned for up to three years, while pursuant to the currently valid CrC-1, the imprisonment ranges from six months up to five years. As of 2012, the punishment for breaching the prohibition of restrictive agreements (not, however, in other cases of competition law breaches) can also be remitted if (i) the perpetrator informed the authorities of the agreement before it was detected or before he or she knew that it was detected, (ii) the perpetrator cooperated in the inspection of the breach and the elimination of its effects, and (iii) the perpetrator did not force others to cooperate or further partake in restricting competition.[495] The reason behind such provision lies in the fact that these types of competition law breaches are most difficult to detect and prove, and success is often dependent upon the cooperation of persons who took part in the restrictive practice.[496] Without such leniency as set up in Article 225/2 of the CrC-1, the perpetrators would not be willing to cooperate.[497]

320. Apart from the leniency regime regulated in Article 225/2 of the CrC-1 (in cases of restrictive agreements), the court may also (in all cases) reduce the sentence below the prescribed minimum period (i.e., below the six-month period)[498] or (if the perpetrator pleads guilty under the circumstances set out by the law) impose a monetary fine instead of imprisonment.[499] The minimum reduced sentence in the case of Article 225 of the CrC-1 is one month.[500] In fixing the sentence, the court considers all circumstances which have an influence on the grading of the sentence (mitigating and aggravating circumstances), and in particular: the degree of the perpetrator's culpability; the motives for which the offence was committed; the intensity of the danger or injury caused to the property protected by law; the circumstances in which the offence was committed; the perpetrator's past behaviour; his or her personal and pecuniary circumstances; his or her conduct after the

494. Prior to 1995, the CrC of the (Yugoslav) Republic of Slovenia of 1977 was in force. As competition law had at the time not yet developed, it did not incriminate any similar acts.
495. Article 225/2 of the CrC-1 and Art. 52 of the CrC-1.
496. Grilc & Bajec, *225. člen*, 751.
497. *Ibid.*
498. Articles 50 and 51 of the CrC-1.
499. Articles 50 and 51 of the CrC-1. Pursuant to Art. 47 of the CrC-1, a monetary fine is imposed in daily amounts (which cannot exceed EUR 1,000) and ranges from a minimum of ten to a maximum of 1,500 daily amounts (as the criminal offence under Art. 225 of the CrC-1 is a criminal offence committed out of greed). The number of daily amounts is fixed by the court in accordance with the general rules on sentencing (save those regarding the perpetrator's financial situation). The court fixes the daily amount by taking into account the perpetrator's income, value of his or her property, and his or her family expenditures (e.g., financial support of minor children). In fixing the daily amount, the court bases its decision on the data not older than one year.
500. Article 51/1/4 of the CrC-1. See also Grilc & Bajec, *225. člen*, 751.

committing of the offence and especially whether he or she recovered the damages caused; and other circumstances referring to the personality of the perpetrator and the anticipated effect of the sentence on his or her future life in social environment.[501]

321. In addition to imprisonment or monetary fine, there are accessory sentences and safety measures that could in principle be imposed on the perpetrator also in cases of offences under Article 225 of the CrC-1. For example, a safety measure of prohibition from performing an occupation from one up to five years could be imposed.[502]

322. One of the elements of this criminal act is a large pecuniary benefit obtained by the perpetrator, or a large pecuniary damage caused to another undertaking. According to Article 99/9 of the CrC-1, a large pecuniary benefit or damage is the amount exceeding EUR 50,000. Damages to other undertakings (who are not the prime protegees of antitrust) and the perpetrator's benefit (not only the damages sustained by the victim(s)) are of relevance in determining the criminal act.[503]

323. The wrongdoers of this criminal act would most plausibly be directors or other persons in charge of undertakings pursuing restrictive practices. Their intent to commit this offence will have to be proven – given the nature of the offence, proving intent should not pose particular difficulties to the prosecutors, at least not in cases of restrictive agreements.[504]

324. According to Article 34 of the CrC-1, attempt to unlawfully restrict competition is also punishable.[505] In that case, the sentence must be applied within the limits prescribed in Article 225 of the CrC-1, or it may be reduced.

325. Criminal prosecution of the criminal acts regulated in Article 225 of the CrC-1 may take place within ten years after the offence had been committed.[506]

B. Criminal Liability of Legal Persons

326. As of 1995 when the CrC of 1994 entered into force, a legal person itself, too, can be held liable for one of the criminal offences committed by a perpetrator (a natural person) in the name of, on behalf of or in favour of the legal person.[507] Article 42 of the CrC-1 sets out the basic rules of the legal person's criminal liability, while detailed rules are regulated in the Liability of Legal Persons for Criminal

501. Article 49 of the CrC-1.
502. Article 71 of the CrC-1.
503. Cf. Grilc & Bajec, *225. člen*, 750.
504. *Ibid.*, 750-751.
505. See Grilc & Bajec, *225. člen*, 754–755, who opine that attempt of committing a crime of Art. 225 of the CrC-1 is not possible.
506. Article 90 of the CrC-1.
507. Article 33 of the CrC of 1994, now (slightly amended) Art. 42 of the CrC-1 of 2008.

Offences Act of 1999 (LLPCOA)[508] which provides for a catalogue of criminal offences for which legal persons can be held liable. The offences regulated in Article 225 of the CrC-1 are among them.[509]

327. According to the LLPCOA, a legal person is liable for the criminal offence: (a) if the natural person was, by committing the offence, carrying out an unlawful decision, order or endorsement of the legal person's management or supervisory bodies; (b) if the management or supervisory bodies of the legal person influenced the perpetrator or enabled him or her to commit the criminal offence; (c) if the legal person has at its disposal unlawfully obtained property benefit or uses objects obtained through the offence; or (d) if the legal person's management or supervisory bodies have omitted due supervision of the legality of the actions of employees subordinate to them.[510] The liability of a legal person does not exclude criminal liability of natural persons.[511] A legal person can be held liable for a criminal offence even if the perpetrator is not criminally liable for the committed criminal act (the legal person's liability is therefore not fully accessory to the perpetrator's; the legal person's liability has its own legal basis on the ground of the legal person's own contribution to the criminal act).[512] If the perpetrator intentionally initiated a criminal offence but did not complete it, the legal person is also liable for the attempt, and the punishment applied against it shall be the same as for the completed criminal offence, although a reduced punishment may also be imposed.[513] In the case of co-perpetration of legal persons each legal person is liable as though it was the only party besides the perpetrator liable for the criminal offence.[514] The Republic of Slovenia and local communities may not be held liable for a criminal offence under LLPCOA.[515]

---

508. Sl. *Zakon o odgovornosti pravnih oseb za kazniva dejanja (ZOPOKD)*, Official Gazette RS, No. 59/99, with further amendments.
509. Article 25 of the LLPCOA.
510. Article 4 of the LLPCOA. According to Art. 6 of the LLPCOA, a bankrupt legal person, too, may be liable for a criminal offence regardless of whether it was committed before the initiation of bankruptcy proceedings or during them. In this case, however, a punishment is not imposed but instead, only the confiscation of property benefits or the safety measure of confiscation of assets are imposed. If a legal person has been liquidated before the legal completion of criminal proceedings, it may be deemed liable, and the punishment and other sanctions are imposed on the legal person which is the legal successor of the legal person that has committed the offence, if its management or supervisory bodies knew of the committed criminal offence prior to the liquidation of the convicted legal person. A legal person which is the legal successor of a convicted legal person but whose management or supervisory bodies were not aware of the committed criminal offence, can only be convicted to the confiscation of property benefits or the safety measure of confiscation of assets. Same goes if the legal person is liquidated after the completion of criminal proceedings.
511. Article 5/1,2 of the LLPCOA.
512. Jakulin, *Odgovornost pravnih oseb* ..., 218. Art. 5/4 of the LLPCOA further states that if a legal person has no other body besides the perpetrator who could lead or supervise the perpetrator, the legal person is liable for the committed criminal offence within the limits of the perpetrator's guilt ((only) in this case its liability is fully accessory to the perpetrator's).
513. Article 8 of the LLPCOA. If the management or supervisory body voluntarily prevented the perpetrator from completing the initiated criminal offence, the punishment of the legal person may be withdrawn.
514. Article 10 of the LLPCOA.
515. Article 2 of the LLPCOA.

328. A criminal offence committed by a legal person (e.g., an undertaking who has abused its dominant position which resulted in a large pecuniary benefit or damage) is punishable by a fine of EUR 10,000 to EUR 1 million,[516] while in those cases where the legal person's criminal offence has caused damage to another's property, or provided the legal person with unlawful proprietary benefit, the highest limit of the fine imposed may be 200-times (sic!) the amount of the damage caused or illegal gain obtained through the criminal offence.[517,518] The legal person may also be punished by confiscation of property,[519] termination of the legal person,[520] and prohibition of disposal with its shares for a period of one to eight years.[521,522] Safety measures in the form of publication of the judgment[523] and prohibition of a specific

516. Article 13 of the LLPCOA. According to Art. 17 of the LLPCOA, the court may impose a suspended sentence to a legal person instead of a fine, where the court may fix a fine of up to EUR 500,000 on the legal person and, at the same time, order that the sentence will not be imposed if the legal person does not commit a further criminal offence within a term defined by the court, which may not be shorter than one year, and longer than five years.
517. Article 13 of the LLPCOA.
518. According to Art. 22 of the LLPCOA, the enforcement of a fine falls under the statute of limitations when three years have lapsed since the date of the final judgment by which the punishment was imposed.
519. Article 77 of the CrC-1. According to Art. 14 of the LLPCOA, half or more of the legal person's property or its entire property may be confiscated in cases of criminal offences, punishable by a five or more years of imprisonment (as is the case of offences under Art. 225 of the CrC-1). In the case of bankruptcy proceedings resulting from the imposing of a punishment of confiscation of property, creditors may be paid off from the confiscated property. In the case of criminal offences for which in addition to a fine the confiscation of property is prescribed, Art. 16 of the LLPCOA provides that the court must ensure that the fine does not exceed half of the property of the legal person.
520. According to Art. 15 of the LLPCOA, termination of a legal person may be ordered if the activity of the legal person was entirely or predominantly used for the carrying out of criminal offences. In addition to termination, the court may also impose a punishment of confiscation of property. When terminating the legal person, the court proposes the initiation of liquidation proceedings.
521. Article 15b of the LLPCOA, which was inserted in the LLPCOA in 2008 (regulating a sanction of prohibition of trading with financial instruments on a regulated market), but was amended in 2012 so as to regulate prohibition of disposal of the shares the legal person holds. A sanction of prohibition of participation in public procurement tenders was also inserted in Art. 15a of the LLPCOA, but was deleted in 2012.
522. According to Art. 22 of the LLPCOA, enforcement of these types of punishment falls under the statute of limitations when five years have elapsed since the date of the final judgment with which the punishment was imposed.
523. According to Art. 19 of the LLPCOA, the safety measure of publication of the judgment is applied by the court in cases where it would be beneficial for the public to be informed of the judgment, and especially if publication of the judgment would contribute to removing danger to life or limb or the securing of safety of traffic or some economic good. The court must consider, with regard to the importance of the criminal offence and the need for the public to be informed of the judgment, whether the judgment should be published in the press, broadcast by radio or television or by several of the listed means of public information simultaneously, and whether the explanation of the judgment should be published in full or in excerpt form; the court must see that the means of publication enable the informing of all those in whose interest it is necessary to publish the judgment. According to Art. 22 of the LLPCOA, the enforcement of a safety measure falls under the statute of limitations when six months have elapsed since the final judgment with which the measure of publication of the judgment was imposed.

commercial activity[524] may also be imposed on the legal person. In addition, the following legal consequences of a conviction may come into effect for a legal person: prohibition of activity performed on the basis of licenses, authorizations or concessions granted by state bodies, and prohibition of acquisition of licenses, authorizations or concessions, granted by state bodies.[525] Security measures are also available to prosecutors to secure enforcement of certain types of punishments as well as to prevent repetition of the offence.[526]

329. In fixing the punishment, the court has to consider (in addition to the general rules for fixing punishments set out in CrC-1) the legal person's economic strength. If after the committing of a criminal offence the management or supervisory body voluntarily reports the perpetrator, the legal person may be given a reduced punishment. Further, if it voluntarily and immediately orders the restitution of unlawfully obtained property benefits or provides indemnification for damages caused through the offence or reports information on the grounds for liability for other legal persons, the legal person's punishment may be withdrawn.[527]

330. Limitation of criminal prosecution of a legal person accords to the one prescribed for natural persons committing the offence under Article 225 of the CrC-1.[528] The LLPCOA provides that proceedings are as a rule initiated and carried out against the legal person together with proceedings against the perpetrator for the same criminal offence.[529] In unified proceedings, a single charge is lodged against the accused legal person and the accused natural person, and a single judgment is issued. The state prosecutor may decide not to request the initiation of criminal proceedings against a legal person if the circumstances of the case show that this would not be expedient because the legal person's participation in the criminal offence was insignificant, because the legal person does not have any property or has so little property that this would not even suffice to cover the costs of the proceedings, because bankruptcy proceedings have been initiated against the legal person, or

524. According to Art. 20 of the LLPCOA, this safety measure means prohibiting a legal person from producing certain products or doing business in certain plants or prohibiting a legal person from involving itself in certain transactions in the traffic of goods and services, or in other commercial transactions. It may be applied to a legal person if its further involvement in a given commercial activity would present a danger to life or limb or be harmful to the commercial or financial business of other legal persons or to the economy, or if the legal person has already been punished in the last two years for the same or a similar criminal offence. It may be applied for a term of six months to five years from the time the judgment becomes legally binding. According to Art. 22 of the LLPCOA, the enforcement of a safety measure falls under the statute of limitations when the term for which the measure of prohibition of a specific commercial activity was applied to a legal person has elapsed.
525. Article 21 of the LLPCOA.
526. Article 41 of the LLPCOA.
527. Article 11 of the LLPCOA.
528. Article 22 of the LLPCOA.
529. Article 27 of the LLPCOA. Proceedings against a legal person alone may only be initiated or carried out in cases where it is not possible to initiate or carry out proceedings against the perpetrator for reasons specified by law, or when proceedings against the perpetrator have already been carried out. The court may, however, decide until the closure of the hearing that due to important reasons or reasonableness, the proceedings against the legal person are conducted separately.

because the perpetrator of the criminal offence is the sole owner of the legal person against which it would be necessary to initiate proceedings.[530]

331. Although the analysed criminal acts of natural and legal persons have been regulated in the CrC since 1995 and in the LLPCOA since 1999, the provisions have to date almost never been applied. It is therefore yet to be seen how the prosecutors and the courts are to deal with them. The only case known to the authors is the prosecution of Telekom Slovenije d.d. and its CEO relating to the *Sinfonika* case. The District State Prosecutor's Office started the criminal case against them charging them with committing an unlawful act of creating a monopolistic position according to Article 231 of the Penal Code, during the period between 19 April 2001 and 31 December 2003 by concluding subscription contracts for Centrex telecommunication services. Criminal procedure started on the grounds of the legal complaint made by distributors of in house switchboards – Kron Telekom, Sinfonika, Iskra Prins, Pro Com, Telefax, Telego, In life – who have also claimed in the proceeding that because of this behaviour they were damaged for the total amount of EUR 12,202,753.68. In January 2009, the District Court of Ljubljana dismissed the indictment proposal. It decided that the act, which was the subject of the indictment, is not a criminal act.[531]

332. There is no doubt that to foster competition culture in Slovenia, criminal enforcement has to strengthen. Relevant criminal law, however, should be rewritten in close cooperation with competition and corporate lawyers in order to incriminate properly relevant breaches of competition law, and to prescribe reasonable sanctions for the criminal offences committed by legal persons. Due regard should in particular be given to formulating a clear and consistent set of rules of sanctioning natural and legal persons for breaches of competition law in order to lift the veil of proper co-application of the PRCA-1 on the one hand, and the CrC-1 and LLPCOA on the other.

II. Other Application of Criminal Law to Relevant Conducts

333. As Article 225 of the CrC-1 incriminates specifically crimes against competition, other provisions of the CrC-1 listing criminal acts are not relevant to anticompetitive conducts.

III. Role of Prosecutors

334. State prosecutors have an important role in criminal law proceedings where they file and present criminal charges.[532]

530. Article 28 of the LLPCOA.
531. http://seonet.ljse.si/Default.aspx?doc=SEARCH&doc_id=35131.
532. State Prosecutor Act (Sl. *Zakon o državnem tožilstvu (ZDT-1)*), Official Gazette RS, No. 58/11, with further amendments.

335. State prosecutors have to date unfortunately been inactive in prosecuting offences against competition what could be mostly attributed to the lack of initiative and knowledge in competition law cases. Poor quality of the text of Article 225 of the CrC-1, as well as of the LLPCOA, could also be detected as an obstacle to efficient prosecution of these crimes. As, according to the available information, thus far no criminal proceedings have been initiated in cases of competition law breaches,[533] the first set of reasons is the most plausible cause of the current state of criminal enforcement of competition law in Slovenia.

IV. Competent Criminal Courts

336. As the imprisonment sanction for the criminal offence under Article 225 of the CrC-1 is higher than three years, district courts of general jurisdiction are competent to hear the cases at the first instance.[534] A panel of three judges, of which two are lay judges, decides these cases. In second instance, cases are heard before higher courts by panels of three judges, while the Supreme Court as the third instance court hears the cases in panels of five judges.[535] A district court investigating judge takes part in the pre-trial investigations.[536]

337. Territorial jurisdiction is in principle vested in the court in whose territory the criminal offence was committed or attempted. If it was committed or attempted in the territories of different courts or on the border between these territories, or the territory in which the offence was committed or attempted cannot be ascertained, the competent court is the court which, upon request filed by the authorized prosecutor, had instituted proceedings first or, if proceedings have not been instituted, the court at which the request to institute proceedings was filed first.[537]

338. If the territory in which the offence was committed is not known or is outside the territory of the Republic of Slovenia, the competent court is the court in whose territory the accused permanently or temporarily resides.[538] That court retains jurisdiction even after the place of the commission of the criminal offence has become known. If, however, neither the place of commission of a criminal offence nor the permanent or temporary residence of the accused are known, or are both situated outside the Republic of Slovenia, the competent court is the one in

533. Cf. Grilc & Bajec, *225. člen*, 755.
534. Articles 99 and 101 of the Courts Act (Sl. *Zakon o sodiščih (ZS)*), Official Gazette RS, No.19/94, with further amendments; also Art. 25/1 of the Criminal Procedure Act (Sl. *Zakon o kazenskem postopku (ZKP)*), Official Gazette RS, No. 63/94, with further amendments.
535. Article 25/1-3 of the Criminal Procedure Act.
536. Article 25/4 of the Criminal Procedure Act.
537. Article 26 of the Criminal Procedural Act.
538. According to Art. 29 of the LLPCOA, in cases where under the Criminal Procedure Act the territorial jurisdiction of the court is dependent on the place of residence of the accused, but proceedings are only being brought against an accused legal person, the competent court is the court which has jurisdiction over the area in which the head office of the legal person is located, or where the branch office of an accused foreign legal person is located.

whose territory the accused was caught or reported him- or herself.[539] If it is impossible to determine which court has territorial jurisdiction in a specific case, the Supreme Court designates one of the courts of real jurisdiction as the court competent to conduct the proceedings.[540]

539. Article 29 of the Criminal Procedure Act.
540. Article 31 of the Criminal Procedure Act.

Part II. The Application of the Prohibitions

Chapter 1. Restrictive Agreements

§1. Horizontal Agreements

I. Cartels

A. *Price Fixing*

339. Price fixing in the ambit of horizontal agreements is seen as the most heinous form of restriction of competition. By concluding a price fixing agreement in a highly concentrated oligopolistic market with a homogenous product and high barriers to entry, the colluding undertakings will be able to completely eliminate price competition, whereas the consumers will consequently lose their freedom of choice. By concluding price fixing agreements, the colluding undertakings try to enlarge the pool of monopolistic profits; hence they usually reach an agreement on a price higher than in the absence of collusive behaviour. Price fixing agreements come in many shapes and nuances – in addition to the basic vanilla type of direct transactions price setting, one should not overlook agreements on rebates, premiums and discounts, bid rigging in public procurement procedures, agreements on target prices, agreements on supply costs, etc. All the above types of restrictive agreements have the possibility to result in consequences equal to those of direct setting of transaction prices.

340. As already pointed out, Article 6 of the PRCA-1 expressis verbis prohibits direct or indirect fixing of purchasing or selling prices or any other trading conditions, and is therefore mirroring Article 101 TFEU.

1. *GZS*

341. Following the complaint by Piano, a small independent book publisher, the CPO found that certain provisions of General conditions of operation of Slovenian book market restrict competition in this market.[541] Slovenian Chamber of Commerce ('SCC') is an independent expert-business organization established on the

541. CPO's decision No. 306-21/2005-92 of 1 Feb. 2006, available at (in Slovene): http://www.varstvo-konkurence.si/fileadmin/varstvo-konkurence.si/pageuploads/ijz066.pdf.

basis of special law with the purpose of developing of market economy, free enterprise and stimulating competition. The membership in SCC was, at the time of this decision, obligatory for basically all legal or natural persons evolved in business operations in Slovenia. In the SCC framework there exists special industry-wide Association for print and media ('APM') with obligatory membership for all subjects doing business in this area. As part of APM there exists Expert Association of Publishers and Book Sellers ('EAPBS') which adopted General conditions of operation of Slovenian book market ('General conditions'). The General conditions were published in the Official Gazette of Republic of Slovenia and were obligatory for all book market participants. In case of violation, there existed a system of sanctions and damages enforced through bodies of SCC. In its decision the CPO found that the General conditions represent decisions by associations of undertakings and that the provisions regulating uniform price and fixed discounts violated the PRCA-1 and are therefore null and void.

B. Market/Client Allocation

342. Territorial market division provides the colluding undertakings with absolute control over their respective geographic market. The agreement to allocate markets will usually be a corollary of a direct price fixing agreement. Hence, market allocation in the ambit of horizontal restrictive agreements undoubtedly stands as one of the hardcore restrictions of competition.

C. Production/Innovation Limitation

1. Bank Association of Slovenia

343. The Bank Association of Slovenia ('BAS')[542] is an economic interest grouping whose main goals are fostering of activities of its members, enhancing of the results of banking activities and implementing of good business customs and business ethics. For these purposes the BAS pursues various activities, such as representing common interests of its members before various governmental and other bodies, organizes the exchange of credit standing information, etc. All major Slovenian banks are members of the BAS. After internal BAS working group consultations, the Supervisory Board of the BAS in March 2005 adopted the decision with which it appeals to its member banks to denounce the contracts on Standing Order/Direct Debit ('Standing Order') for purchases payable by instalments at the point of sale provided by merchants, in order to foster the implementation process of the BAS own new joint banking product – BanKredit. In its decision the CPO declared

542. CPO's decision No. 306-62/2005-59 of 15 Nov. 2006, operative part of the decision is available at (in Slovene): http://www.varstvo-konkurence.si/zakonodaja-in-dokumenti/ostali-dokumenti/arhiv-odlocb/odlocba49/.

null and void a decision of the BAS since it restricts competition on market for purchases payable by instalments (credit) at the point of sale. In explanation of its decision the CPO found that the relevant markets for banking services are traditionally divided to retail banking, corporate banking, investment banking and financial markets. In this particular case it was considering the restrictions on instalment payments at the point of sale and concluded that it is not appropriate to distinguish between instalment payments and credits for the purpose of defining relevant market, since from consumer perspective both payment instruments pursue the same goal. Moreover, because of the following elements: (i) place of taking on the credit – point of sale, (ii) credit repayment period, (iii) purpose of credit – purchase of particular goods, (iv) special characteristics of the credit and (v) costs of credit, the CPO found that it is appropriate to distinguish a market for purchases payable by instalments (credit) at the point of sale as a separate relevant service market. It is interesting to note that it quoted these special elements as the reason why it concluded that SSNIP test was not appropriate for this case. The CPO also found that the object of the provisions of the BAS decision on denouncing the contracts on Standing Orders in process of implementation of new joint banking product – BanKredit, was abolition of effective provision of services for purchases payable by instalments and therefore exclusion of competitors (points of sale) in regard of offering the services of instalment payments (credit) at the point of sale. Moreover, it found that this was done at considerable expenses and effective elimination of choices for consumers.

2. *ASNSH*

344. The Association of Slovenian Natural Health Spas ('the ASNHS')[543] is a business association of thirteen natural health spa providers in Slovenia. The ASNHS goal is to foster business activities of its members. The membership is voluntary, and the members are equal in decision-making of the association and have to comply with its decisions. The ASNHS adopted several decisions providing that the expansion of health spa activities to particular additional standard under the Framework Agreement with the Health Insurance Institute of Slovenia ('the Institute') for particular health spa provider, was not allowed without the conclusion of the General Assembly of the ASNHS that (i) the existing capacities are not sufficient for implementation of particular health care programme or (ii) the providers already holding the particular standard agree with that. When under investigation the ASNHS submitted that its decisions are not infringing the predominantly, because the healthcare activity of natural spas is not a market activity, since it is operated as non-profit public service in the framework of public healthcare network. The CPO did not accept these arguments as it considered that market activity consists of two elements: (i) carrying out of activity for other persons against remuneration and (ii) execution of such activity on the market. Although finally paid for by the Institute, there is no doubt that the activity of natural health spas is carried

543. CPO's decision No. 306-83/2005-18 of 19 Jan. 2006, operative part of the decision is available at (in Slovene): http://www.varstvo-konkurence.si/index.php?id=6726.

out for other persons against remuneration and not for free or in form of non-market charge such as obligatory contribution or tax. Moreover, there exist the demand and supply for such activities which is crucial for market to exist and the fact that the prices are regulated in the Framework Agreement is not of critical importance for such finding. The CPO also found that implementation of disputed decisions limits expansion of activity on the relevant market to agreement of existing participants, which represents elimination of competition in respect of a substantial part of the services in question. In its decision the CPO therefore concluded that the subject decision of the ASNHS represent decisions by associations of undertakings on the conditions of conducting business on the market, which have as their object or effect the prevention, restriction or distortion of competition in RS and are therefore null and void.

D. Group Boycott

345. Group boycotts represent a rather difficult theoretical concept of competition law. Sharing some of its basic characteristics with a disputed notion of (unilateral) refusal to deal, it is not perfectly clear which of its modalities should be perceived as anti-competitive by object (or per se in American antitrust terms). A non-critical glance at the case law of the European court's docket could lead to a mistaken conclusion that any and all forms of 'negative' coordinated behaviour between horizontal competitors should be declared illegal by object. It is our firm belief that European competition law should follow the insights of American antitrust in this area and acknowledge the different range of (anti) and (pro) competitive effects that different types of collective negative actions (group boycotts) may result in. Here we point especially to the definite characterization of such actions by the US Supreme Court, where certain forms of concerted refusals to deal are dealt with through the rule of reason standard even though they might prima vista be perceived as cartelization (e.g., efficient and even inefficient joint refusals to deal in joint ventures even if the joint venture partners have market power, but the refusal to deal was efficient, or at least harmless, to competition).[544] Group boycotts where participants of the boycott hold no significant market power should also be considered through the rule of reason standard. Currently, we can report of no published decisions of the CPA in the field of concerted refusal to deal.

E. Collusion on Other Objects

1. Bid Rigging: *ER Maribor*

346. In its decision issued on 21 May 2015, the CPA found GH Holding, TAMES d.o.o. and Begrad d.d. guilty of direct or indirect price setting in a public procurement procedure for construction works on the new Emergency Room of the

544. Hovenkamp, *Antitrust*, 33.

University Clinic in Maribor.[545] CPA discovered that the said undertakings filed a coordinated bid where one of the undertakings (Begrad) abstained from filing its own bid in return for a role of a subcontractor of the remaining two undertakings. The Agency relied heavily on the jurisprudence of the European courts and the Commission, borrowing especially from the theoretical conceptualizations of 'concerted practices' – an Article 6 PRCA agreement between the respective undertakings was thus inferred and imputated on the basis of a claimed 'market contact' and not direct evidence of collusion.

F. Applying Dissimilar Conditions to Similar Transactions

347. The discriminatory type of restrictive collusive behaviour is rarely seen in practice as the persecution of price or non-price discrimination will usually fall into the ambit of the abuse of dominance. However, discrimination can also be a trait of collusive behaviour, i.e., agreements between undertakings, especially in cases where discrimination between cartel clients result (or will probably result) in market division (allocation). Here, the most frequent type of behaviour is differentiation between different groups of clients on the basis of different levels of discounts or rebates on the one hand[546] and different mark-ups on the other.

348. Article 6 of the PRCA-1 expressis verbis prohibits application of dissimilar conditions to similar transactions resulting in restraint of competition, and is therefore mirroring Article 101 TFEU.

II. Information Exchange Practices

A. Nova Ljubljanska Banka, Banka Celje, Nova KBM, Abanka Vipa

349. This case started in May 2006, when the CPO started the proceedings on finding whether decisions of four major Slovenian banks (with combined market share of Slovenian retail banking market around 80%) on introduction of new ATM fee for withdrawing cash to their retail customers, represents restrictive agreement in violation of the PRCA.[547] In 1998, most of the Slovenian banks set-up a company Bankart for the purposes of executing of processing of ATM and payment cards business activities. Bankart manages the ATM network for most business and savings banks in Slovenia. The role of Bankart in mutual settling of interchange fee among banks is to provide required technology support and to make the settlements of compensations that are mutually calculated among banks in connection with

545. Decision No. 3060-5/2013-102 of 21 May 2015.

546. See ECJ judgment in C-73/74 *Groupement des Fabricants de papiers peints de Belgique v. Commission.*

547. CPO's decision No. 306-14/2006-100 of 26 Feb. 2007, available at (in Slovene): http://www.varstvo-konkurence.si/fileadmin/varstvo-konkurence.si/pageuploads/ijz033.pdf.

usage of ATMs in a form of monthly reports. The report covers bilateral net positions among banks, which are the basis for executing monthly settlements for the transactions performed in each past month. The particularity of the ATM network in Slovenia compared with abroad is that it has only one processor – Bankart – i.e., all ATMs are part of one network. Until introduction of the new ATM fee for withdrawing cash to their retail customers (which is charged always when a customer uses an ATM owned by other bank) the interchange fee covering the ATM transaction on ATMs of other banks was charged only among banks and was not directly transferred to their customers. In its decision the CPO found that the four banks acted in concert when they, on the same day (20 February 2006) and in exactly the same amount (SIT 80.00), introduced a fee for their customers for withdrawing of cash with domestic debit card on the ATMs of other banks. This practice represents a concerted practice on conditions of performing business on the market which have as their object or effect the prevention, restriction or distortion of competition in Republic of Slovenia. One rather surprising particularity of the subject decision by the CPO is that it stopped it proceedings against a fifth bank, Banka Koper, which was also a part of initial proceedings, on the ground that it found that Banka Koper got information about intended introduction of subject ATM fees from mass media and not on the basis of cooperation with its competitors. Consequently, its activities in this regard represented parallel behaviour which could be introduced as reasonable response on the actions of its competitors and therefore could be a consequence of normal development of market relations.

III. Cooperation Agreements

A. Research and Development Agreements and Specialization

350. In cases where horizontal competitors cooperate in view of purveying or supplying a new service or good, a thorough analysis of objective necessity of input for the provision of a new integrated service is to be carried out.[548] Cooperation between competitors is generally illegal or at least frowned upon (*de minimis*), however, in certain situation it is exactly such cooperation that results in new goods or services, which would have not been supplied had it not been for the cooperation in question. As such cases bring with them an inherent danger of illegal anti-competitive behaviour (hidden or overt) in the forms of cartelization or abuse of dominance, a special legal framework has been adopted for their analysis in the European Union. The said framework deals mainly with the issue of proper economic effects-based analysis of potential efficiencies of specialization and R&D agreements as seen through the spectrum of Article 100/3 TFEU. The framework consists of the following pieces of secondary legislation: Commission Regulation (EU) No. 1217/2010 of 14 December 2010 on the application of Article 101(3) of the TFEU to certain categories of agreements on research and development (hereinafter 'Regulation 1217/2010') and Commission Regulation (EU) No. 1218/2010

548. Specialization is also partly covered in Pt. C of this chapter.

of 14 December 2010 on the application of Article 101(3) TFEU to certain categories of specialization agreements and concerted practices (hereinafter 'Regulation 1218/2010') and the Guidelines on the application of Article 101 TFEU to horizontal cooperation agreements (hereinafter 'the Guidelines').

351. The European Commission guidelines suggest that each case is to be analysed in terms of its economic context in which it is necessary to take into account (a) the nature of the agreement, (b) the total market power of companies and (c) other structural factors. These elements affect the fact that the horizontal cooperation can reduce the competition to such an extent that a negative impact on the market is to be expected (on prices, levels of service, innovation, diversity/quality of goods/ services). The Commission primarily notes that in most cases of horizontal cooperation where the undertakings involved lacked market power, no anti-competitive effects or consequences were to be established (such a perception coincides with the spirit of the modernization of European antitrust issues, brought about by Regulation 1/2003). One of the fundamental objectives of the applications of a more economically oriented approach was the relief of the Commission's burden, which has instead enabled it to focus on the worst forms of antitrust violations, such as cartels and other agreements that harm consumers by fixing prices, sharing markets or reducing the amount of product, innovation or the variety/quality of goods/services.

352. The Commission's guidelines focus on six types of cooperation between competitors (actual or potential), which potentially generate efficiencies. However, the guidelines are not clear as to the consequences for more complex types of cooperation such as strategic alliances, linking a series of different areas and cooperation mechanisms. In addition, the guidelines also do not apply in the case of existing sectoral legislation.

353. In the Guidelines, the Commission notes (paragraphs 13 and 14) that some horizontal agreements contain varying degrees of cooperation (e.g., joint research, development and commercialization of the results) – in such cases it is the centre of gravity approach that determines which part of the guidelines are to be used in the case, wherein determining the centre of gravity requires: (i) identification of the starting point of cooperation (e.g., when total production is realized only if the joint research and development are successful, the centre of gravity shall be deemed to be the R&D agreement); and (ii) taking into account the degree of integration of the different functions which are combined (e.g., in the case of an the agreement providing for a full integration in the area of production and only a partial integration of some R&D activities. In this case, the centre of gravity of the cooperation would be the joint production).

B. Standardization

354. In antitrust, standardization can take different forms. Standard setting or rulemaking practices exercised by standard setting bodies, associations of professionals[549]or standards set through an agreement between independent undertakings can be perceived as anti-competitive, when their aim is to prevent access to market to new entrants or achieve exit of an existing market player. As pointed out, standards can take different forms, from basic technical demands[550] to strict quality standards,[551] and trigger antitrust attention in cases where standard setting activities take place in the ambit of a broader anti-competitive behaviour of involved undertakings, where too detailed and definite standards could result in hampering of innovation through/technical) market foreclosure and in cases of standard setting procedures are not transparent and exclude relevant market players.[552] Of course, standardization can also result in anti-competitive effects even in cases when there is voluntary action on the part of the industry, especially in cases where the standards have took over the role of industry practice and access thereto is vital for entry into the market and in cases where the standards agreed upon by the industry as a whole become the norm, i.e., there are no deviation from the set standard while the choice and innovation are limited.[553] No current jurisprudence in the area of standardization could be found in publicly accessible sources of information in Slovenia. We believe, however, that in dealing with potential issues regarding standardization, the national CPO would closely follow the Guidelines as there exist no national best practices or policy papers on the issue.

C. *Joint Production*

355. In the Guidelines, joint production agreements are divided into four main groups – first, the typical joint production agreement down the lines of a joint venture with a goal of producing new type of output and second, the horizontal subcontracting agreements, which can be further subdivided into unilateral specialization agreements, reciprocal specialization agreements and pure subcontracting agreements. Generally, joint production agreements have the potential of resulting in anti-competitive effects, especially in the form of price setting, output reduction or market foreclosure, all due to coordinated behaviour between the parties to a joint production agreement. Of course, such anti-competitive effects are feared especially where the parties to an agreement are direct competitors and/or one or both of the parties have a high degree of market power. As certain forms of specialization agreements have abundant pro-competitive effects, they benefit from the safe harbour provided by the Commission Regulation (EU) No. 1218/2010 of 14 December 2010 on the application of Article 101(3) of the Treaty on the Functioning of the European Union to certain categories of specialization agreements.[554]

549. Hovenkamp, *Antitrust*, 34.
550. E.g., standards set for computer chip components or a common specification of screw thread to ensure that camera tripods produced by one manufacturer could couple with a camera produced by a third party manufacturer, Ashurst, *Co-operation agreements between competitors*.
551. Quality standards set forth by designated national standard-setting bodies, e.g., SQ standard (Slovenian Quality, http://www.szko.si/sq-%E2%80%93-slovenska-kakovost/zakaj-pridobiti-znak-sq/).
552. These types of behaviour are deemed anti-competitive by object.
553. Slaughter & May, *The EU Competition Rules on Horizontal Agreements*, 33.
554. 'Specialisation Block Exemption'.

Of course, the comfort of the safe harbour is revoked in cases where the specialization agreements include one of the following hardcore restrictions:

(a) the fixing of prices when selling the products to third parties with the exception of the fixing of prices charged to immediate customers in the context of joint distribution;
(b) the limitation of output or sales with the exception of:
  - provisions on the agreed amount of products in the context of unilateral or reciprocal specialization agreements or the setting of the capacity and production volume in the context of a joint production agreement; and
  - the setting of sales targets in the context of joint distribution.
(c) the allocation of markets or customers.

356. No current jurisprudence in the area of standardization could be found in publicly accessible sources of information in Slovenia. We believe, however, that in dealing with potential issues regarding standardization, the national CPO would closely follow the Guidelines as there exist no national best practices or policy papers on the issue.

D. Joint Purchasing

357. Joint purchasing agreements can lead to different efficiencies, most notably in joint buyer power resulting in constraints on large sellers' market power, intensified competition in the purchasing market and consequently lower prices, innovation and higher level of choice. Granted, such agreements also have the potential to negatively affect competition in different markets and on different levels of production/trade. The analysis of competition authorities should first be focused on joint purchasing agreements between direct horizontal (inter-brand) competitors, as these enable express or tacit collusion between the parties thus directly diminishing downstream competition. In addition, horizontal agreements can negatively impact downstream competition indirectly through affecting upstream competition[555] (high prices for outsiders, decreased competition between suppliers). The Guidelines provide a safe harbour clause for agreements between purchasers not exceeding 15% joint market share both upstream and downstream – the threshold is intensely criticized due to the too narrowly construed markets and above all due to the fact that purchasing agreement are generally beneficial for competition and can adversely affect the market structures only in cases of significant market power in the downstream market.[556]

358. No current jurisprudence in the area of standardization could be found in publicly accessible sources of information in Slovenia. We believe, however, that in

555. Koponen, *Joint Purchasing Agreements*.
556. Cf. The competitive effects of buyer groups (OFT Economic Discussion Paper, RBB Economics), January 2007, available at: http://www.rbbecon.com/downloads/2012/12/oft863.pdf.

dealing with potential issues regarding standardization, the national CPO would closely follow the Guidelines, as national best practices or policy papers on the issue do not exist.

E. *Joint Selling*

359. Agreements on joint commercialization cover a wide array of business practices, most commonly joint selling, distribution, promotion, after-sales services, advertising, etc. Commercialization agreements can result in serious anti-competitive consequences, in particular price fixing, limitation of output, territorial market division, collusion on the basis of strategic information exchange. As usual, the level of potential threat of anti-competitive behaviour of parties to a commercialization agreement correlates to the level of jointly held market power. As in other cases of agreements between competitors, the Guidelines in absence of a block exemption provide for a safe harbour for all cases where the jointly held market share does not exceed 15%. Of course, the presumption of legality of such agreements is invalidated in cases of hard core restrictions agreed upon by the parties to a joint selling agreement.

360. No current jurisprudence in the area of standardization could be found in publicly accessible sources of information in Slovenia. We believe, however, that in dealing with potential issues regarding standardization, the national CPO would closely follow the Guidelines, as national best practices or policy papers on the issue do not exist.

§2. Vertical Agreements

I. Distribution (Exclusive Distributorship, Exclusive Dealing, Selective Distribution)

361. The notion behind the Slovenian legislative regime of vertical restraints mirrors the one set forth by the European Union. This is an expected turn of events, as the Slovene legislator (apart from erroneous translations and conceptual misunderstandings) rarely departs from the safe harbour of verbatim translation of primary and secondary EU legislation. In addition, the analysis of the Agency's docket reveals that we are yet to have a procedure concerning vertical restraints in Slovenia. We, therefore, propose not to spend much time and effort on an encyclopaedic presentation of main notion of vertical restraints as regulated in Slovenia but rather to point out certain general conceptual facts regarding the restraints themselves, and, more importantly, their potential positive or negative consequences for the competition process and thus for consumer welfare. With nothing but a simplified analysis of the (economic) effects brought along by vertical restraints, we would like to address two historically different lines of approach to vertical schemes as they can be identified in the United States and the European Union, whereby the former jurisdiction deferred to the findings of economic theorists almost from the onset and (apart from the extremely stern decision regarding per se illegality of RPM's in Dr Miles Medical[557]) treated vertical schemes through a very mildly mannered rule of reason standard, taking into consideration potential economic efficiencies, while the latter jurisdiction took a different stance and vilified almost all forms of vertical schemes, disregarding the economic reality and using competition law for the attainment of political goals (internal market). As the venerable, almost a hundred years old judgment in Dr Miles was overruled in 2007, the US Supreme Court took a step many have longed, but, on the other side, many have feared. In Leegin,[558] the Court has essentially stricken down the concept of per se illegality of retail price maintenance agreements in vertical distribution schemes. The decision was met with contention from certain illustrious antitrust scholars, their main argument resting on the recognition of a diminished potential for price competition between retailers 'locked in' into a distribution scheme, finally leading to higher (or at least 'no lower') prices for final consumers.[559] Conversely, those closer to the Chicagoans felt elated as the Court has removed another 'obstacle' from the path to greater allocation efficiency.[560] Both views deserve merit. It is undoubtedly true that the defeat of the per se rule for setting minimum retail prices to one's distributors or retailers diminishes the level of legal clarity in the area. If all RPM schemes are to be looked at through the rule of reason prism, and hence pro-competitive effects are to be looked for, there are no clear-cut answers to what is prohibited and what is legal anymore. This, however, is a dangerously dogmatic (dare I say European) argument in its nature and thus lacks proper value. On the other hand, one can be extremely attracted to the validity of the 'diminished consumer welfare' argument because – as will be shown in a below table – enforcement of minimum RPM schemes inevitably leads to a halt on the price competition between retailers or distributors. It should not be forgotten that the most appreciable efficiency effect that RPM schemes (working together with exclusive distribution) result in is the elimination of the free rider problem. More to the point, the elimination of competition on prices between sellers or between distributors also eliminates the lack of consumer information, or, as Elzinga and Mills put it: 'The economic logic of RPM is to redirect retailers' competitive activities from prices to customer service.'[561] Acknowledging the risk of overgeneralization one could claim that what consumers potentially lose

557. *Dr. Miles Medical Co. v. John D. Park & Sons Co.*, 220 U.S. 373 (1911).
558. *Leegin Creative Leather Products, Inc. v. PSKS, Inc.*, 551 U.S. 877 (2007).
559. Cf. Lande Robert, *The Effect will Behigher Price for Consumer Goods, and I Think that is Undesirable*, cited in Savage, *Paging Dr. Miles …*, 16. Cf. also the American Antitrust Institute Amicus Brief: '*Treating resale price maintenance as "inherently suspect" is consistent with the economic learning cited in Leegin as well as common sense because the direct and intended effect of RPM is to raise prices to consumers, which is precisely what the complaint alleges in this case*', Brief of the American Antitrust Institute as Amicus Curiae in Support of Respondent, S. Ct. No. 06-480, available at: http://www.antitrustinstitute.org/files/AAI-%20Leegin%20v%20%20PSKS,%20amicus%20brief%20FILED%202-26-07_022620071820.pdf.
560. Cf. Elzinga & Mills, '*The Court's Opinion in Leegin Enables the Institution of Antitrust to Examine and Distinguish those Instances When RPM Adds to or Reduces Consumer Welfare on a Case by Case Basis Rather than Summarily Rejecting the Well-Established Economic Arguments about RPM 's Potential Procompetitive Effects*', Elzinga & Mills, *Leegin and Procompetitive Resale Price Maintenance*.
561. *Ibid.*

due to the absence of competition on prices, they might gain through an increase in quality and quantity of pre- and after-sale services. Hence, RPM schemes should not be frowned upon, as they result in a more informed consumer who can take more informed decisions about his/her purchases. Such a conception, however, appears to stem from a viewpoint that certainly commences to lose its validity. The schism between discounters, vilified for their 'low price-garage sale-no information' strategy on the one hand and highly trained, motivated, salon building distributers on the other is not as black and white as it was. This is mainly so due to the extremely fast development of the Internet, which enables everybody to attain as much information on certain products as they wish. This is where, I think, the validity of the 'more information, less free riding' notion falters. It could probably be argued that today's average consumer no longer needs as much information and pampering with high-gloss brochures, test-drives or comparisons as he or she can obtain all this information on the Internet. The information efficiency set aside, not much else speaks in favour of RPM schemes, lest we invoke the brand value dissolution argument, which, however, has nothing to do with antitrust. Leegin has also had a profound effect on EU competition law – the 2010 vertical restraints package certainly has taken into account the prevailing ideas regarding the necessity for an economics-based analysis of market effects of certain types of vertical schemes. In addition, the 2010 Block Exemption Regulation (hereinafter 'BER') stands as a confirmation of the new European approach towards competition law that slowly turns from regulation towards policy: in line with the regime already known from Regulation 1/2003, the hardcore restrictions set forth in Article 4. BER are not to be perceived as per se violations of Article 101 TFEU and can thus also enjoy the exception provided for by Article 101/3 TFEU if and when enough pro-competitive results can be shown.[562]

362. In general, the last twenty years mark a dramatic change in the area of vertical restraints of competition in the European Union. The concept of vertical restraints and the perception thereof by the Commission has evolved under the influence of economic theories, shifting from an overtly and intensely negative perception towards an economic-based approach, acknowledging potential economic efficiencies borne by the restraints. Generally, competition law and policy in the field deals with the two main concepts of vertical restraints, the issue of pricing vertical restraints, i.e., resale price maintenance schemes, and, on the other hand, the mechanisms – also called non-pricing vertical restraints – used by manufacturers or

---

562. Cf. Commission Guidelines on Vertical Restraints, C(2010) 2365, 225:

> Most notably, where a manufacturer introduces a new product, RPM may be helpful during the introductory period of expanding demand to induce distributors to better take into account the manufacturer's interest to promote the product. RPM may provide the distributors with the means to increase sales efforts and if the distributors in this market are under competitive pressure this may induce them to expand overall demand for the product and make the launch of the product a success, also for the benefit of consumers. Similarly, fixed resale prices, and not just maximum resale prices, may be necessary to organise in a franchise system or similar distribution system applying a uniform distribution format a coordinated short-term low price campaign.

suppliers to control the process of product distribution. Such types of vertical schemes can commonly be defined as vertical territorial divisions, location clauses, vertical customer divisions, exclusive distribution clauses, single branding clauses, territorial exclusivity clauses, areas of primary responsibility clauses, selective distribution clauses, full line purchasing or selling obligations, etc. The pivotal issue at hand is whether the vertical schemes (vertical agreements, concerted practices or decisions by undertakings) are anti-competitive at all? The first signals of 'effects-based approach' in the European Union can be traced back to the late nineties, when the Commission commenced with actual analysis of vertical schemes effects on market structures and consumer welfare. The concept of vertical restraints and the perception thereof by the Commission has evolved under the influence of economic theory. A quick glance at the effects of vertical restraints shows that they can almost never result in anti-competitive consequences in the absence of market power, mainly due to the fact that an undertaking cannot obtain or maintain market power simply by choosing to enact a special distribution regime or by starting a resale price maintenance scheme. Conversely, setting up a distribution scheme can actually result in economic efficiencies, internalization (elimination) of double marginalization costs and consequently a more intense inter-brand competition process resulting in higher level of consumer welfare. In the following diagram we show a simplified chart of positive and negative consequences resulting from different types of vertical schemes.

Form	+	–	*Effects*
exclusive distribution	better information for consumers	fewer outlets	restriction of INTRA-BRAND competition
territorial exclusivity	Better information for consumers +incentive to invest	fewer outlets	restriction of INTRA-BRAND competition
single-branding	Better information for consumers +incentive to invest	increasing transaction costs	restriction of INTER-BRAND competition
RPM schemes	getting rid of the FREE RIDER problem, better information for consumers	policing a cartel	restriction of INTRA-BRAND competition, intensifying INTER-BRAND competition

363. The latest vertical restraints package thence somewhat correlates to the latest developments in this area of competition law (antitrust) in the United States. Economic theory is now at the forefront, vertical restraints are to be analysed for potential pro-competitive efficiencies, there is no place for the clear-cut per se rule any longer. The Commission, however, still has certain doubts regarding an all-out positive perception of RPM schemes – this undoubtedly stems from a cautious wording[563] in the Guidelines – and is therefore still a step behind the colleagues from across the pond.

364. The main issues regarding restrictive agreements (concepts, procedure, illegality tests) were already dealt with in other parts of the monograph, while the practice of the SCPA in the area is rather scarce (agreements) and, above all, mirrors the concepts, doctrine and phenomenology of the one currently valid in the European Union. In addition, the Slovene theoretical writing in the area is not particularly rich, and – again – has not sidestepped from the well-established EU concepts.

II. Technology Licensing

365. Agreements consisting of licensing of technology (know-how as well as all traditional intellectual property rights, such as patents, utility models, design rights, semiconductors, etc., as well as software copyright) can definitely produce efficiencies but can also be extremely anti-competitive, especially when concluded between actual or potential competitors with high levels of market power. In certain circumstances – e.g., an innovation market with two main competitors jointly holding up to 85% of market share – an agreement to mutually license all patents can result in a complete foreclosure of such a market, whereby actual or potential competition loses all power to curb potential anti-competitive behaviour by the parties to a patent licensing agreement. As already pointed out, technology transfers can lead to efficiencies, as they enable sharing of accrued knowledge among a wider set of market participants, thus potentially resulting in higher level of innovation, lower prices, etc. In EU competition law, the area is covered by the fairly recent Technology Transfer Block Exemption Regulation[564] (hereinafter 'TTBER'), which covers a wide ambit of transfer of technological knowledge (know-how, patents, utility models, design rights, supplementary protection certificates, and software copyrights for their use beyond mere reproduction and distribution), but expressly excludes from its regime technology licensing in the context of R&D and specialization agreements that fall within the scope of the respective separate Block Exemption Regulations for these types of agreements, and in the context of the set-up of technology pools. The new regime also excludes from its coverage software licensing agreements in the context of mere reproduction and distribution of software copyright protected products, 'pure' copyright and trademarks. As other block exemption regulations, the TTBER provides for a safe harbour and also enumerates hardcore restrictions which automatically remove the block exemption shield from

563. See the previous footnote.
564. Commission Regulation (EU) No. 316/2014 of 21 Mar. 2014 on the application of Art. 101(3) of the Treaty on the Functioning of the European Union to categories of technology transfer agreements.

over an agreement. Article 4 of the TTBER 2014 provides for a 'classic' list of hardcore restrictions,[565] whereas Article 5 lists restrictions that are to be excluded from the ambit of safe harbour without the prejudice to the agreement as a whole.[566] The 2014 TTBER sets forth the same levels of joint market share as provided for in the 2004 TTBER. Thus, agreements between parties that together hold less than 20%[567] or 30%[568] of market share can be covered by the exemption from the TTBER 2014.

366. As Slovenia (similarly to most EU Member States) has no national primary or secondary legislation covering a relatively narrow field of competition law regime of intellectual property rights – or better – technology transfer, this subchapter will deal only with a condensed presentation of the current regime on the EU level. We should also add that – due to an unfortunate position of the CPA that chose not to publish every and all of its decisions – there are no cases from the area of tech transfer to report on. We do, however, offer a brief description of a recent case invoked against the Commission by a Slovenian pharma-giant Krka.

A. *Patent Licensing*

367. In the hierarchy of industrial property rights patents undoubtedly rank first. Entitlements deriving from a patent enable its holder to defend his or her position of monopoly over commercial use of an invention for a limited period of time (usually twenty years). As this part of the monograph deals only with issues regarding situations whereby rights stemming from patents are transferred from the licensor to the licensee with a licensing agreement, we will not delve into the complex subject matter of social and economic justifications of all industrial property rights, in particular patents. Be it enough to say that the current system of patent law in European Union Member States and the United States paradoxically cripples innovation in many areas of science, causes obscenely high direct and opportunity costs throughout the whole economy and is co-responsible for the rise in the level of inequality among men and nations. As for the competition regime regarding potential anti-competitive consequences of patent licensing agreements, the 2014 applies

565. Restriction of a party's ability to determine its prices when selling products to third parties; the limitation of output, except limitations on the output of contract products imposed on the licensee in a non-reciprocal agreement or imposed on only one of the licensees in a reciprocal agreement; the allocation of markets or customers (with exceptions); the restriction of the licensee's ability to exploit its own technology rights or the restriction of the ability of any of the parties to the agreement to carry out research and development, unless such latter restriction is indispensable to prevent the disclosure of the licensed know-how to third parties.
566. Any direct or indirect obligation on the licensee to grant an exclusive licence or to assign rights, in whole or in part, to the licensor or to a third party designated by the licensor in respect of its own improvements to, or its own new applications of, the licensed technology; any direct or indirect obligation on a party not to challenge the validity of intellectual property rights which the other party holds in the Union, without prejudice to the possibility, in the case of an exclusive licence, of providing for termination of the technology transfer agreement in the event that the licensee challenges the validity of any of the licensed technology rights.
567. Agreements between competitors or potential competitors.
568. Agreements between non-competing undertakings.

as regards the already described safe harbour and hardcore restrictions. Certain modifications of the 2004 TTBER in the field of patent licensing however were put in place in the current system. For example, the issue of patent pools has been approached in a different manner; there is now a clear safe harbour that covers the creation of the pool and its subsequent licensing out. As far as payment settlements are concerned, the Commission expresses apprehension regarding potential anti-competitive effects of certain clauses settlements in patent disputes. It is now clear that the 'pay-for-delay' clauses can result in anti-competitive consequences. In Slovenia, the pharma-giant Krka has been accused and also found guilty of anti-competitive technology agreements. On 9 July 2014, the European Commission issued a decision finding the infringement of European antitrust and setting fines in the total amount of EUR 427.7 million for French pharmaceutical company Servier and five generic companies, including Krka.[569] Servier sought protection against generic entry by concluding five patent settlement agreements with the (most) advanced generic contenders: Niche/Unichem, Matrix, Teva, Krka and Lupin between 2005 and 2007. The settlements consisted of significant payments, or other inducements, to the generic companies, and the obligation for them not to challenge Servier's patents and not to enter the market (directly or indirectly) for a number of years. The settlement agreements with Krka and Lupin also included an assignment (transfer) of certain patents to Servier. Krka was fined with EUR 10 million for participating in the cartel. In September 2014, Krka attacked the Commission's decision by filing a nullity action with the General Court in Luxembourg. Finally, in December 2018, the General Court annulled the fine imposed on Servier and Krka.[570]

B. *Trademark Licensing*

368. As already pointed out in the previous subchapters, 'pure' trademark licensing is not covered by the TTBER; its regime will come into play only in cases where licensing of a trademark represents a part of a broader agreement on technology transfer. Thus, a simple trademark license agreement, concluded in view of transferring from licensor to licensee solely the right to use in commercial transactions a trademark attached to a good or service, should be analysed in light of Article 101 TFEU. It is interesting, however, that the new regime deviates from the one in 2004 TTBER whereby it covers also the 'mixed' agreements, i.e., transactions where technology rights are transferred together with a trademark, even if the trademark license is the main objective of the parties.

C. *Know-How and Trade Secret Licensing*

369. If agreements covering transfer of know-how are covered by the current TTBER (as already pointed out, the TTBER exhaustively lists types of technology

569. Decision C(2014) 4955 final of 9 Jul. 2014 in case AT.39612 – Perindopril (Servier).
570. Case T-684/14, *Krka v. Commission*, Judgement of 12 Dec. 2018.

rights it covers, know-how being among them), the issue regarding trade secrets is not so clear. The TTBER does not mention trade secrets and also does not include them in its exhaustive list of technology that is to be governed by its regime. Generally, trade secrets can play an important role in competition law, especially in leniency procedures, where the question of access to corporate statements (and thus also potential trade secrets) of whistleblowers stands as one of the central issues; this issue, however, is outside the scope of this subchapter. As far as transfers of know-how are concerned, the prevailing opinion before the enactment of TTBER 2014 was that EU institutions dealing with such issues should refer to the 2004 TTBER. This question now being moot due to the express inclusion of know-how transfers into the ambit of TTBER 2014, there are still uncertainties regarding the application of competition law to the area of trade secret transfers. We believe that the transactional issues of trade secrets should and can be dealt with by the existing competition law rules, with that we think not only of Article 101 TFEU but also of analogous application of the 2014 TTBER. Problems undoubtedly appear more in the area of dominance, where no secondary legislation on the subject exists in the European Union – with the proposal of the Trade secrets Directive being the only legal instrument near on the horizon we fear that the clarification of the issue is still far away.

Chapter 2. Dominant Undertakings' Prohibited Practices

370. As can be understood from Part I, Chapter 4, §6 of this monograph on abuse of dominant position exploitative as well as exclusionary abuses are proscribed by Slovenian competition law.

371. The example of exploitative abuse of dominant position as set out by the PRCA-1 is the following: (i) 'directly or indirectly imposing unfair purchase or selling prices, or other unfair trading conditions', that is, unfairly high prices. Invoicing an additional amount to specific customers was considered to be contrary to the PRCA-1.[571]

372. The examples of exclusionary abuse of dominant position as set out by the PRCA-1 include, inter alia, the following ones: (i) 'unjustifiably increasing or reducing prices' that is, predatory pricing, (ii) 'applying discriminative conditions to equivalent transactions with other trading partners, thereby placing them at a competitive disadvantage' that is, discrimination and refusal to deal and (iii) 'imposing supplementary obligations which, by their nature and according to commercial usage, are not related to the subject-matter of the contracts' that is, tying.

373. Charging the same type of service at different rates in order to support a subsidiary was also considered to be contrary to the PRCA-1.[572]

§1. Exploitative Practices

374. As already explained above, these kinds of abuses lead to direct decrease in consumers' benefits and the dominant undertaking direct gain is on consumer's expense, which would not be possible had the undertaking not been dominant. Such practices include:

I. Excessive/Unfair Pricing

375. This practice is included in exemplary list of Article 9/4 of the PRCA-1. Abuse of dominant position includes, inter alia, 'directly or indirectly imposing unfair purchase or selling prices, or other unfair trading conditions'. It is evident from the definition that such an abusive behaviour also includes prohibition of a wider concept of unfair trading conditions.

---

571. See, for example, the *Pogrebno podjetje Maribor* case, Decision No. 3073-04/01 of 18 Aug. 2003, available at (in Slovene): http://www.varstvo-konkurence.si/fileadmin/varstvo-konkurence.si/pageuploads/ijz054.pdf; and the *Žale and Mojmir* case, Decision No. 3072-1/2004 of 28 Apr. 2005, not available online.

572. See, for example, the *Telekom Slovenije/Medinet* case, Decision No. 3072-14/02 of 19 Nov. 2004, available at (in Slovene): http://www.varstvo-konkurence.si/fileadmin/varstvo-konkurence.si/pageuploads/ijz018.pdf.

376. Even without specific impact on competitors' market entry, prices charged by dominant firms may be excessive and therefore infringe Article 9/4 of the PRCA-1, if they have no reasonable link with the underlying economic value of the service provided. The latter will normally be established on the basis of costs that can be attributed to a certain service based on an appropriate cost methodology. The concept of excessive prices can be used in retail markets as well as wholesale markets.

377. The PRCA-1 entails no definition on excessive pricing (i.e., price which is above the level of competition), or how it should be assessed. The SCPA follows the case law of the European Commission, the General Court of the EU and the CJEU in this regard – consequently its assessment is based on the comparison with: (i) the price otherwise present on the competitive market, (ii) the price on other relevant markets (so-called benchmarking), or (iii) taking into account the 'economic value' of the product – comparison between the price, incurred costs and economic value of the product, though non-costs factors may also be taken into consideration as they increase the value of the product for the customer. One should bear in mind that even the EU case law contains no rules as to which costs are to be taken into consideration – their amount, value of 'threshold value' above which the difference between price and value would be deemed excessive.

378. In the case *Pogrebno podjetje Maribor*[573] the SCPA found that invoicing an additional amount to specific customers was considered to be contrary to the competition law. In this case the leasing of graves subject to simultaneous order of a funeral, or purchase and installation of a gravestone, all from one dominant firm was considered contrary to provisions of the PRCA-1.[574]

379. A similar decision was adopted in case *Žale and Mojmir.*[575] Žale, having a dominant position on the relevant market for funeral services in Ljubljana, charged for its funeral services higher prices, if the deceased's last place of residence was not in Ljubljana.[576]

II. Discrimination

380. In general, discrimination is described as 'applying discriminative conditions to equivalent transactions with other trading partners, thereby placing them at a competitive disadvantage' without a valid reason for such treatment. This practice is also included in exemplary list of Article 9/4. The assessment of discrimination must be complex with underlying economic analysis of all the relevant circumstances.[577]

573. Decision No. 3073-04/01 of 18 Aug. 2003, available at (in Slovene): http://www.varstvo-konkurence.si/fileadmin/varstvo-konkurence.si/pageuploads/ijz054.pdf.
574. Fatur & Podobnik, *Competition Law in Western Europe and USA: Slovenia*, s. 4.3.
575. Decision No. 3072-1/2004 of 28 Apr. 2005, not available online.
576. Janežič, *Getting the Deal Through – Dominance, Slovenia*, 180, point 19.
577. Grilc in Grilc et al., *PRCA-1 Commentary*, 162.

381. In Telekom Slovenije and Medinet[578] Telekom Slovenije being the exclusive supplier of certain telecommunication services, charged lower rates than the ones set out in its price list when services were provided to its subsidiary. The CPO considered this as contrary to competition law.

382. In Kolosej,[579] proceedings against Kolosej kinematografi, a company which operates cinemas, were initiated upon the request of a company, Blitz Film & Video Distribution, engaged in film distribution, alleging discriminatory terms and conditions. The CPO established that Kolosej imposed discriminatory contractual terms and conditions on its movie distributor.

383. On similar grounds, in case *Pošta Slovenije*,[580] proceedings against the national postal service operator, Pošta Slovenije, were initiated.

384. In the *Slopak* case,[581] the CPO established that Slopak, holding a dominant position on the market for packaging waste (not communal waste), violated the PRCA by restricting its customers in relation to their choice of alternative service providers, which diminished the possibilities of Slopak customers cooperating with competitors engaged in the collection of waste-packing material. Slopak was the leading packaging waste processing service provider in the Slovenian market. It held a dominant position on the market for packaging waste (not communal waste) processing services in Slovenia with a market share exceeding 80%. This was combined with its monopoly position and 100% market share on the market for packaging waste (communal waste) processing services. The case was initiated ex officio after the CPO received a complaint from the competitor Interseroh.

385. The CPO for the first time acting under Article 102 TFEU found Slopak was abusing its dominant position in the packaging waste (not communal waste) processing market in Slovenia from January 2005 to the adoption of the decision in December 2006 by preventing service users from switching to competing service providers, either indirectly with its dealings or directly on the basis of the provisions of the Agreement on transfer of obligation in accordance with Article 15 of the Rulebook on handling packaging and packaging waste ('Agreement'). The abusive practices consisted primarily of:

578. Decision No. 3072-14/02 of 19 Nov. 2004, available at (in Slovene): http://www.varstvo-konkurence.si/fileadmin/varstvo-konkurence.si/pageuploads/ijz018.pdf.
579. Decision No. 306-66/2006-52 of 26 Jul. 2007, available at (in Slovene): http://www.varstvo-konkurence.si/fileadmin/varstvo-konkurence.si/pageuploads/informacija_javnega_znacaja/ijz108.pdf.
580. Decision No. 306-35/2005 of 28 May 2008, available at (in Slovene): http://www.varstvo-konkurence.si/fileadmin/varstvo-konkurence.si/pageuploads/ijz015.pdf.
581. Decision No. 306-125/05 of 21 Dec. 2006, available at (in Slovene): http://www.varstvo-konkurence.si/fileadmin/varstvo-konkurence.si/pageuploads/ijz056.pdf.

- Linking the transfer of obligations of handling of packaging waste which is not communal waste, with the handling of the one which is communal waste, combined with demanding a transfer of entire quantity of the packaging of the service user to Slopak with defined sanctions for deviating from forecasted yearly quantities in connection with enforcing an unjustifiably long twelve-month termination period for the indefinite duration contracts.
- Demanding the service users to enter into Slopak's system in case that the packaging, the service users were putting into circulation on Slovenian market, had a green dot mark.

386. To remedy the infringements the CPO imposed the following measures on Slopak:

- In a three-month term, Slopak had to settle its relations with the service users in the way that it offered them a separate agreement for transfer of obligations regarding handling of packaging waste which is not communal waste, and regarding handling of packaging waste which is communal waste. These new agreements had to specify the quantities of the packaging waste which shall be transferred. Furthermore, in this connection, it could not enforce the termination period provisions for under the existing Agreements.
- In a three-month term, Slopak had to change the existing Agreements with service users in the way that the termination would be possible at the end of each quarter, with the termination period until the end of the current year.
- In a one-year term, Slopak had to arrange the relationship with other systems in regard the use of the green dot mark.

387. It is interesting to note that on the basis of its decision that Slopak violated Slovenian competition legislation, the CPO, as the competent body for prosecuting minor offences, also issued a decision on an offence where it fined Slopak and its authorized officer for the total amount of EUR 129,360.71, which was by far the highest fine issued by the CPO up to that date.

388. The CPO ended the proceedings against Slopak in the part regarding the possibility of cross-subsidization since at that time available information did not support this allegation.

389. The CPO also dealt with abuse of dominant position by discrimination in the *SAZAS* case,[582] establishing that SAZAS, the Society of Composers, Authors and Publishers for Copyright Protection in Slovenia, which has a legal monopoly on collective management of copyrights to music authors, abused its dominant position by sharing collected funds among its members based on non-transparent, subjective and retroactively set rules adopted by certain members only, thereby placing

582. Partial Decision No. 306-35/2009-108 of 8 Apr. 2011, available at (in Slovene): http://www.varstvo-konkurence.si/fileadmin/varstvo-konkurence.si/pageuploads/informacija_javnega_znacaja/202_306-35-2009_sazas.pdf.

some authors at a competitive advantage.[583] On 8 April 2009, the CPO initiated a case against SAZAS which provides for granting licenses to the users who wish to use copyright musical works in public, collection of royalties for the public use of music within the territory of the Republic of Slovenia, and the distribution of the collected royalties to the authors or holders of respective copyrights. In the assessment of the case the CPO established that the markets concerned are collective management of copyrights to authors and the licensing of public performance music copyrights to users. The CPO found that SAZAS has a legal monopoly on both markets due to the legislation in the Republic of Slovenia.

390. The CPO established that SAZAS set and divided collected fees among authors in a non-transparent way which led to discrimination among authors. The CPO held that SAZAS has established a non-transparent system according to which only few authors have a right to decide on the rules on the distribution of the collected royalties to authors. With this system SAZAS has favoured some authors, especially those who were included in the decision-making process of distribution of the collected royalties. Furthermore, the CPO established that SAZAS also discriminated the same type of users by (i) setting and performing the rules for public performance of music copyrights, part of which are also tariffs, in a non-transparent manner, and (ii) dictating the condition of use to users.

391. On 8 April 2011, the CPO issued a partial decision in administrative proceedings finding that SAZAS had abused its dominant position by sharing collected funds among its members based on non-transparent, subjective and retroactively set rules adopted by certain members only – thereby granting some authors a better competitive position on the market. With its decision the CPO also imposed obligations on SAZAS regulating relations between the Society's members. The CPO held that all these established activities constituted a breach of Article 9 of the PRCA-1 as well as Article 102 TFEU, since the infringement by SAZAS has an effect on the whole territory of Slovenia and has effect on services provided by and for companies from other EU Member States, it has an effect on the substantial part of internal market. The CPO's decision was upheld by the Supreme Court in January 2014. The CPA also conducted a separate minor offences proceedings and issued on 20 June 2014 a minor offence decision imposing SAZAS and 14 of SAZAS's responsible persons a fine for the abuse of dominant position of total EUR 177,500.[584]

---

583. *Ibid*; OECD, Directorate for Financial and Enterprise Affairs, Competition Committee: Annual Report on Competition Policy Developments in Slovenia 2011 of 16 Oct. 2012, No. DAF/COMP/AR(2012)42, 5, 6.

584. See Press Release on the CPA's website, 15 Sep. 2014 (in Slovene): http://www.varstvo-konkurence.si/informacije/novica/avk-izdala-prekrskovno-odlocbo-s-katero-je-pravni-osebi-sazas-in-njenim-14-odgovornim-ose-95/.

392. On 5 September 2017, the CPA stopped the proceedings in part of allegations regarding SAZAS' activities towards the users who wished to use copyright musical works in public.[585]

393. In the *SODO* case,[586] the CPO found that SODO, the electricity distribution system operator in the Republic of Slovenia, had abused its dominant position in the market for the management of the electric energy distribution network by charging only some electric power producers connected to distribution network held by specific distributing companies for excessive electric energy received and thus applying discriminative conditions to companies.

§2. Exclusionary Practices

394. As already explained above, these kinds of abuses cover practices by a dominant firm that tends to impair the opportunities of competitors based on considerations other than competition on the merits. Such practices include:

I. Predation

395. Predation, as well as competitive conduct, frequently eliminates competitors. Competitive conduct produces exit from the market when a competitor can no longer keep up with the efforts of other companies to offer superior products or lower prices. The distinguishing feature of predation is that it takes aim deliberately at competitors and potential competitors in an effort to inhibit their capacity to compete. Thus, the pay-off from predation is expected to flow not from increased consumer satisfaction but from reduced competition, which in turn harms consumers.

396. Although consumers may gain from initially lower prices in the short run, they might lose much more in the long run, if the dominant undertaking is able to create the suitable market conditions for charging significantly higher prices than the market price. Moreover, predation can also have harmful effect on available choices and the quality of the goods. Consequently, predation is commonly defined as 'unjustifiably reducing prices'.

397. One should, however, bear in mind that not every decrease in price is predation as it can be also consequence of the lower production costs, globalization, new technologies, licences, etc.[587]

---

585. Decision No. 306-35/2009-178 of 5 Sep. 2017, available at (in Slovene): http://www.varstvo-konkurence.si/fileadmin/varstvo-konkurence.si/pageuploads/informacija_javnega_znacaja/Sklep_306-35-2009-178.pdf.
586. Decision No. 306-5/2011-22 of 9 Aug. 2012, available at (in Slovene): http://www.varstvo-konkurence.si/fileadmin/varstvo-konkurence.si/pageuploads/informacija_javnega_znacaja/Odlocba_306-5-2011-22_-_preciscena.pdf.
587. Grilc in Grilc et al., *PRCA-1 Commentary*, 154.

398. In order to establish whether the pricing is predatory or not, an economic analysis of costs must be conducted with a special regard to average variable costs. If the pricing is below such costs then it is most likely we are dealing with the case of predation, though there are some other possible exculpatory reasons. If the price is above the average variable costs, then the intention to eliminate competition from the market must be proven, a rather difficult task in practice. However, court practices assume such an intent if no objective reasoning for setting such prices is found.[588]

399. The CPO also investigated in *Mobitel/WWI* (*Mobitel I*),[589] whether Mobitel, the largest Slovenian mobile phone service provider, abused its dominant position by tying subscribers that purchased subsidized mobile phones for excessively long periods. The CPO established that Mobitel did not abuse its dominant position when charging very low price for on-net calls, that is, calls within its own network, since such calls were charged at rates that exceed costs.[590] Mobitel was a subsidiary of Telekom Slovenije, Slovenian national telecommunication incumbent at the time of this decision (the merger with the parent company has taken place in July 2011 as described below in case *Mobitel II*), and leading public mobile phone service operator. It held a dominant position on the market for mobile telecommunications services in Slovenia with a market share exceeding 70%. This case started in 2003, when mobile phone operator Western Wireless International ('WWI') complained to the CPO about abusive pricing practices, cross-subsidizing of different telecommunication services and restrictive contract conditions of its rival, Mobitel. In its decision on the case, the CPO:

(1) Rejected the claim of WWI that Mobitel is abusing its dominant position by cross-subsidizing of different telecommunication services.
(2) Accepted the following commitments proposed by Mobitel:
   - regarding the length of period of customers commitments when buying subsidized mobile phone, (a) to cut the necessary period of contract to twelve months, (b) to cut the number of necessary annexes to 1 and (c) to cut the periods of existing contracts to 1 May 2007 the latest;
   - regarding the locking of the subsidized mobile phones, (a) not to lock them anymore, (b) to un-lock with no charges the phones of all existing customers, (c) to un-lock with no charges subsidized mobile phones after twenty-four months when used for prepaid package and (d) no to lock non-subsidized mobile phones;

588. *Ibid.*
589. Partial Decision No. 3072-4/03-184 of 13 Jun. 2005, available at (in Slovene): http://www.varstvo-konkurence.si/fileadmin/varstvo-konkurence.si/pageuploads/ijz008.pdf, and Supplementary Decision No. 3072-4/03-206 of 20 Dec. 2005, available at (in Slovene): http://www.varstvo-konkurence.si/fileadmin/varstvo-konkurence.si/pageuploads/ijz052.pdf.
590. The competitors on the mobile service market were alleging that Mobitel's on-net prices were too low/predatory, which in combination with higher off-net costs, very big Mobitel's customer base and contractual limitations allegedly prevented them to effectively compete for new/Mobitel's customers.

– regarding the costs premature termination of the contracts, to inform every customer when buying subsidized mobile phone on the size of connected advantages and the size of the costs of premature termination of the contracts.

(3) Rejected the claim of WWI that Mobitel is abusing its dominant position by imposing unfair and under-cost prices, particularly for the calls originating and terminating in its own network, by holding that in case of retail market for mobile telecommunications the use of average variable costs as a benchmark for the prima facie decision on existence of predatory prices is inappropriate. Furthermore, it decided that in retail market for mobile telecommunications Fully Allocated Cost model in more appropriate than Long Range Incremental Cost Model for analysis of the level of the prices.

400. The CPO also initiated an investigation against a service provider that allegedly submitted bids on public tenders with unjustifiably low prices.[591]

401. In case *Certus, avtobusni promet Maribor*,[592] the CPO initiated an investigation against a bus company for having offered free-of-range transport for certain routes (VAT and some other costs were apparently not considered) while at the same time it was performing public transport services and was allegedly receiving state subsidies for it.[593]

402. In *Mobitel II* (*Itak Džabest*)[594] the CPO established that Telekom Slovenije (previously Mobitel) acted in predatory manner by imposing the 'Itak Džabest' package on under-cost prices that were lower from the costs incurred.[595] This case was initiated in the beginning of 2009, when the CPO received a complaint from the mobile phone operator Tušmobil, the third biggest mobile operator, entering Slovenian market in 2006, claiming that its competitor, Telekom Slovenije (previously Mobitel, who entered the market in 1991 and merged with its parent company in July 2011, making Telekom Slovenije its universal legal successor), is abusing its dominant position with predatory pricing and price squeeze practices in breach of Article 9 of the PRCA-1 and Article 102 TFEU.

403. After conducting an in-depth investigation the CPO issued a decision on February 2012, finding that Telekom Slovenije has been abusing its dominant position in the retail mobile telecommunications service market from November 2008 to June 2010, by offering the Itak Džabest package to mobile phone users for prices

591. See, for example, the CPO's decision in *GZS*, Decision No. 306-21/2005-92 of 1 Feb. 2006, available at (in Slovene): http://www.varstvo-konkurence.si/fileadmin/varstvo-konkurence.si/pageuploads/ijz066.pdf.
592. CPO's decision No. 3073 – 2/01, not available online.
593. Janežič, *Getting the Deal Through – Dominance, Slovenia*, 180, point 22.
594. Decision No. 306-14/2009-239 of 13 Feb. 2012, operative part of the decision is available at (in Slovene): http://www.varstvo-konkurence.si/ostali-dokumenti/arhiv-odlocb/odlocba228/.
595. *Ibid.* See, for example, OECD, Directorate for Financial and Enterprise Affairs, Competition Committee: Annual Report on Competition Policy Developments in Slovenia 2012 of 3 Oct. 2013, No. DAF/COMP/AR(2013)35, 7, 8.

set too low and therefore infringed Article 9 of the PRCA-1. Since such behaviour of Telekom Slovenije made it more difficult also for the potential operators from other EU Member States to enter the Slovenian market and thus affected trade between Member States and consequently infringed Article 102 TFEU.

404. The CPO established that Telekom Slovenije had a 60% market share at the end of August 2009 which is deemed as dominant position according to Article 9 of the PRCA-1. Despite the gradual decrease in its market share (it fell down by 10% from 2008 to 2010), it was still sufficiently high. Moreover, taking into account the fact that Telekom Slovenije had enjoyed such a position for a longer period of time on the telecommunications market, where economies of scale and network effects are of special importance, it only indicates that Telekom Slovenije has the power to act freely without regard to other competitors.

405. The CPO established that Telekom Slovenije acted in predatory manner by imposing the Itak Džabest package on under-cost prices, that were lower from the costs incurred, in particular charging lower prices for on-net calls (calls terminating in its central network) than for the off-net calls (calls terminating in other networks). The Itak Džabest package was specifically aiming at the young population of mobile phone users, between age of 15 and 30, that presented an important segment of more than 20% of Slovenia's population and having certain specific characteristics (above average use of mobile phone, keeping up with the development of technology, price sensitivity resulting in over average tendency to seek for the most affordable provider). With such unfair selling prices Telekom Slovenije gained new users and made it more difficult for the other equally efficient competitor to gain new users and not suffer loss by doing so.

406. In accordance with Article 40 of the PRCA-1, the CPO ended the proceedings against Telekom Slovenije in the part regarding the possibility of creating price squeeze by charging Tušmobil more for the data transfer than it charged its final users. It concluded that such behaviour did not materially contribute to the infringement and thus the continuance of the proceedings in this part is not relevant for the final decision.

407. In 2013, the Supreme Court annulled the CPO's decision and returned the case to the CPA, which has to reopen the administrative procedure. It considered inter alia that the CPO incompletely established relevant facts, since it gave no reasons for the method, which was used to calculate the incremental costs. However, the Supreme Court upheld the CPO's definition of the relevant market since it explicitly rejected the applicant's assertion of incorrect definition of the relevant market. The Supreme Court stated that a transparent calculation of negative margin per subscriber is crucial in cases like this one, where there is no clear and direct evidence of a 'predation strategy'. Therefore, the CPA should establish more precisely all the relevant elements on which the cost/price analysis is based. While accepting that the cost/price analysis is an element in deciding whether a price is predatory, the Supreme Court noted that it was also relevant what the effects of the introduction and sale of the contested package would likely to be on the elimination of competitors which (in the long run) harms the consumers. Therefore, in order to establish whether the pricing is predatory or not, the Supreme Court considered that not only the intention of predator must be proven but mostly its effect on the market.[596]

II. Tying

408. Tying practices can infringe Article 9 of the PRCA-1 as one of the 'leveraging' non-price abuses, by using market power to influence conditions of competition in related markets. Most of decisions condemning tying obligations involve contractual tying. Contractual tying is defined as 'imposing supplementary obligations which, by their nature and according to commercial usage, are not related to the subject-matter of the contracts' and is one of the examples that the PRCA-1 expressly sets out as an abuse of dominant position in its Article 9/4. It is clear however that this is not the only possible legal basis for tying abuses under Slovenian and EU competition policy and that they are not limited to contractual tying. They can cover all business practices with similar effects, including 'technical' tying and even situations where the products concerned are linked by natural or normal commercial use.

409. Tying constitutes one of the foreclosures of the market as the demand is shifted away from the competitors. The size of demand being tied, and the identity of customers being tied will constitute determining factors in assessing the potential for foreclosure. There is no definition of 'tied demand' in national law, but the SCPA would naturally follow the understanding of the European Commission, which defines it as demand for which 'rivals cannot compete'.[597] Since market distorting foreclosure becomes more likely if tied customers represent a large proportion of the tied market and since the identity of tied customers will also be relevant (in terms of their importance for successful entry), the close economic analysis of the market will be required, which will include other relevant factors also in assessing dominance.[598] The factors having effect on the assessment of the situation and the presence of which may limit the foreclosure effect will be product differentiation, costumers having strong preference for the products of competitors, the ability of competition to offer competing incentives, etc. The reaction of customers to tying and the change in market share will also be considered indicators of the foreclosure effects.[599]

596. See the Supreme Court Judgment No. G 9/2012 of 26 Nov. 2013, available at (in Slovene): http://www.sodisce.si/znanje/sodna_praksa/search.php?q=G%205/2008&database%5BSOVS%5D=SOVS&_submit=i%EF%BF%BD%C3%A8i&showType=table&order=score&direction=asc&rowsPerPage=20&page=4&id=2012032113061462.

597. See: http://ec.europa.eu/dgs/competition/economist/article82.pdf.

598. *Ibid.*

599. *Ibid.*

410. Such was the prior mentioned *Pogrebno podjetje Maribor* case,[600] where the leasing of graves subject to simultaneous order of a funeral, or purchase and installation of a gravestone, all from one entity (having a dominant position) was considered contrary to competition law.

411. In case of *Telekom Slovenije* (ISDN/ADSL),[601] the SCPA held that Telekom's abusive practices with regards to unjustifiable technological tying/bundling of ISDN and ADSL telecommunications services constitute an abuse of dominate position.[602] The Supreme Court later found procedural errors in decision and sent it back to the authority for re-examination. In the new proceedings the SCPA adopted a decision,[603] which found anti-competitive conduct on the part of the Telekom Slovenije from December 2002 to September 2005. However, in this case a minor offence procedure already expired therefore no fine would be imposed.

412. The CPA concluded in case of *Geoplin*[604] that Geoplin, incumbent gas importer and supplier in the Republic of Slovenia, abused its dominant position on the market of gas supply to large industrial customers by concluding long-term contracts with industrial customers connected to the transmission network which included contracted quantities of gas to be taken over for the whole contract period as also obligation to take delivery of minimum quantities. The CPA held that industrial customers connected to the transmission network were entirely tied to Geoplin. Geoplin attacked the CPA's decision before the Administrative Court of RS that quashed the CPA's decision and returned the case back to the CPA.[605] Following the re-examination of the case, the CPA finally accepted the proposed commitments in 2017.[606]

600. CPO's decision No. 3073-04/01 of 18 Aug. 2003, available at (in Slovene): http://www.varstvo-konkurence.si/fileadmin/varstvo-konkurence.si/pageuploads/ijz054.pdf.

601. See the CPO's case *Telekom Slovenije* (ISDN/ADSL,) Decision No. 3072-2/2004-81 of 31 Mar. 2008, not available online.

602. Fatur & Podobnik, *Competition Law in Western Europe and USA: Slovenia*, s. 4.3.

603. See the CPA's decision No. 3072-2/2004-132 of 25 Oct. 2013, available at (in Slovene): http://www.varstvo-konkurence.si/fileadmin/varstvo-konkurence.si/pageuploads/informacija_javnega_znacaja/ijz178.PDF. According to a recent Telekom's public announcement the Administrative Court in November 2015 decided in favour of the Telekom that the CPA's decision of 25 Oct. 2013 is to be set aside and the matter returned to the CPA for a retrial.

604. See Press Release on the CPA's website of 14 Jan. 2015: 'Geoplin abused its Dominant Position on the Market of Gas Supply by Prohibited Contractual Clauses', http://www.varstvo-konkurence.si/en/information-centre/news/geoplin-abused-its-dominant-position-on-the-market-of-gas-supply-by-prohibited-contractual-2/. Decision No. 306-43/2012-162 of 23 Dec. 2014, operative part of the decision is available at (in Slovene): http://www.varstvo-konkurence.si/ostali-dokumenti/arhiv-odlocb/odlocba306/.

605. See Press Release on the CPA's website of 2 Jun. 2015 (in Slovene): http://www.varstvo-konkurence.si/informacije/novica/sodba-upravnega-sodisca-rs-v-zadevi-geoplin-izjava-za-javnost-113/.

606. Decision No. 306-43/2012-466 of 10 Nov. 2017, available at (in Slovene): http://www.varstvo-konkurence.si/fileadmin/varstvo-konkurence.si/pageuploads/informacija_javnega_znacaja/Odlocba_306-43-2012-466-preciscena.pdf.

III. Rebates

413. Rebates and discounts of the dominant undertakings in exchange for ensuring business with customers are considered abuse of a dominant position, if the undertaking having a dominant position ties customers (even if by their own wish) with obligations or their promise in order to gain their orders and if the obligation stipulated has no qualification or if it is taken on the subject of rebates. The same applies for fidelity rebates – which mean conditional discounts regardless of the quantities ordered in exchange for fidelity.[607] Such rebates are incompatible with competition as the benefits given cannot be justified on the quantity of business conducted, but are rather based on disarming the costumers and foreclose the market for competitors. Such an abusive behaviour is especially typical for developing markets giving competitive advantages with means other than concluded transactions.[608]

414. In *Europlakat* case,[609] the CPO initiated an investigation against the largest Slovenian provider of outdoor advertising Europlakat for allegedly abusing its dominant position on the market for providing outdoor advertising space in the Republic of Slovenia, by offering basic and additional discounts for lease of 'outdoor' advertising space and by doing so bind the customers to itself and discriminate them against each other.

415. In 2007, the CPO initiated an ex officio case against Mercator,[610] a retail company with the largest market share in the Slovenian retail market, for alleged abuse of its dominant position on the procurement market for daily consumer goods regarding its contract clauses in annual supply agreements. Mercator had included in its supply agreements unfair rebates which were not cost based and were not passed on to the final consumers. In addition, it had also charged the suppliers for the provision of services which were not essential to the agreement. The market concerned was the procurement market for daily consumer goods. The CPO has decided not to define separate markets within this group, since based on the obtained evidence, practice described above is common on a number of markets for daily consumer goods. Since the infringement concerned the biggest retailer in Slovenia and could have effect on all of its suppliers of daily consumer goods, which are also companies from other EU Member States, apart from the effect on the territory of Slovenia, it could have an effect on substantial part of internal market.

416. After the initiated procedure, Mercator offered commitments which were supposed to eliminate the circumstances leading to the likelihood of the existence of alleged infringements. The commitments offered were of behavioural nature and

607. Grilc in Grilc et al., *PRCA-1 Commentary*, 162.
608. *Ibid.*, 163.
609. Decision No. 306-140/2007-247 of 23 Feb. 2011, available at (in Slovene): http://www.varstvo-konkurence.si/fileadmin/varstvo-konkurence.si/pageuploads/informacija_javnega_znacaja/ijz125.pdf.
610. Decision No. 306-178/2007-189 of 26 Jun. 2009, available at (in Slovene): http://www.varstvo-konkurence.si/fileadmin/varstvo-konkurence.si/pageuploads/ijz073.pdf.

introduced a number of clauses that Mercator had to include in its supply agreements. They also prescribed the duty of Mercator to manage the relations with its suppliers in a written form and to make the text of the commitments public. This would allow the CPO to monitor the retail market for possible future infringements of competition rules. The CPO had decided that the offered commitments were sufficient and concluded the case with the commitment decision.[611]

417. In the *Pro Plus* case,[612] the CPA adopted a decision in April 2013 finding that a leading broadcasting and Internet media company in Slovenia, part of multinational enterprise CME, had abused its dominant position in the market for TV advertising via exclusivity clauses and conditional loyalty rebates. In particular, the CPA concluded that Pro Plus abused its dominant position with requiring individual advertisers to devote their entire advertising budget exclusively to Pro Plus in return for granting rebates. The decision was upheld by the Supreme Court of RS in December 2013.[613]

IV. Refusal to Deal

418. Refusals to deal by a dominant undertaking without objectively justified reasons is considered as 'applying discriminative conditions to equivalent transactions with other trading partners, thereby placing them at a competitive disadvantage', which is listed exemplary in Article 9/4 of the PRCA-1.

419. As in most practices of interest in competition policy, refusals to deal come in many different forms. For example, the dominant company may simply refuse to supply the essential product, charge a prohibitively high price, or make the bottleneck product incompatible with products offered by competitors.

420. The core of the problem in cases involving 'refusals to deal' is that a single company has monopoly power over a key input, product, or network. Consider the standard example of a 'vertical refusal to deal'. By refusing access to the input product in a vertically integrated dominant company, it extends its monopoly from the market, for the essential input, to the potentially competitive downstream market. It follows that an extreme form of refusal to deal exists when a facility in question is essential – its duplication is not possible or is very complicated due to physical, geographical or legal barriers, or is unwanted due to public policy and without access

611. Summary of the *Mercator* case based on OECD, Directorate for Financial and Enterprise Affairs, Competition Committee: Annual Report on Competition Policy Developments in Slovenia 2009 of 4 Oct. 2010, No. DAF/COMP/AR(2010)16, 5.

612. Decision No. 306-90/2009-169 of 24 Apr. 2013, available at (in Slovene): http://www.varstvo-konkurence.si/fileadmin/varstvo-konkurence.si/pageuploads/informacija_javnega_znacaja/201_306-90-2009_Pop_TV.pdf.

613. See the Supreme Court of RS Decision No. G 7/2013 of 15 Apr. 2014, available at (in Slovene): http://www.sodisce.si/znanje/sodna_praksa/vrhovno_sodisce_rs/2012032113066402/.

to which the competitor cannot perform services for their clients. Leading examples are ports, airports, energy and other distribution systems of common goods.[614]

421. The circumstances that must exist in order to define a position of an undertaking as essential facility are mostly economic in nature. The main problem is making a decision whether a certain facility is essential. Among other things one has to assess, similarly as in the case of refusal to deal, if the denial of access will substantially affect competition and no objective justification exists for such conduct of the dominant undertaking. Factors taken into consideration with such an assessment are also plans of undertaking regarding future investments and innovations, especially if the essential facility resulted from previous innovations. The process of deregulation and liberalization is of a special importance for this doctrine, especially in the telecommunications sector.[615]

422. In *Luka Koper*[616] case, an operator of the seaport of Koper refused without justification to allow its competitor access to the port, therefore making it impossible for the competitor to perform towing and mooring activities. Regarding the towing services, Luka Koper claimed that it had no available space in the port, while its daughter company Adria Tow was given access to the port and had freely performed the towing services. Moreover, the demand for towing services was on the rise in the past years. Regarding the mooring services, Luka Koper had prolonged its decision to allow access to the workers of its competitor to the port in order to perform mooring, until the legal basis was changed, and the services were included as the exclusive rights of the concessionaire (Luka Koper). Mooring activities were also performed by Luka Koper's daughter company, in this case Luka Koper INPO. On 29 July 2008 a new decree entered into force, which gave the authority to decide on access to the port infrastructure to its owner, the Government of Republic of Slovenia.

423. Three relevant markets defined in order to examine the behaviour of Luka Koper were the market for organization of port services, market for towing services and market for mooring services. Although separate from the first market, the second and third markets are affected by the actions of the dominant company on the market for organization of port services in which Luka Koper enjoyed de facto monopoly through its subsidiaries. The CPO concluded that refusing the access to the port infrastructure by Luka Koper had the effect of excluding all competition on the markets for towing and mooring services in the port of Koper and therefore constitutes a breach of Article 9 of the PRCA-1 as well as of Article 102 TFEU.[617]

---

614. Grilc in Grilc et al., *PRCA-1 Commentary*, 160.
615. *Ibid.*
616. Decision No. 306-1/2008-84 of 15 Oct. 2009, available at (in Slovene): http://www.varstvo-konkurence.si/fileadmin/varstvo-konkurence.si/pageuploads/ijz085.pdf.
617. Summary of the *Luka Koper* case based on OECD, Directorate for Financial and Enterprise Affairs, Competition Committee: Annual Report on Competition Policy Developments in Slovenia 2009 of 4 Oct. 2010, No. DAF/COMP/AR(2010)16, 6.

424. In the case *Gasilska oprema*,[618] the CPO established that Gasilska oprema, a wholesale company for fire extinguishers and related equipment, had a dominant position on the upstream market of sale of new fire extinguishers. Although Gasilska oprema was not directly involved in after-sales services and maintaining of fire extinguishers, the CPO held that it was indirectly present on the downstream market through its right to conclude or not to conclude a contract for after-sales services and maintenance of the fire extinguishers trade mark Pastor.[619] The CPO concluded that Gasilska oprema abused its dominant position by (i) terminating the contract for after-sale services of fire extinguishers brand Pastor concluded between complainant and Gasilska oprema, because the complainant has obtained an authorization to maintain competitor's fire extinguishers, and (ii) maintaining in force the contracts for maintenance of the fire extinguishers trade mark Pastor subject to abstention from selling competitors' fire extinguishers and maintaining competing brands of fire extinguishers. The CPO's decision was upheld by the Supreme Court of RS in June 2013.[620]

V. Price Squeeze

425. Price squeezes are not specifically mentioned in Article 9/4 of the PRCA-1. The SCPA tends to follow the practice as developed under Article 102 TFEU.

426. In principle, the price squeeze may occur when a vertically integrated monopolist sells an upstream input to its competitors from the market of the production of a downstream product sold to end users. The vertically integrated monopolist has a possibility of reducing the margin between the input price charged to competitors and the price charged in the downstream market for the end product incorporating that particular input. With such behaviour competition concerns arise when the margin is negative or too small to enable downstream competitors to achieve a sufficient profit level, so as to make entry difficult or to encourage exit.

427. The CPO dealt with an alleged abuse of dominant position by price squeeze in the *Mobitel II (Itak Džabest)* case,[621] establishing that Telekom Slovenije (Mobitel at the time), the largest Slovenian mobile phone service provider, abused its dominant position by pricing its Itak Džabest package below costs with the purpose of strengthening or preserving its market power on an important part of the retail mobile telecommunications market. After in-depth enquiry it decided to drop the price squeeze part of complaint and proceeded only with assessing predation.

618. Decision No. 306-93/2008-267 of 8 Nov. 2010 in *Gasilska oprema*, available at (in Slovene): http://www.varstvo-konkurence.si/fileadmin/varstvo-konkurence.si/pageuploads/informacija_javnega_znacaja/Odlocba_306-93-2008-267_-_preciscena.pdf.

619. OECD, Directorate for Financial and Enterprise Affairs, Competition Committee: Annual Report on Competition Policy Developments in Slovenia 2010 of 11 Oct. 2011, No. DAF/COMP/AR(2011)33, 5, 6.

620. See the Supreme Court of RS Decision No. G 47/2010 of 11 Jun. 2013, available at (in Slovene): http://www.sodisce.si/vsrs/odlocitve/2012032113061464/.

621. Decision No. 306-14/2009-239 of 13 Feb. 2012, operative part of the decision is available at (in Slovene): http://www.varstvo-konkurence.si/ostali-dokumenti/arhiv-odlocb/odlocba228/.

Chapter 3. Concentrations

428. Some of the main issues regarding concentrations (concepts, procedure, illegality tests) were already dealt with in other parts of the monograph (Part I, Chapter 3, §3; Part I, Chapter 4, §7; Part III), while the practice of the SCPA in the area is rather one-sided and, above all, mirrors the concepts, doctrine and phenomenology of the one currently valid in the European Union. In addition, the Slovene theoretical writings in the area are not particularly rich, and – again – have not sidestepped from the well-established EU concepts.

§1. Horizontal Mergers

429. Basic features of horizontal mergers make them relatively simple to assess and analyse. A merger of two or more undertakings in the same relevant (product and geographical) market always results in a lessening of the number of competitors in the respective markets, therefore its potential to negatively impact competition is clear. Not all horizontal mergers are anti-competitive, however, as their consequences for the market depend on many parameters, largely on the market power of the merging companies, their financial capabilities, quality and size of their competitors, potential competition and its timely entry into the market, etc.

430. There is no specialized secondary legislation or policy papers on horizontal mergers in Slovenia at the time. The CPA thus operates in the broad limits set forth by the PRCA-1 and Regulation 139/2004, while also taking into account the Commission's Guidelines on the assessment of horizontal mergers under the Council Regulation on the control of concentrations between undertakings.[622]

431. Mergers and other forms of concentrations of competitors in their respective relevant markets can represent a threat to the proper functioning of such market precisely because of the conditions that they create. Concentrations (horizontal mergers in particular) tend to create factual situations that enable business behaviour characteristic of decisions made independent of market realities. Corporate bonds between former independent rivals namely result in a state of diminishing competition; undertakings that acted as competitors are thus joined by merger and cease to compete. The consequences of market concentrations caused by mergers can be divided into two basic categories, namely unilateral effects and collusive (coordinated) effects. Unilateral effects can be identified when a merger of two or more undertakings results in a new single undertaking with considerable market power.

432. Unilateral effects therefore stem from post-merger market conditions which enable the newly formed undertaking to retain and even enlarge its market power through its business practices (e.g., raising prices, limiting production, etc.) which

622. OJ C 31, 5 Feb. 2004, 5–18.

are more or less independent as regards the market, the consumers and the remaining competitors. The level of unilateral effects in horizontal mergers also depends largely on produce differentiation and spatial competition. Whereas the use of term 'unilateral effects' is common to certain jurisdiction, the Commission has in its Guidelines decided to coin the term 'non-coordinated' effects. Non-coordinated effects can be defined as negative consequences of mergers in all cases where the merger results neither in a single powerful firm nor in an oligopolistic, cartel conducive market structure. In the Guidelines the Commission defines the non-coordinated effects as effects 'eliminating important competitive constraints on one or more firms, which consequently would have increased market power, without resorting to coordinated behavior'.[623] The designation of non-coordinated effects itself lacks precision to an extent: the definition of non-coordinated effects the Commission sets forth in the Guidelines could (and should) already be covered by the 'classical' unilateral effects doctrine[624] (especially so in cases of mergers of companies with highly differentiated products), the only prerequisite being the understanding that unilateral effects can and do occur also in the absence of a creation of a post-merger dominant undertaking and not only in single firm dominance post-merger scenarios.

433. Collusive (coordinated) effects on the other hand come into play in cases of mergers which result in a highly concentrated market structure whereby tacit or overt collusion between the merger and the remaining companies is almost imminent.

§2. VERTICAL MERGERS

434. Contrary to horizontal mergers, their vertical counterpart is not perceived as inherently threatening to competition. There are, however, different theories of harm that vertical mergers can result in. First, the foreclosure theory posits that certain vertical mergers will deprive non-integrated undertakings of the input or outlet they require for their business. The entry barriers theory focuses on the potential competitors and their ability to enter into a vertically integrated market. Both theories of harm hold water only in conditions of high market power, extensive integration (foreclosure) or high volume of trade by vertically integrated companies (entry barriers). In addition, other non-coordinated effects (acquisition of confidential information about market) can occur. As for coordinated effects, vertical mergers can result in market conditions that facilitate coordination, collusion, eliminate or neutralize mavericks, etc. At the union level, the Commission has published the Guidelines on the assessment of non-horizontal mergers, which mirror the effects-based approach of the reformed European antitrust. The Commission perceives vertical mergers as largely positive, efficient and pro-consumer welfare in their consequences. The guidelines follow the methodology of the horizontal merger

623. Guidelines, para. 22(a).
624. Cf. Ridyard, *The Commission's New Horizontal Merger Guidelines – An Economic Commentary.*

guidelines as the potentially negative effects of vertical mergers are divided into two main groups (non-coordinated and coordinated effects).

435. There is no specialized secondary legislation or policy papers on non-horizontal mergers in Slovenia at the time. The CPA thus operates in the broad limits set forth by the PRCA-1 and Regulation 139/2004, while also taking into account the Commission's Guidelines on the assessment of non-horizontal mergers.

§3. MARKET/PRODUCT EXTENSION MERGERS

436. Market and/or product-extension mergers make part of a broader group of conglomerate mergers. Their main characteristic is the cooperation of two or more non-competing undertakings, whereby in the market extension type one will detect a merger of two or more undertakings that sell the same product or service in different geographic markets, whereas in the product-extension type, the products or services of the merging undertakings can be marketed, supplied, sold by the same channels or means or to the same consumers, thus achieving efficiencies for the merged companies. Potential competition concerns of product/market extension mergers are mainly similar to those of non-horizontal mergers, whereby a product-extension merger consisting of two dominant players in their respective markets could result in reduction or dissuasion of potential competition and higher barriers to entry.[625] There is no specialized secondary legislation or policy paper on non-horizontal mergers in Slovenia at this time. The CPA thus operates in the broad limits set forth by the PRCA-1 and Regulation 139/2004, while also taking into account the Commission's Guidelines on the assessment of non-horizontal mergers.

§4. PURE CONGLOMERATE MERGERS

437. A conglomerate merger is a merger between firms that neither compete in the same market nor operate at different levels of the supply chain. The anti-competitive potential of pure conglomerate mergers is almost non-existent, except for certain possibilities connected to the business practices of bundling and tying. It is therefore of particular interest that in contrast to its US counterparts, the European Commission continues to express some suspicion towards pure conglomerate mergers, mainly concentrating on potential foreclosure scenarios stemming from business practices encouraging consumers to buy a larger number of products as a package. Unfortunately, the Commission here yet again uses unfortunate wording which attests to its ongoing care for competitors.[626] There is no specialized secondary legislation or policy paper on conglomerate mergers in Slovenia at the time. The

625. Cf. *FTC v. Procter & Gamble Co.*, 386 U.S. 568 (1967).
626. Cf. Para. 93 of the Guidelines:

> Companies engage in tying and bundling in order to provide their customers with better products or offerings in cost-effective ways. Nevertheless, in certain circumstances, these practices

SCPA thus operates in the broad limits set forth by the PRCA-1 and Regulation 139/2004, while also taking into account the Commission's Guidelines on the assessment of non-horizontal mergers.

§5. Joint Ventures

438. In line with the merger control reform in the European Union the regime of Article 10 of the PRCA-1 also covers all forms of full-function joint ventures, their main characteristic being the formation of a joint venture, permanently operating as an autonomous economic entity. To be caught by the provision of Article 10 of the PRCA-1, the created joint venture undertaking must perform, on a lasting basis, all the functions of an autonomous economic entity thus bringing about a lasting change in the structure of the undertakings concerned.[627] To be deemed fully functioning, joint ventures must satisfy a relatively wide range of criteria. The existence of a separate staff and management structure entrusted with daily operations of the joint venture is a precondition. The same requirement applies as far as the ability to gain access to sufficient financial resources and ownership of movable and immovable property. A full-function joint venture cannot be established in cases where the joint venture performs solely one specific function within the parent companies' business activities without access to the market (joint venture acting as a distributor of products or services of parent companies). In cases where the said criteria are not met, a joint venture will be analysed and assessed using Article 6 of the PRCA-1. If the SCPA determines that the conditions referred to in Article 6/3 of the PRCA-1 are not met, it shall issue an order declaring the concentration incompatible with competition rules and prohibit the concentration.

---

may lead to a reduction in actual or potential rivals' ability or incentive to compete. This may reduce the competitive pressure on the merged entity allowing it to increase prices.

627. Commission Notice on the concept of full-function joint ventures under Council Regulation (EEC) No. 4064/89 on the control of concentrations between undertakings (98/C 66/01).

Part III. Administrative Procedure

Chapter 1. Administrative Investigations Before the Antitrust Authority

§1. Initiative

I. General Sectors Inquiry

439. When price rigidity or other circumstances indicate the possibility of impeding or distorting competition on Slovenian territory,[628] the SCPA may conduct a study of a particular sector or certain types of agreements in multiple sectors.[629] In order to acquire the data required for the study, Articles regulating the SCPA's request for data submission and investigation apply mutatis mutandis.[630] The SCPA may publish a report on the study excluding data which constitute business secrets and other confidential data, and invite interested third parties to submit their comments. The SCPA may use the data obtained in the course of conducting research in procedures contemplated within the PRCA-1.

II. Ex officio Investigations

440. The CPA initiates administrative proceedings ex officio by issuing an order on the commencement of the proceedings if it finds that it is probable that European antitrust (Article 101 or 102 TFEU) and/or Slovenian antitrust (Article 6 or 9 of the PRCA-1) has been breached.[631] While the previous PRCA (i.e., the PRCA of 1999 which was in force until 2008) allowed for proceedings to be initiated upon a motion by the parties, the presently valid legislation makes room solely for the ex officio initiation. Initiation of the proceedings is in absolute discretion of the CPA. Such system is supposed to accord to a greater extent to the purposes of public enforcement of competition law, and to make competition law administrative proceedings more similar to typical inspection proceedings. The SCPA may obtain

---

628. It must be stressed here Slovenia has not yet transposed the ECN+ Directive (Directive (EU) 2019/1 of the European Parliament and of the Council of 11 Dec. 2018 to empower the competition authorities of the Member States to be more effective enforcers and to ensure the proper functioning of the internal market (Text with EEA relevance.), *OJ L 11, 14.1.2019, 3–33).*
629. Article 26 of the PRCA-1.
630. That is, Arts 27 to 32 of the PRCA-1.
631. Article 23 of the PRCA-1.

information on allegedly anti-competitive behaviour by its own activities (e.g., when performing studies of a particular sector or certain types of agreements according to Article 26 of the PRCA-1; on the basis of answers obtained on the CPA's request for information in accordance with Article 27 of the PRCA-1; from media) or by persons informing the CPA thereof prior or after the proceedings are initiated.[632] The new regime – while not explicitly regulating such course of action – nevertheless still permits the parties which have information on allegedly anti-competitive behaviour, to inform the SCPA thereof. On the basis of such information, the SCPA then decides whether the proceedings are initiated or not. Even after it has initiated proceedings, the SCPA may invite via its webpage any person having relevant information as to the case, to forward it to the SCPA.[633]

441. As of April 2014, the CPA is vested with an explicit competence within the field of unfair trading practices in the food supply chain as the amendment to the Agriculture Act provided that the newly established Slovenian Ombudsman protecting the relationships in the food supply chain[634] is to report to the CPA of every practice in the food supply chain which is prohibited by Article 61f of the Agriculture Act. Apart from setting out the ombudsman's reporting obligation, Article 61d of the Agriculture Act does not provide for any further details as to how the CPA is to respond to such reports nor as to what the ombudsman's role in the proceedings is.

III. Complaints

442. The PRCA of 1999 allowed for the proceedings to be initiated ex officio by the CPO or upon a complaint lodged by a natural or legal person. In case a complaint was lodged, and the party could show legitimate interest and the probability of the infringement, the CPO had to institute the proceedings and the complainant automatically became a party to the proceedings (having, inter alia, access to the file). If the complainant could not satisfy these prerequisites, the CPO would regard the complaint inadmissible leaving the complainant with an option of instituting administrative dispute proceedings requesting the initiation of the proceedings.

443. As of 2008, the proceedings may be initiated ex officio only, what is supposed to accord to a greater extent to the purposes of public enforcement of competition law, and to make competition law administrative proceedings more similar to typical inspection proceedings. The SCPA may obtain information on allegedly anti-competitive behaviour by its own activities or by the parties which can inform the SCPA thereof prior or after the proceedings are initiated.[635] Such complainants can be of great importance to the SCPA as they might possess focal information as

632. Article 16/2 of the PRCA-1. See, for example, the *Akton v. Telekom Slovenije* case presented in Pt. I, Ch. 5, §2, II B 2 of this monograph.
633. Article 24/4 of the PRCA-1.
634. See the Ombudsman's webpage (in Slovene only): http://www.varuhverigehrane.si/.
635. Article 16/2 of the PRCA-1. See, for example, the *Akton v. Telekom Slovenije* case analysed in Pt. I, Ch. 5, §2, II B 2 of this monograph.

to the allegedly anti-competitive conduct. They may request that their identity is not revealed if they show that otherwise they might sustain material loss.[636] The SCPA may also ask the interested parties to provide it with information as to the practices of the undertaking(s) under investigation by the SCPA. It does so by publishing the invitation on its webpage after the proceedings have been initiated.[637]

444. Persons wishing to protect their legal interests may intervene in the proceedings in order to be more actively involved in the case.[638] It must be stressed that according to the SCPA and the Supreme Court of RS, a mere economic interest does not suffice for being granted the status of an intervener.[639] Only a person safeguarding his or her right or legal benefit within the proceedings concerned may intervene before the SCPA. A specific relationship of the person to the administrative matter pending before the SCPA must exist, whereby this relationship must be regulated by a substantive regulation from which it derives whether a person has a right or a legal interest in the administrative matter before the SCPA. To be granted the status of interveners, the persons having legal interest must file a request within thirty days after the SCPA's order has been published on the SCPA's webpages.[640] If they are granted such status,[641] they have equal rights and obligations as the parties unless the law provides otherwise.[642] In contrast to the parties, they may, for example, not have access to confidential data, they cannot offer corrective measures, etc.

445. In case European antitrust is breached, complainants may lodge a complaint with the European Commission as set out in Regulation 1/2003 and Regulation 773/2004,[643] and in the Notice on the handling of complaints by the Commission.[644]

636. Article 17 of the PRCA-1.
637. Article 24 of the PRCA-1.
638. Article 16/3,4,5 of the PRCA-1.
639. See, for example, the Supreme Court of RS Judgment and Decree No. G 2/2013 of 26 Mar. 2013, available at (in Slovene): http://sodnapraksa.si/search.php?q=varstvo%20konkurence&database[SOVS]=SOVS&_submit=i%C5%A1%C4%8Di&order=date&direction=desc&page=2&id=2012032113053723, where the Supreme Court upheld the CPA's order that undertakings having a mere economic interest in retaining their contractual relationship with the undertaking (dairy) targeted by another undertaking (another dairy) that notified the CPA of the concentration may not intervene in the proceedings before the CPA (they claimed that there is a danger that the dairy concerned would stop purchasing milk from them). Such position of the Supreme Court has been taken already in its judgment No. G 55/2011 of 27 Jun. 2012, available at (in Slovene): http://www.sodisce.si/znanje/sodna_praksa/search.php?q=G%2035/12&database%5BSOVS%5D=SOVS&_submit=i%EF%BF%BD%C3%A8i&showType=table&order=date&direction=asc&page=59&id=2012032113046283.
640. The SCPA must immediately inform the parties of such request.
641. The SCPA may assess their request on a special hearing.
642. Article 43 of the GAPA. For details, see Kerševan & Androjna, *Upravno procesno pravo*, 135–137.
643. Commission Regulation (EC) No. 773/2004 of 7 Apr. 2004 relating to the conduct of proceedings by the Commission pursuant to Arts 81 and 82 of the EC Treaty (Text with EEA relevance), OJ L 123, 27 Apr. 2004, 0018–0024.
644. Commission Notice on the handling of complaints by the Commission under Arts 81 and 82 of the EC Treaty (Text with EEA relevance), OJ C 101, 27 Apr. 2004, 0065–0077.

§2. POWERS

I. Requests for Information

446. Article 27 of the PRCA-1 states that prior to issuing an order on the commencement of the proceedings, the SCPA may request information from any undertaking or partners, members of management or supervisory boards and employees of the undertakings. It may do so by simply sending a letter to the relevant person whereby the form and the content of such letter is not set out in the legislation. The addressees of such letters are not obliged to respond and cooperate with the SCPA, but the SCPA might take their attitude into account when setting fines after finding antitrust infringement.

447. In addition to such simple request, the SCPA may also request information by issuing a special order, which must include the legal basis, the purpose of the request, specification of the requested information, a reasonable deadline for forwarding the information as well as the fine that may be imposed for providing inaccurate, incomplete or misleading information or for failure to provide information within the specified time. No special legal remedy against such order is available and the parties may challenge it only within judicial protection assessing the final decision.[645] Undertakings must provide the SCPA with all requested documentation (in doing that, they may inform the SCPA which data is confidential). They are, however, not obliged to admit the infringement of competition rules. The SCPA decides itself which of the two types of the request is more appropriate in the given circumstances.[646]

448. The SCPA may issue an order imposing a fine of up to EUR 50,000 if the undertaking provides inaccurate, incomplete or misleading information or fails to provide information within the specified time. The deadline for payment of the fine may not be shorter than fifteen days, and not longer than one month. In such cases, the SCPA will issue an order specifying a new deadline for provision of information, and impose further fines to undertakings which continue to refuse to cooperate until the sum of the fines from individual orders reaches 1% of the undertaking's total turnover in the preceding business year. These orders have the quality of enforcement titles.

449. One of the cases in which the CPO set fines pursuant to Article 27 of the PRCA-1, was the *Engrotuš/Špar/Mercator* cartel case (in which the CPO eventually accepted commitments[647]). In July 2008, the CPO send to undertaking Engrotuš d.d. (that was investigated with three other undertakings for breaching Articles 6 of the PRCA-1 and 81 TEC by performing practices of jointly assessing the requests by their suppliers for higher prices of the goods supplied, and of refusing to deal with the suppliers had they offered their goods to other merchants) a simple

645. Article 55/3 of the PRCA-1.

646. For further details, see Bratina & Kocmut in: Grilc et al., *PRCA-1 with Commentary*, 303–312.

647. See Pt. I, Ch. 5, §1, I C of this monograph.

request to provide the CPO with a following set of information: (i) all electronic correspondence (save personal correspondence) during 1 January 2006 and 7 July 2008 between seven undertaking's employees and any of the undertaking's suppliers from the list; (ii) all electronic internal correspondence of these seven employees from this period (save personal correspondence), in which keywords 'Hofer', 'Lidl' 'Leclerc', 'price list', 'price increase' and 'simultaneous price increase'; (iii) all electronic correspondence from this period(save personal correspondence) between these employees and anyone employed at Spar Slovenija d.o.o., Mercator d.d., 'Hofer or Aldi' and 'Rudninis or Leclerc'; (iv) copies of electronic calendars or other media with a monthly list of business meetings of these employees in this period. After ineffective correspondence between the CPO and the undertaking (as to the extension of the deadline to submit information as well as the instructions as to how to submit the requested information), the CPO in September 2008 eventually issued an order on the basis of Article 27 of the PRCA-1 requesting the information.[648] The undertaking requested the Administrative Court of RS to order that the effects of the CPO's order are temporarily stayed, but was eventually not successful.[649] After further ineffective correspondence between the CPO and the undertaking (again as to the extension of the deadline to submit information, and the instructions as to how to separate personal correspondence from the one to be submitted – the undertaking claimed that it cannot submit the requested information as it might contain personal data, and referred to the Information Commissioner's decision of July 2008 prohibiting the CPO to read personal correspondence[650]), the CPO issued an order in January 2009 setting a fine in the maximum amount of EUR 50,000 (to be paid in twenty days after receiving the order) for not sending complete information.[651] The undertaking attacked the order before the Supreme Court of RS that issued a judgment in June 2009.[652] Although the Supreme Court stressed that the undertaking could indeed have excluded the personal information from the information to be submitted to the CPO, it set aside the CPO's order on the grounds that the CPO did not prove that the addressee of its order possessed the requested information nor that it submitted inaccurate, incomplete or misleading information or failed to provide information within the specified time.

450. As has already been analysed in more detail in Part III, Chapter 1, §1, I of this monograph, the SCPA may conduct a study of a particular sector or certain types of agreements in multiple sectors when price rigidity or other circumstances indicate the possibility of impeding or distorting competition on Slovenian territory.

---

648. Order No. 306-182/2007-211 of 11 Sep. 2008.
649. Order No. U 2068/2008 of 24 Nov. 2008. The Administrative Court first issued the interim order but the Supreme Court set it aside and returned the case back to the Administrative Court.
650. For further details see the following paragraphs.
651. Order No. 306-182/2007-365 of 6 Jan. 2009.
652. Judgment No. G 3/2009 of 30 Jun. 2009, available at (in Slovene): http://sodnapraksa.si/?q=G%203/2009&database[SOVS]=SOVS&database[IESP]=IESP&database[UPRS]=UPRS&_submit=i%C5%A1%C4%8Di&page=0&id=63930.

II. Investigative and Search Powers

451. Before 10 May 2014 when the latest PRCA-1 amendment entered into force following the Constitutional Court's decision of April 2013 finding unconstitutionality of the first sentence of Article 28/1 of the PRCA-1 regulating inspections of the SCPA, the SCPA had powers to perform investigative activities on an undertaking against which a procedure has been initiated once an order for inspection has been issued by the SCPA. Namely, prior to the 2014 amendment, the PRCA-1 (obviously by analogy with the system of the European Commission's powers of inspection) did not provide for a court order the SCPA would have to acquire for performing inspections (save in cases of inspections of premises of other undertakings or of residential premises where, as explained below, such order was required already prior to the 2014 amendments).

452. Constitutionality of such regulation was assessed by the Constitutional Court of RS on the motion by the Supreme Court of RS who was assessing in a series of administrative judicial review proceedings, inter alia, the CPO's dawn raids performed without a court order. The Supreme Court stated that Articles 28 and 29 of the PRCA-1 regulating inspections in the premises of investigated undertakings could be in breach of Articles 36 and 37 of the Slovenian Constitution safeguarding the inviolability of dwellings and communications privacy. According to Article 36 of the Constitution, the dwellings may only be entered and searched against the will of the resident on the basis of a court order and in the presence of two witnesses,[653] while according to Article 37 of the Constitution, only a law may prescribe that on the basis of a court order the protection of the privacy of correspondence and other means of communication and the inviolability of personal privacy be suspended for a set time where such is necessary for the initiation or performance of criminal proceedings or for reasons of national security. The decision of the Constitutional Court was issued in April 2013[654] finding that (i) the first sentence of Article 28/1 of the PRCA-1 is unconstitutional, (ii) the Slovenian parliament is to abolish the unconstitutionality in one year after the Constitutional Court's decision is published in the OJ of RS, and (iii) the provision in question is further applied until the unconstitutionality is abolished. As in the focal competition law cases inspections of investigated undertakings have been performed by the CPO without court orders, the ratione temporis of the Constitutional Court's decision acknowledging the PRCA-1's unconstitutionality, is of great importance.

453. Following the Constitutional Court's decision, Slovenian legislator amended in 2014 the relevant provisions of the PRCA-1. Article 28/1 of the

653. Subject to conditions provided by law, an official may enter the dwelling or other premises of another person without a court order, and may in exceptional cases conduct the search in the absence of witnesses, where this is absolutely necessary for the direct apprehension of a person who has committed a criminal offence, or to protect people or property.

654. Decision No. U-I-40/12-31 of 11 Apr. 2013, available (in Slovene) at: http://odlocitve.us-rs.si/sl/odlocitev/US30070.

PRCA-1 now caters for intense procedural safeguards and states that the CPA performs an inspection in the undertaking with regard to which administrative proceedings were initiated (i) on the basis of the undertaking's consent (and, if required, the consent of the person whose data are being investigated), or (ii) on the basis of a reasoned written court order and in the presence of two witnesses over the age of 18.

454. Article 28/3 of the PRCA-1 specifies that the court issues the order for inspection on proposal of the CPA if it finds that the 'justified reasons for suspicion' exist that the undertaking breached Slovenian or European antitrust and that it is probable that the inspection will provide evidence relevant for the proceedings. If inspection refers to electronic devices and devices connected to them or/and electronic data carriers, such as phone, telefax, computer, optical media, memory cards and other electronic data carriers, as well as data on electronic devices stored by the undertaking with the provider of information technology services, such as leasing servers services and cloud services, the CPA must show the probability that electronic devices in question contain data relevant for the proceedings. Article 28/4 of the PRCA-1 vests jurisdiction for issuing court orders in these cases with the District Court in Ljubljana which is to issue the order in forty-eight hours after receiving the CPA's proposal. The CPA's proposal must contain the following: determination of premises, documentation, electronic devices to be inspected; reasoned grounds for inspection; the evidence or information searched; circumstances requiring an investigative act and how it is to be performed; deadline for performing the inspection. According to Article 28/5 of the PRCA-1, cases of issuing court orders for inspection are considered urgent and are to be handled by the court as priority.

455. The Information Commissioner of RS has also challenged the constitutionality of the PRCA-1 before the Constitutional Court after the CPO had obtained e-mails of the employees in the *Mercator/Spar/Engrotuš* cartel investigation.[655] According to the Information Commissioner, parts of Article 29/2 of the PRCA-1 listing the SCPA's powers of inspection were unconstitutional. The Commissioner focused on the power of the SCPA to conduct inspection of electronic mail.[656] In October 2013, the Constitutional Court of RS issued the decision dismissing the Commissioner's request on grounds that by interfering in cases pending before other state institutions empowered to assess these cases (the CPO in the case), the Commissioner had exceeded the limits of its jurisdiction vested with it by the law and may not require assessment of constitutionality before the Supreme Court of RS.[657]

655. Decision of the Information Commissioner prohibiting the CPO the use of the e-mails and the discs seized during dawn raids, is available at (in English): https://www.ip-rs.si/fileadmin/user_upload/Pdf/odlocbe/Odlocba__mercator___tus_in_Spar-eng.pdf.

656. In July 2008, the Information Commissioner issued a highly debated Decision on communication privacy and electronic mail regarding competencies of the CPO regarding the investigation of the *Spar Slovenija/Poslovni sistem Mercator/Engrotuš* cartel (available at (in English): https://www.ip-rs.si/fileadmin/user_upload/Pdf/odlocbe/Odlocba__mercator___tus_in_Spar-eng.pdf).

657. Decision No. U-I-92/12 of 10 Oct. 2013, available at (in Slovene): http://odlocitve.us-rs.si/usrs/us-odl.nsf/o/55DE3F95953BDE53C1257C0C00314C9D.

456. According to Article 28/2 of the PRCA-1, the court order must be served at the commencement of the inspection personally on the undertaking against which the inspection is being carried out. The CPA's order initiating the proceedings against the undertaking may be served together with the court order.

457. Both in the fields of antitrust and merger control, the powers of inspection empower the authorized persons[658] to:

- enter and inspect premises, land and means of transport at the registered office of the undertaking and at other locations at which the undertaking itself or another undertaking authorized by the undertaking concerned performs the activity and business for which there is probability of an infringement of Slovenian or/and European competition rules;[659]
- examine the books, contracts, papers, business correspondence, business records and other information relating to the business of the undertaking, irrespective of the medium on which they are stored;
- take or obtain in any form copies of, forensic copies of or extracts from business books and other documentation using photocopying devices and computer equipment of the undertaking or the SCPA;[660]
- seal any business premises and business books and other documentation for the period of the inspection and to the extent necessary for the inspection;
- seize items and business books and other documentation for a period no longer than twenty working days;
- ask any representative or member of staff of the undertaking to give an oral or written explanation of facts or documents relating to the subject-matter and purpose of the inspection and record it;[661]
- examine papers disclosing the identity of persons;
- perform other actions in line with the purpose of the inspection.

458. The investigated undertakings must allow authorized persons access to premises, business books and other documentation. Authorized persons may also conduct inspections against the will of the undertakings using assistance of the police were it established that an undertaking refuses to permit the authorized person, or interferes with, any entry into the premises or denies access to business books or other documentation or obstructs or otherwise interferes with an inspection.[662] In

658. I.e., the employees of the SCPA or persons appointed by the SCPA (specialized organizations, public institutions or individuals may perform investigations unless this would be contrary to public interest or to the interests of the parties).
659. Article 29 of the PRCA-1 sets out the rules on inspection in cases of antitrust breaches, while Art. 48 of the PRCA-1 refers to these rules in cases of merger investigations. In merger control proceedings, inspections may be performed in the undertakings taking part, as well as in those likely to have taken part in a concentration.
660. If, for technical reasons, it is not possible to make photocopies with photocopying devices or computer equipment of the undertaking or of the SCPA, authorized persons may take away business books and other documentation for the time required to make photocopies.
661. When a written explanation is requested by the authorised person, the latter shall set a deadline for its submission.
662. The cost and damages incurred by such access are borne by the investigated undertaking.

view of the highly invasive nature of the described practices, the SCPA and its authorized personnel are bound by the principle of proportionality and should ensure that all performed measures are proportionate to the pursued aims of the investigation and are time-limited. Hence, an inspection shall, as a rule, be carried out between 6 am and 10 pm. Authorized persons must carry out the inspection in such a manner as to cause minimum disturbance to the undertaking's operations. Furthermore, privileged communication, i.e., communication between the investigated undertaking and its attorney regarding the investigation at hand, is outside the ambit of the inspection.[663]

459. The person using the inspected electronic device must enable the authorized person access to the device, submit encryption keys or passwords, and provide explanation on how to use the device. Inspection of electronic devices must be performed so as to interfere as little as possible with the rights of persons who are not subject to inspection, to protect secrecy or confidentiality of data and to omit causing disproportionate harm, doing all that also by regular extraction of irrelevant data. If the device is used by a person who reasonably expects that privacy of the contents will be guaranteed has the right to be present during the inspection of the device.

460. To secure efficient conduct of inspection, the PRCA-1 provides for severe penalties for legal and natural persons obstructing authorized personnel in the exercise of their powers of inspection. Hence, the SCPA may issue an order imposing a penalty payment on the undertaking[664] amounting to up to 1% of its total turnover in the preceding business year for legal persons, and an order imposing a penalty payment amounting up to EUR 50,000 for natural persons[665] obstructing an inspection. In February 2012, the CPO fined Slovenian media company Pro Plus with EUR 105,000 (i.e., 0.2% of its total turnover) for obstructing the CPO's inspection at its premises on 11 August 2011.[666] The inspection that was carried out within the proceedings investigating Pro Plus's abuse of dominant position in the market of television advertising. In this particular case, the penalty could be set to up to approx. EUR 530,000 representing 1% of the Pro Plus's total turnover in the preceding year. The CPO explained that in setting the penalty, it paid due regard to the fact that after initial problems it had had carrying out the inspection (supposedly, the CPO's agents were allowed to seal the premises only after an hour and a half after entering the premises as one of the employees, referring to the absence of the management, refused to cooperate with the agents), cooperation was eventually nevertheless guaranteed (the CPO even asked the police to assist it), and that that was the first time the CPO had ever fined an undertaking for obstructing investigation.

663. When in doubt whether a particular communication is privileged, it is seized and handed to the Supreme Court of RS who assesses its nature.
664. It is deemed that the undertaking is obstructing the inspection if the inspection is obstructed by the undertaking's management, members of the supervisory board or its staff.
665. I.e., in cases where a natural person's conduct is not deemed a conduct of the undertaking.
666. Vogrinec, *Oviranje preiskave po ZPOmK-1*, 9.

Pro Plus filed a lawsuit with the Supreme Court of RS[667] claiming, inter alia, that the CPO should have imposed the penalty in the minor offences proceedings, not in regular administrative proceedings, but the Supreme Court did not share this view and stated that penalizing undertakings for obstructing inspection as set out in Article 31/2 of the PRCA-a is not the minor offences proceedings setting fines which is regulated in other parts of the PRCA-1. It rejected the plaintiff's action and thus upheld the CPO's decision.[668] It stressed that the inspected undertaking must show at least minimal cooperation, e.g., by opening the doors to the inspectors to enter the business premises and perhaps also to show them where the documentation is located.

461. Another case in which the CPA set a fine for obstructing investigation was the *Geoplin* case. Undertaking Geoplin d.o.o. was investigated for abuse of dominant position and refused on 17 and 18 July 2013 to cooperate with the CPA's investigators. In October 2013, the CPA set a fine of 0.2% of the undertaking's total turnover in the preceding business year.[669]

462. The SCPA is also empowered to enter and inspect premises of other undertakings not under investigation, and residential premises of the members of the investigated undertaking's management or supervisory boards as well as of other staff or associates of the investigated undertaking if there are reasonable grounds to suspect that documentation relating to the subject-matter of the inspection is being kept in these premises.[670] In contrast to inspections of the investigated undertaking's premises, the PRCA-1 explicitly set out that the SCPA must obtain a court order before performing such inspections even before the 2014 amendment entered into force.[671] When residential premises are inspected, two witnesses must be present during the inspection. Otherwise, general rules of the PRCA-1 on inspections apply.

463. In accordance with Regulation 1/2003 and Regulation 139/2004, the SCPA may also perform inspections for the European Commission or other competition authorities of the Member States of the EU, or may assist them in performing

667. As during the inspection the CPO seized electronic mail of the employees, Pro Plus filed also a complaint with the Slovenian Information Commissioner alleging that the CPO had breached its communication privacy. The Information Commissioner issued its opinion on 11 Sep. 2011, available (in Slovene) at: https://www.ip-rs.si/varstvo-osebnih-podatkov/iskalnik-po-odlocbah-in-mnenjih/odlocbe-in-mnenja-varstvo-osebnih-podatkov/?tx_jzvopdecisions_pi1%5BshowUid%5D=2066&cHash=7e7acd55a1ca5ed420a73a02a0faead8.

668. Judgment No. G 10/2012 of 26 Nov. 2013, available at (in Slovene): http://sodnapraksa.si/search.php?q=varstvo%20konkurence&database[SOVS]=SOVS&_submit=i%C5%A1%C4%8Di&order=date&direction=desc&page=1&id=2012032113062489.

669. Vogrinec, *Oviranje preiskave po ZPOmK-1*, 9.

670. Article 33 of the PRCA-1. The PRCA of 1999 regulated such inspections in much more general terms enabling a wider scope of other premises to be inspected.

671. The PRCA-1 states that court orders are issued by the 'competent court in Ljubljana' and has not been amended with the 2014 amendments, whereas the District Court in Ljubljana has been explicitly vested with jurisdiction of issuing court orders in cases of inspection of business premises of the undertaking against which the CPA proceedings were initiated.

inspections on the territory of Slovenia.[672] Slovenian authorities, for example, assisted the European Commission in performing investigative acts in Novo mesto in the premises of the Slovenian pharmaceutical undertaking Krka d.d. Following the pharmaceutical sector inspections in January 2008, the Commission performed a series of dawn raids in the pharmaceutical companies in November 2008 and was accompanied by the CPO's personnel (who supposedly arranged also for the presence of Slovenian police whose assistance was eventually not required).[673] Antitrust proceedings were initiated on 2 July 2009.[674] On 9 July 2014, the European Commission issued a decision finding the infringement and setting fines in the total amount of EUR 427.7 million for French pharmaceutical company Servier and five generic companies (Niche/Unichem, Matrix (now part of Mylan), Teva, Krka and Lupin) for curbing entry of cheaper versions of cardiovascular medicine.[675] Krka was fined with EUR 10 million for participating in the cartel.[676] Krka has attacked the Commission's decision by filing a nullity action with the General Court in Luxembourg.[677]

III. Cooperation with Other State Institutions

A. *Cooperation in Drafting the Competition Policy*

464. Article 12 of the PRCA-1 states that the SCPA submits its opinions on general issues under its competence to the National Assembly of the Republic of Slovenia and to the Government of the Republic of Slovenia. Article 121 of the PRCA-1 which came into force in 2011 and is applied by 1 January 2013, also provides that the SCPA cooperates in drafting the competition policy.

B. *Cooperation in Bilateral and International Relations*

465. Article 121 of the PRCA-1 provides a new also for the SCPA's involvement in bilateral relations and international organizations. Although these tasks have previously not been explicitly set out in the PRCA-1, the CPO has as of its establishment been taking part in different bilateral and international competition policy activities. The CPA has continued with this practice.[678]

466. According to Article 121 of the PRCA-1, the director of the CPA has to report on the cooperation within the EU to the CPA's Council and to the relevant

672. See Art. 22 of Regulation 1/2003 and Art. 35 of the PRCA-1, and Arts 12–13 of Regulation 139/2004 and Art. 48 of the PRCA-1.
673. http://europa.eu/rapid/press-release_MEMO-08-734_en.htm?locale=en; http://www.finance.si/230773/Uradno-Evropska-komisija-Colari%C4%8Devo-Krko-sumi-kartelnega-dogovarjanja.
674. http://ec.europa.eu/competition/antitrust/cases/dec_docs/39612/39612_841_8.pdf.
675. http://ec.europa.eu/competition/elojade/isef/case_details.cfm?proc_code=1_39612.
676. http://europa.eu/rapid/press-release_IP-14-799_en.htm.
677. See Pt. I, Ch. 5, §1 of this monograph.
678. http://www.varstvo-konkurence.si/mednarodno-sodelovanje/.

ministry. Within public enforcement of European antitrust, the SCPA cooperates with the European Commission and with national competition authorities of EU Member States (i.e., within the European Competition Network – ECN)[679] according to the rules as set out in Regulation 1/2003 and the Commission Notice on cooperation within the Network of Competition Authorities.[680] Such cooperation takes the form of, inter alia, exchange of information and documents, consultation with the Commission on cases involving the application of European antitrust, assistance to the Commission when performing investigative tasks in Slovenia, etc. National competition authorities and the European Commission cooperate also within the system of referrals as set out in the EU Merger Regulation (Regulation 139/2004). The SCPA also takes part in the discussions within the European Competition Authorities (ECA), an informal association of NCAs of the European Economic Area.[681]

467. The SCPA is also a member of International Competition Network (ICN).[682] Being a member of OECD[683] and WTO,[684] it has also taken part in addressing issues of competition law in the ambit of these organizations.

C. *Cooperation with National Courts Applying European Antitrust*

468. Article 15 of Regulation 1/2003 and Article 63 of the PRCA-1 provide for a cooperation of the SCPA (as well as the European Commission and national competition authorities of other Member States of the EU) with Slovenian courts applying European antitrust. After the 2017 amendments of the PRCA-1, Article 63 also covers the cooperation between the CPA and Slovenian courts when the latter apply Slovenian antitrust.[685]

469. According to the currently valid rules, the Slovenian courts applying European or Slovenian antitrust must immediately inform the CPA (and, in the case of European antitrust, the European Commission) of initiation of such proceedings as well of any decisions issued applying European or Slovenian antitrust.

470. The courts also have to inform the CPA of any opinion of the European Commission delivered to the courts in accordance with Article 15/1 or Article 15/3 of Regulation 1/2003. Further, under Article 15/3 of Regulation 1/2003, the SCPA itself may provide Slovenian courts applying European antitrust with a non-binding amicus curiae opinion on the application of European antitrust. Article 63, as

679. http://ec.europa.eu/competition/ecn/index_en.html.
680. Commission Notice on cooperation within the Network of Competition Authorities (Text with EEA relevance), OJ C 101, 27 Apr. 2004, 43–53.
681. https://ec.europa.eu/competition/publications/eca/.
682. http://www.internationalcompetitionnetwork.org/.
683. http://www.oecd.org/competition/.
684. http://www.wto.org/english/tratop_e/comp_e/comp_e.htm.
685. For further details, see Vlahek, *Amicus curiae*.

amended in 2017, adds that in such cases, the court must send a copy of such written statement to the CPA and the parties. Article 63 now states also that the CPA may issue written opinions to Slovenian courts on their request and sets out detailed rules on how the cooperation between the CPA and the courts under Regulation 1/2003 and Article 63 of the PRCA-1 takes place. The 2017 PRCA-1 amendment to Article 63 added the provision stating that the Commission and the CPA may send a written opinion anytime until the judgment is rendered.

471. The SCPA may also be used as a communications channel between the Slovenian courts and the European Commission. The CPA and the courts had supposedly agreed to such cooperation as regards the courts' obligation to inform the Commission of the judgments applying European antitrust as set out in Article 15/2 of Regulation 1/2003. As the agreed cooperation was not implemented in practice, the courts have decided (after a decade of inactivity with that regard) to start informing the Commission of the judgments directly. According to Article 63 of the PRCA-1 as amended in 2017, this cooperation takes place between the CPA and the courts.

472. Prior to the 2017 PRCA-1 amendment, Article 63 of the PRCA-1 did not provide for any cooperation between the SCPA and the courts when the courts applied Slovenian antitrust, save in cases of damages actions where Article 62/4 (as in force before the 2017 amendment) obliged Slovenian courts to inform the SCPA (only) of every action requesting damages for breaches of Slovenian or European antitrust. It did not, however, oblige the courts to inform the SCPA of the judgments rendered applying Slovenian antitrust.

D. Exchange of Information

473. According to the PRCA-1, the SCPA's employees, members of its bodies, and persons cooperating with the SCPA in the implementation of its tasks, must treat confidential information as confidential in compliance with the rules determining protection of such information.[686] The SCPA may, however, disclose confidential information to administrative bodies, other state authorities and holders of public authorizations in the Republic of Slovenia on the basis of their substantiated written request. Likewise, it may disclose information to the European Commission and national competition authorities of EU Member States in accordance with Regulation 1/2003, as well as to authorized authorities of foreign states in cases determined by international treaties binding on Slovenia.[687] It must also disclose all relevant information to the bodies enforcing the SCPA's decisions.[688]

474. The PRCA-1, on the other hand, also obliges state authorities, local community authorities, holders of public authority and other persons and organizations

686. Article 13a of the PRCA-1.
687. Article 13b/1,2 of the PRCA-1.
688. Article 13b/3 of the PRCA-1.

with access to information required for the SCPA's decision-making, to provide the SCPA, at its request, the required information free of charge.[689]

§3. RIGHT OF DEFENCE

I. Content and Notification of Opening Decisions

475. Administrative proceedings are initiated when the SCPA issues an order on the commencement of the proceedings. The order is of a purely procedural nature and does not encroach upon the relevant parties' rights, hence no judicial protection against it is granted. As the order represents the initial phase of proceedings against the alleged anti-competitive behaviour, the undertaking to which the order applies and becomes a party to the proceedings at its issuance,[690] should be thoroughly informed of the grounds for the commencement of the proceedings. To this goal, the PRCA-1 provides that the order shall contain thorough information regarding the initiation of the proceedings, including the description of the alleged anti-competitive behaviour providing grounds for the commencement of the proceedings, specification of the provisions of the PRCA-1 for which a probability has been demonstrated that they have been breached; and the grounds for the commencement of the proceedings.[691]

476. To satisfy the condition of publicity, the PRCA-1 also provides that the extract of the order is published on the SCPA's website.[692] The extract contains information as to the parties to the proceedings, the reasons and the legal basis for initiating the proceedings, as well as the invitation to any person having any relevant information as to the subject matter of the proceedings. Should the need arise to amend the proceedings to include an additional infringement or undertaking, the SCPA shall issue an order amending the order on the commencement of the proceedings.

II. The Proceedings: Hearings, Access to File, Briefs, Etc.

A. *Privileged Communication*

477. According to Article 32 of the PRCA-1, letters, notifications and all other communication between the undertaking against which the proceedings have been initiated, and their counsel, are deemed privileged and may not be subject to inspection of the SCPA to the extent that such communication pertain to the proceedings

689. Article 14 of the PRCA-1.
690. Article 16 of the PRCA-1.
691. Article 24 of the PRCA-1. For further details regarding the content and effect of the order, see Bratina & Galič in Grilc et al., *PRCA-1 Commentary*, 297–286.
692. Article 24 of the PRCA-1. Those decisions and extracts that are published online, are available in Slovene only. See: http://www.varstvo-konkurence.si/en/antitrust/decisions/, http://www.varstvo-konkurence.si/en/concentrations-of-undertakings/notified-concentrations-and-decisions/.

in question. The quality of privileged communication is to be established by the authorized personnel of the SCPA at the request of the party. If it is ascertained that the undertaking's request that the communication be characterized as privileged, is utterly unfounded, the document (or its copy) containing such communication must be sealed in an envelope, signed by the authorized person and the undertaking or its counsel, and filed with the Administrative Court of RS in Ljubljana in assessment of its character. The court must issue its decision within fifteen days. There is no judicial remedy available against such decision. If the court finds that the document contains privileged communication, it sends it to the party, if not, it sends it the SCPA. In accordance with Article 31 of the PRCA-1, the SCPA may impose fines amounting up to 1% of the undertaking's total annual turnover in the preceding business year if it establishes that the claim of privileged communication equals an obstruction of the inspection.

B. Right to Be Heard

478. The PRCA-1 follows the traditional audiatur et altera pars principle, which is set out in Article 19 of the PRCA-1.[693] While the SCPA as a rule decides without a hearing (unless an official conducting the proceedings determines that a hearing is to be conducted in order to establish or to clarify essential facts), it is explicitly forbidden to issue a decision based on facts and evidence in respect of which the undertaking against which proceedings have been initiated, or the party notifying a concentration, have not been given the opportunity to reply. This principle is, inter alia, enshrined in the instrument of statement of objections and the possibility of the parties to express their views on it.

479. As has been stressed in Part I, Chapter 5, §1, VI of this monograph, this principle is not observed within the interim measures regime set out in Article 38 of the PRCA-1 as the PRCA-1 does not provide for a party against which interim measures are ordered to be heard before the order for interim measures is issued. It has been interpreted by the SCPA that the interim measures regime observes the adversarial principle as the respective party has a right to challenge the order issuing interim measures ex post facto before the Supreme Court of RS.[694] Such interpretation falls short of the constitutional safeguards stemming from Article 22 of the Constitution of RS and the jurisprudence of the Constitutional Court of RS. The Supreme Court of RS has also stated in 2010 in clear and unequivocal terms that an invasive measure such as ordering interim measures cannot be issued in a non-adversarial procedure.[695] According to the Supreme Court of RS, the adversarial

693. Galič & Kocmut in Grilc et al., *PRCA-1 Commentary*, 254.

694. The Supreme Court is to assess the SCPA's order without delay and in any case within fifteen days after the action has been filed with the court.

695. Decision No. G 8/2010 of 20 Apr. 2010, available at (in Slovene): http://www.sodisce.si/vsrs/odlocitve/2010040815244809/.

nature of the proceedings will manifest in particular in the right to be heard and to make statements, less in the right to access to file which may be reserved to later stages of the proceedings.

C. Access to File

480. Article 18 of the PRCA-1 grants the parties to the proceedings the right to access and review the case file, as well as to make transcriptions or copies of the documents contained therein.[696] However, the accessibility does not extend to the following documentation: internal documentation of the SCPA including its correspondence with the European Commission and the competition authorities of the EU Member States; confidential data;[697] data containing identity of the persons who have provided the SCPA with information but have requested that their identity is not revealed; minutes of the SCPA's deliberations; drafts of the SCPA's decisions.

481. Parties are entitled to inspect, transcribe and photocopy the documents of the file under the supervision of the SCPA's official from the moment the proceedings are initiated. In the interest of the proceedings, the director of the SCPA may suspend access to file up until the statement of objections is issued.[698] The parties may file a request to access to file in writing or in person. Although as of 2008 the PRCA-1 provides for the possibility of accessing the file via means of electronic information system, such option has to the author's knowledge to date not been available to the parties.

482. If a party to the proceedings is not granted access to the file, it may start judicial proceedings reviewing the SCPA's order denying access, or it may challenge the order within judicial proceedings reviewing the SCPA's final administrative decision.[699]

483. To prevent potential fishing expeditions and other types of strategic behaviour, the regime clearly excludes persons submitting complaints, initiatives or messages claiming anti-competitive conduct from the scope of the definition of a party. Article 16 of the PRCA-1 provides explicitly that only undertakings against which the proceedings have been initiated, and persons notifying of a concentration, are parties to the proceedings, while the complainants are not. Experts have access to

696. The party itself bears the costs of the copying services. Currently, the parties make use of the photocopying services offered by a private company having its office in the building where the SCPA has its headquarters. Photocopying is made in the presence of a SCPA official.

697. Article 3 of the PRCA-1 determines what constitutes confidential data (the definition has been broadened in 2009 to cover a wider range of information beside business secrets). The undertaking stating that certain data is confidential, must provide proof of that. Where the SCPA determines that disclosure of confidential data to parties under investigation is necessary for guaranteeing their right to be heard, it may decide to allow access to such data.

698. Article 18/3 of the PRCA-1. No legal remedy against the Director's decision is available.

699. Kocmut in Grilc et al., *PRCA-1 Commentary*, 246, referring to the case law of the Supreme Court of RS (Decision No. I Up 556/2004) and the Administrative Court of RS (Decision No. U 1027/2003).

file to the extent necessary for providing their expert opinions.[700] Interveners demonstrating legal interest sufficient to substantiate entry into the proceedings also have access to the file (save confidential data).

484. Provisions of the PRCA-1 regulating access to file are to be applied during the administrative proceedings before the SCPA as well as in judicial review proceedings before the competent courts.[701]

D. Hearings

485. In contrast to Regulation 1/2003 and Regulation 773/2004 where hearings before the European Commission are regulated in detail, the currently valid PRCA-1 merely provides that the SCPA decides without an oral hearing unless the official conducting the proceedings determines that a hearing needs to take place in order to clarify or to establish essential facts.[702] In such cases, general rules of the GAPA on conducting hearings apply.[703] According to the PRCA of 1999, the CPO conducted hearings on request of the parties or on its own motion. The PRCA's first amendments of 2004, however, set aside the possibility of the parties to request an oral hearing. The PRCA-1 of 2008 additionally narrowed the CPO's possibilities to conduct oral hearings to cases where essential facts need to be established or clarified.

486. In judicial review proceedings, the court reviews (in principle) the SCPA's decision without holding a hearing.[704]

E. Briefs

487. The PRCA-1 does not set out any rules regarding the briefs of the parties. Therefore, general rules of the GAPA apply.[705]

III. Statement of Objections

488. By issuing the statement of objections, the SCPA informs the parties concerned in writing of the objections raised against them in all those cases where the SCPA intends to issue a decision finding infringement of European and/or Slovenian antitrust. According to Article 36 of the PRCA-1, the statement of objections must present the SCPA's findings as regards the facts and evidence relevant for the

700. Article 18/4 of the PRCA-1.
701. Article 60 of the PRCA-1.
702. Article 21 of the PRCA-1.
703. For further details, see Kerševan & Androjna, *Upravno procesno pravo*, 264–269.
704. Article 59 of the PRCA-1.
705. For further details, see Kerševan & Androjna, *Upravno procesno pravo*, 161-172.

decision. If the statement contains confidential data, such data is deleted from the copies of the statement handed out to other parties under investigation. According to the general rules on administrative procedure, the SCPA may issue a partial statement of objections in all those cases where it has initiated the proceedings alleging various infringements but has afterwards focused on one or part of them only. In such cases, the statement of objections as well as the final decision may be issued with regard to these infringements only.[706]

489. The SCPA must set a reasonable time-limit of up to forty-five days within which the parties may inform it in writing of their views as to the objections raised by the SCPA.[707] Such time-limit is deemed reasonable as the parties are informed of the proceedings as of the issuance of the SCPA's order on the initiation of the proceedings and have, in principle, unlimited access to the case file already before the statement of objections is issued. Until the expiration of the set time-limit, the parties may also offer commitments.[708]

490. Although statement of objections is regulated in the PRCA-1 only as of 2008, the CPO had been issuing them before that on the basis of general provisions of the GAPA enabling the parties to be informed of the evidentiary status of the proceedings and to comment on it.

IV. Final Hearing and Decision

491. As has already been emphasized, the SCPA decides without holding an oral hearing unless the official conducting the proceedings determines that a hearing is to take place in order to clarify or to establish essential facts. In such cases, general rules of the GAPA on conducting hearings apply.[709]

492. Within antitrust enforcement, the SCPA may issue the following substantive decisions if it determines that the undertakings concerned have breached European and/or Slovenian antitrust: decisions finding an infringement of Articles 101 or 102 TFEU and/or Articles 6 or 9 of the PRCA-1, or decisions accepting commitments. If the SCPA does not find an infringement, it must terminate the proceedings by issuing an order.[710]

706. As was the case in a telecommunications case *Mobitel* where the CPO issued a partial decision in June 2005 accepting commitments regarding the alleged abuse of the undertaking's dominant position on the retail market of public mobile services.
707. If the comments are received by the SCPA at a later date, the SCPA is at liberty to take them into account or not. A time-limit set by the SCPA in practice is approx. twenty days. In determining what a reasonable time-limit would be in a particular case, the SCPA takes into consideration all relevant circumstances of the case. See Bratina in Grilc et al., *PRCA-1 Commentary*, 372–373.
708. See Pt. I, Ch. 5, §1, I C of this monograph.
709. For further details, see Kerševan & Androjna, *Upravno procesno pravo*, 264–269.
710. See Pt. I, Ch. 5, §1, I C of this monograph.

493. According to Article 22 of the PRCA-1, all decisions and orders that may be judicially reviewed, must state reasons for the SCPA's decision. If decisions and orders by which the proceedings are brought to an end, contain confidential data, such data is deleted from the copies handed out to other parties. The SCPA may request the parties to label those parts of the decision which it deems confidential. As of 2008, the SCPA must publish on its webpages all operative parts of its decisions and orders by which the proceedings are brought to an end.[711] As of 2009, it must also publish all final administrative and minor offences decisions, as well as all final orders bringing proceedings to the end. Confidential data is left out. Unfortunately, the CPO and the CPA have not been particularly transparent in publishing their decisions, searching the decisions in general is not very user-friendly. After the transformation of the CPO into the CPA, the webpages have been updated only to a minimum extent and have only recently become more valuable and useful to their users.[712]

711. See, e.g., http://www.varstvo-konkurence.si/en/antitrust/decisions/. Operative parts of the CPO's decisions were previously published in the Official Gazette RS.
712. http://www.varstvo-konkurence.si/en/.

Chapter 2. Voluntary Notifications and Clearance Decisions

494. As Slovenia has completely conformed to the competition law of the European Union, the system of public control of Restrictive Business Practices (RBPs) in the form of agreements, concerted practices or decisions by associations of undertakings follows the one from Regulation 1/2003 to the point. Article 1, section 2 of the said regulation provides that 'Agreements, decisions and concerted practices caught by Article 81(1) of the Treaty which satisfy the conditions of Article 81(3) of the Treaty shall not be prohibited, no prior decision to that effect being required.' Thus, the PRCA in its current form has no provisions regulating voluntary notifications of anti-competitive behaviour. Same goes for provisions regarding negative clearance decisions or comfort letters.[713]

713. For details, see Vlahek, *Reforma antitrusta v Evropski uniji.*

Chapter 3. Merger Control

495. Merger proceedings are normally initiated on the basis of notification. In addition, if a suspicious merger was not notified, the SCPA can initiate the proceedings ex officio. While pre-notification discussions are normal, they are not formally regulated. There exists only one regular type of merger notification, which has to be submitted to the SCPA using a special form, the content of which is regulated by Government Decree.[714] In accordance with Article 43 of the PRCA-1, a concentration has to be notified prior to its implementation but not later than thirty days after the conclusion of the contract, the announcement of the public bid, or the acquisition of a controlling interest. That period begins when the first of these events occurs. Apart from concentrations deriving from mergers or acquisitions of joint control where the filing must be done by all parties concerned, the filing must be made by the parties acquiring control over the other undertakings. The filing fee has to be paid by the notifying party at the time of the filing.

496. The SCPA may by decision impose fines not exceeding 10% of the aggregate turnover of the undertaking concerned including affiliated companies, in the previous business year if it: (i) fails to notify of a concentration, or failing to do so within the time-limit pursuant to Article 43; (ii) implements a concentration in breach of Article 44; (iii) fails to comply with undertakings or an obligation imposed by a decision on compatibility of the concentration with competition rules and (iv) implements a concentration declared incompatible with competition rules or does not comply with any measure ordered pursuant to Article 53, aimed at dissolving consequences of concentration. Fines ranging from EUR 5,000 to EUR 10,000 can also be imposed on persons who are responsible for that legal entity. If there exist aggravating circumstances the fine can be elevated to range from EUR 15,000 to EUR 30,000.[715] There is no exact method defining the calculation of the level of fines, therefore the general rules of penalization apply.

497. The role of efficiencies in merger assessment is not entirely clear. In the past, it seems certain concentrations might be approved on their basis, although the SCPA never made a formal reference to efficiencies in its decisions. Accordingly, in cases *Union/Laško*[716] and *Europlakat/Metropolis Media*,[717] the SCPA approved a concentration although the analysed concentration would create a dominant position in the market and could significantly lessen effective competition. In this particular case the concentration, without any conditions, even in the absence of any mechanism for ensuring that any efficiency benefits would be passed on to consumers, was allowed.

---

714. English version available at: http://www.varstvo-konkurence.si/fileadmin/varstvo-konkurence.si/pageuploads/Decree.pdf.
715. See Art. 74 of the PRCA-1.
716. CPO's decision in *Union/Laško* merger, Decision No. 3071-1/02-369, available at (in Slovene): http://www.varstvo-konkurence.si/fileadmin/varstvo-konkurence.si/pageuploads/ijz014.pdf.
717. CPO's decision in *Europlakat/Metropolis Media* merger, Decision No. 306-42/2006-76, available at (in Slovene): http://www.varstvo-konkurence.si/fileadmin/varstvo-konkurence.si/pageuploads/ijz064.pdf.

498. Even under the new PRCA-1, formally there is no exemption of the general prohibition against concentration which would significantly impede effective competition in the territory of the Republic of Slovenia or in a substantial part of it, particularly as a result of the creation or strengthening of a dominant position. However, similar to the EU Merger Regulations, Article 11/2 of the new PRCA-1 of 2008 provides that in making its appraisal, the SCPA shall, among other things, take into account the development of technical and economic progress, provided that it is to the consumers' advantage and does not form an obstacle to competition. While there exists no formal statement of its policy in connection with merger efficiencies, the SCPA, responding to the claims of efficiencies in the *Delo/Večer*[718] case, did make a direct reference to the cumulative conditions as set in paragraph 78 of the EU Merger Guidelines[719] when rebuffing efficiencies claims. This, together with general alignment of a substantive test with EU Merger Regulation, would indicate that the approach of the SCPA will follow the approach as indicated by Commission in its guidelines.

§1. Preliminary Filing Obligations

499. The main provisions dealing with mergers and joint ventures are Article 10 (Definition of concentration) and Article 11 (Appraisal of concentrations) of the PRCA-1. The legislation covers all types of mergers: horizontal, vertical and conglomerate. The wording of Article 11/1 of the PRCA-1 is effectively the same as the wordings of Article 2/2,3 of the EU Merger Regulation, and suggests the application of the SLC test.[720] The wording of Article 11/1 provides:

> Concentration which would significantly impede effective competition in the territory of the Republic of Slovenia or in a substantial part of it, particularly as a result of the creation or strengthening of a dominant position, shall be prohibited.

Article 11/2 of the PRCA-1 corresponds to Article 2/1 of the EC Merger Regulation.

718. CPO's decision in *Delo/Večer* merger, Decision No. 306-195/2008-57, available at (in Slovene): http://www.varstvo-konkurence.si/fileadmin/varstvo-konkurence.si/pageuploads/ijz084.pdf.

719. Council Regulation (EC) No. 139/2004 of 20 Jan. 2004 on the control of concentrations between undertakings (the EC Merger Regulation), OJ L 24, 29 Jan. 2004, 1–22.

720. While the previous wording of Art. 11 also suggested the application of the SLC test, the CPO was, in accordance with Art. 13, obliged to appraise concentrations with a view to establishing whether or not there exists a threat of creating or strengthening of a dominant position, as a result of which effective competition could be excluded or significantly impeded. The relationship between these two provisions was therefore a matter of interpretation. The new wording of Art. 11 now clearly suggests the application of the SLC test and is therefore aligned with the approach on the EU level.

I. Criteria and Thresholds

500. The intention of concentration is in accordance with provisions of Article 42 of the PRCA-1 subject to a notification (merger notification) submitted to the SCPA in the case where:

- the total annual turnover of the undertakings involved in a concentration, together with other undertakings in the group, on the market of the Republic of Slovenia in the preceding business year, exceeded EUR 35 million; and
- the annual turnover of the acquired undertaking, together with other undertakings in the group, on the market of the Republic of Slovenia in the preceding business year, exceeded EUR 1 million; or if in the case of creation of a joint venture, the annual turnover of at least two undertakings concerned in a concentration, together with other undertakings in the group, in the preceding business year exceeded EUR 1 million.

501. However, even if the concentration does not exceed the set thresholds, Article 42/3 of the PRCA-1 provides the SCPA with an option to demand notification from the undertakings concerned, if these undertakings together with affiliated undertakings exceed 60% market share on the market of the Republic of Slovenia.

502. Mergers involving companies headquartered in other jurisdictions are caught if they are within the set thresholds. However, the obligation to notify of concentration under Slovenian competition law does not apply if the merger falls under the EU Merger Regulation (139/2004/EC).

II. Turnover Calculation

503. The PRCA-1 defines 'annual turnover' as net revenues from sales generated by an undertaking over a business year from the sale of products or the provision of services falling within ordinary activities. Article 3 of the PRCA-1 further elaborates on the definitions of annual turnover where group of undertakings and/or financial and insurance institutions are involved in a concentration

III. Market-Share Calculation

504. The PRCA-1 does not include a provision or guidance of how to calculate market shares (which is in line with the relatively abstract nature of the Act), unfortunately, the same is true for all of the other pieces of legislation or official publications by the SCPA, bar a publication procured by the SCPA, which in general terms mentions the importance of market shares and their calculation. This lack of written instructions may pose problems to the undertakings involved in concentrative actions as they cannot be certain, whether their respective calculation of market shares is in line with the one SCPA would or will use to assess whether the concentration is subject to the notification. As the SCPA was (and still is) notoriously understaffed and lacks cadres with focused professional education, it is difficult to imagine that it will conduct its own investigations and market research as to the size of market shares. It is to be expected that the SCPA will therefore rely on publicly gathered and provided data (when available), or side with the information provided by the notifying parties in cases no data is accessible.

IV. Other Relevant Notions

A. *Exception for Financial Institutions*

505. Article 10/4 of the PRCA-1 represents an exception to the general rule and provides that concentration will not arise when banks, insurance companies, savings institutions or other financial institutions, the normal activities of which include transactions and dealing in securities for their own account or for the account of others, hold on a temporary basis business assets that they have acquired in an undertaking with a view to reselling them, provided that they do not exercise voting rights in respect of those business assets with a view to determining the competitive behaviour of that undertaking or provided that they exercise such voting rights only with a view to preparing the disposal of these business assets and that any such disposal takes place within one year of the date of acquisition of these business assets. The period of one year may be extended by order of the SCPA on request when the financial institution can show that the disposal was not reasonably possible within the prescribed period.

B. *Suspensive Effect*

506. The suspension of concentrations set forth in Article 44 of the PRCA-1 is formed along the lines of the communitarian merger control regime. In order to clearly define the obligations of the notifying parties during the appraisal process, the PRCA-1 introduced a separate provision, largely based on the wording of Article 7 of Regulation 139/2004. Article 44 of the PRCA-1 thus prohibits the exercise of rights and obligations arising from the merger. The suspension is triggered by the voluntary notification of concentrative behaviour and thus comes into action *ex lege*.

507. As is the case in the ambit of Article 7 of Regulation 139/2004, the main purpose of the suspensive effect of Article 44 of the PRCA-1 is the ensuring of an efficient merger control in the sense of ensuring the conditions for a coherent pro futuro assessment of the effects of a concentrative structural change or a change in control. The primary purpose of the provision therefore lies in preventing the execution and final implementation of the concentration before the final decision on its (in) compatibility with competition law is issued by the SCPA. As is the case with the provision of Article 7 of Regulation 139/2004, the wording of Article 44 of the PRCA-1 does not provide a clear answer to the question of the ambit and nature of the rights that are not to be exercised. I remain convinced that the teleological and linguistic interpretation of the provision considered leaves no room for doubt – the scope of the suspensive effect has to be limited to the rights that give rise to the structural change in control. It is thence possible to conclude that the suspensive provision of Article 44 of the PRCA-1 applies only to actions that may influence the strategic commercial behaviour of a previously independent undertaking. This is why the provision of Article 44 of the PRCA-1 does not and cannot provide for a suspension of a right to dispose of the shares or assets conferring control.

508. In case of different interpretation, the said article would consist of a conceptually meaningless provision. An undertaking, which has obtained control through an acquisition of shares in another undertaking (consequently both are now parties to a concentration) can change its business behaviour and dispose of the said shares or assets at any time during the appraisal procedure thus restoring the situation prevailing before the implementation of the concentration. The disposal will primarily take the form of a sale of shareholdings or assets. With the disposal, the previously controlling undertaking has divested its control and the concentration is no more.

509. Disposal of controlling shares or assets in the course of appraisal procedure can only have positive effects for the SCPA's position as it eliminates the basic reason for authority's activity, i.e., the existence of concentration. The proposed interpretation of scope and ambit of Article 44 of the PRCA-1 is additionally validated by the comparative regulation. The provisions contained in paragraphs 117–121 of the Commission Consolidated Jurisdictional Notice under Council Regulation (EC) No. 139/2004 on the control of concentrations between undertakings[721] thus provide for a possibility of abandonment of concentrations. In such cases, the Commission shall close the procedures concerning the control of concentrations without a final decision.

510. The Notice introduces additional criteria that must be met by undertakings involved in the concentration, if their actions are to be interpreted as abandonment of concentration. The basic interpretative criterion is that the:

> requirements for the proof of the abandonment must correspond in terms of legal form, intensity, etc., to the initial act that was considered sufficient to make the concentration notifiable. In case the parties proceed from that initial act to a strengthening of their contractual links during the procedure, for example by concluding a binding agreement after the transaction was notified on the basis of a good faith intention, the requirements for the proof of the abandonment must correspond also to the nature of the latest act.[722]

511. The reversion to pre-merger conditions i.e. without a concentration is most easily achieved by disposal of shares, assets, etc., conferring control by means of selling the shares or assets in consideration to third parties. It should be noted that

721. 2008/C 95/01.
722. Notice, para. 119.

it would be completely inappropriate to interpret the requirement to restore the status quo ante so narrowly that it would be fulfilled only by a complete winding-back process. This is especially true in cases where the controlling shares were purchased on a stock exchange as a result of a realization of financial collateral and the original seller or shareholder would be impossible to identify.

512. In view of the aforementioned, the provision of Article 45 Article of the PRCA-1 is unusual and difficult to understand. Perhaps it is conceptually comparable to the provision of Article 8/5 of Regulation 139/2004. The latter enables the Commission to impose provisional measures intended to ensure the restoration or maintenance of effective competition. The provision is interestingly vague, particularly regarding the nature or form of action that the Commission is empowered to introduce, the wording is much more precise, however, regarding the conditions that trigger the introduction of such measures. According to Article 8, the Commission may impose provisional measures in cases where an undertaking has infringed the regime set forth by Article 7 of the Regulation, namely when undertakings concerned either failed to notify a concentration or have commenced to implement a notified (and thus suspended) concentration. It has to be mentioned that the wording of Article 45 of the PRCA-1 only enumerates the first condition, namely the failure to notify, while the second condition is not expressly mentioned.

513. It should be emphasized that the interim measures from Article of the Regulation can only be imposed in accordance with the procedural safeguards set forth in Articles 18 and 19 of the Regulation. Thus, the Commission shall give the persons, undertakings and associations of undertakings concerned the opportunity, at every stage of the procedure up to the consultation of the Advisory Committee, of making known their views on the objections against them. A decision pursuant to Article 8(5) of the Regulation may be taken provisionally, without the persons, undertakings or associations of undertakings concerned being given the opportunity to make known their views beforehand, provided that the Commission gives them that opportunity as soon as possible after having taken its decision.

514. Unfortunately, the regime of Article 45 of the PRCA-1 is devoid of any procedural safeguards. As the PRCA-1 fails to provide for a motion against imposed interim measures to be entertained on the first instance and the right to be heard cannot be effectively guaranteed in the process of judicial review before the Supreme Court (as a general rule there are no oral hearings in procedures before the Supreme Court), the adversarial safeguards have to be guaranteed before the imposition of interim measures under Article 45/5 of the PRCA-1. The SCPA therefore has to ensure to the persons, undertakings and associations of undertakings concerned with the right to be heard, the right to produce statements and the right to access the file.[723]

723. Supreme Court Decision No. G 8/2010 of 20 Apr. 2010, available at (in Slovene): http://www.sodisce.si/znanje/sodna_praksa/search.php?q=sklep%20G%2030/2012&database%5BSOVS%5D=SOVS&_submit=i%EF%BF%BD%C3%A8i&showType=div&rowsPerPage=20&page=1&id=2010040815244809.

515. Article 45/5 of the PRCA-1 specifies the measures that can be imposed. According to its wording, the SCPA may:

> ex officio, by decision prohibit undertakings, competent authorities and holders of public authority from exercising voting, management, property and other rights and obligations arising from the concentration until a decision declaring the concentration compatible with the competition rules has been issued.

516. Another issue arising from the incompetent wording of Article 45/5 of the PRCA-1 that is worth mentioning is the fact that it consists only of proscriptive measures while, in addition, lacking any referral as to the intent of said measures. Looking at the wording of Article 8/5 of the Regulation, it is clear to see that the intent of any interim measures is to restore or maintain conditions of effective competition. The array of proscribed practices is obviously quite broad: the SCPA is empowered to prohibit many types of behaviour related to the right arising from a concentration. To point, the exercise of voting, management, property and other rights arising from the concentration can be banned. It is quite apparent what the reasons are behind the ban on the exercise of voting and management rights, as such a measure can bring to a halt further exercise or implementation of the concentration. Here, the provision of Article 45 of the PRCA-1 does come close to the intention encompassed in the wording of Article 8/5 of the Regulation.

517. Unfortunately, this cannot be said for the remaining two types of rights whose exercise can be prohibited. This is especially true regarding the prohibition to exercise the property rights – while it is possible to envisage a situation where the exercise of property rights could amount to exercise of control over a previously independent company (e.g., allocation of profits), such a prohibition can certainly not extend to a pure divestiture, i.e., the sale of acquired shares or assets as such exercise of property rights amounts in a dissolution or abandonment of the concentration, and therefore in an elimination of the reason for SCPA's actions. A prohibition on sale of acquired shares or assets conferring control is tantamount to a total ban on abandonment of concentration, and by imposing it, the SCPA would thence force an undertaking into a concentration. It therefore must be said that Article 45/5 of the PRCA-1 undoubtedly does not empower the SCPA to impose a ban on disposition with property rights.

518. To deepen the confusion, Article 45/5 of the PRCA-1 extends the personal scope of the prohibitory clause to persons who are not parties to the concentration and even to persons not holding any shares in undertakings effecting the concentration. The ban can thus also be imposed on 'competent authorities and bodies exercising public powers'. This broadening of the personal scope can be interpreted as an additional safeguard, which should prevent any actions that represent the exercise or implementation of rights airing from a concentration by third parties. By prohibiting the Central Securities Clearing Corporation from executing the transfer of shares the SCPA can effectively prevent the completion of concentration in term of the final transfer of shares. It is also possible to foresee situations (especially when the control has already been obtained by means of purchase and transfer of shares) when a measure prohibiting the court to execute an entry into the court registry of, e.g., certain fundamental corporate government changes (changes in membership of management or supervisory body), thus preventing changes in undertaking's legal status amounting to the implementation of the control and the execution of a transaction. We cannot stress enough how important it is to understand that even in cases where the SCPA imposes the (interim) measures upon third parties, such measures necessarily impact the legal status and fundamental rights undertakings involved in the concentration. It is thence imperative to provide them with the procedural and material safeguards as if the measures were imposed unto them.

§2. Structure of Proceedings

I. Preliminary Assessment and Full Investigation

519. The examination of a merger notification is exclusively performed by the SCPA[724] and is divided in Phase I and Phase II stages. In Phase I of the examination, which has to be concluded in twenty-five calendar days, counted from the date of receipt of the complete notification, the SCPA will perform a notification screen and sometimes request for additional information. The merger examination will be finished after Phase I with the issuance of a decision, if the SCPA either: (i) concludes that the concentration notified does not fall within the scope of the provisions of the PRCA-1, or (ii) finds that the concentration, although falling within the scope of the provisions of the PRCA-1, does not raise serious doubts as to its compatibility with competition rules.

520. If, however, the SCPA finds that the concentration falls within the scope of the provisions of the PRCA-1 and raises serious doubts as to its compatibility with competition rules, it will start Phase II of the merger examination and issue an order on the commencement of procedure. In Phase II of the merger examination, which should be concluded in sixty days,[725] the SCPA has very extensive investigation authority[726] and may examine premises, business books, documentation and records to the extent required for identifying all relevant facts. It can also confiscate required documentation or computer equipment of the companies involved for up to twenty days. The SCPA may also request from the management and other employees oral or written explanation on the circumstances with respect to the investigation.[727] The SCPA has also the authority to investigate third parties' premises, but in this case it needs to secure a court order in advance.[728] There is no provision on the obligation

724. The Courts are not directly involved in the merger investigation, but they review the SCPA's decisions.
725. Time limits for investigation is set by the PRCA-1 (Arts 46 and 50), but are only instructive in nature. While the SCPA regularly renders its decision within time limits in Phase I investigations, it is much less effective in Phase II investigations which can take up several mounts, to be finished.
726. See Art. 48 of the PRCA-1.
727. See Art. 29 of the PRCA-1.
728. See Art. 33 of the PRCA-1.

of third parties to answer questions set by the authorities; however, there is a general provision stating that authorized persons can execute other acts, which are in accordance with the objective of the investigation.[729]

521. After Phase II merger investigations, the SCPA can either: (i) issue a decision declaring the concentration compatible with competition rules, if it finds that the concentration is not in contravention of the PRCA-1,[730] or (ii) issue a decision declaring the concentration incompatible with competition rules and prohibit it, if it finds that the concentration is in contravention of this Act. When the SCPA intends to issue a decision declaring a concentration incompatible with competition rules, it must in advance inform the notifying party of its statement of objections. While the burden of proof is on the SCPA, however, the SCPA does not specifically analyse theories of harm (unilateral, coordinated effects, etc.) in its decisions.

II. Time Framework

522. The time limitations for the SCPA action in Phase I and Phase II of the merger appraisal procedure are dealt with in Part I, Chapter 4, §7 of this monograph.

III. Right of Defence

523. General procedural provisions analysed in Part III, Chapter 1, §3 of this monograph apply mutatis mutandis to concentration procedures, while certain issues of particular importance for merger control (e.g., regarding the right to be heard and lack thereof) are dealt with in Part III, Chapter 3, §1, IV B of this monograph.

§3. CLEARANCE AND CONDITIONAL CLEARANCE

I. Conditions and Undertakings

A. Content

524. Remedies (corrective measures) are to be proposed by the undertakings effecting the concentration. The proposal should consist of a precise definition of remedial action (and especially the set of effects eliminating the reasons for incompatibility with competition law) stemming thereof. The SCPA shall adopt such remedies as it considers appropriate to remove serious doubts as to the compatibility of

729. See Art. 29 of the PRCA-1.
730. The notifying party is required to specify and explain all ancillary restrictions included in concentration documents on the notification form and should ask for their assessment. The clearance decision also covers such restrictions.

the concentration with competition rules, taking into consideration their nature, scope and likelihood of effective and timely implementation. Before such adoption, the SCPA has to carry out a detailed economic analysis of the proposed remedies' impact. Such an analysis requires a repeated simulation of the impact caused by an implemented concentration in terms of assessing structural (potential post-merger dominance) and behavioural effects (collusion, non-coordinated effects) and a subsequent simulation of potential beneficial effects on market conditions by the proposed remedies. Such an assessment is relatively straightforward in the event of horizontal mergers with structural remedies as proposed corrective measures. If the notifying parties suggest a divestiture of assets of one of the undertakings involved in the merger, and the proposed buyer has not previously been active in the relevant market, the decision to adopt the proposed remedy is unproblematic. Implementation of such a remedy results in a de-merger and thus a market condition similar to one before the concentration. When behavioural remedies are proposed, the analysis demands higher level of scrutiny; in addition, current aversion towards behavioural remedies (in favour of purely structural corrective measures) on the communitarian level will probably also reflect in the actions of the SCPA, moreover so as the appraisal of behavioural remedies requires complex simulations of remedies' effects on a post-concentration market. These are the reasons why we expect the SCPA to give preferential treatment to structural remedies – it is difficult to imagine an understaffed and undereducated agency to deal with behavioural measures which do not offer 'clean' results in the sense of demergers. In addition, the need for continuous monitoring and control of the implementation and effect of behavioural measures is not to be overlooked.

525. Article 51/6 of the PRCA-1 provides the grounds for control over the compliance with the imposed remedies. Thus, the SCPA may by demand for information require the notifying party to provide a report on the implementation of remedies imposed by the SCPA decision. The monitoring process enables the SCPA to watch over the quality, timeliness and effectiveness of remedies. There is a clear distinction between the monitoring of the compliance with the measures imposed to enable monitoring of the remedies (second indent of Article 51/3 of the PRCA-1) and the control over the implementation of the remedies themselves (first indent of Article 51/3 of the PRCA-1). If the Office finds that the remedies have not been implemented at all, it shall issue a decision imposing measures on the undertakings involved in the concentration to restore the situation prevailing prior to the implementation of the concentration; in particular, through the division of the undertaking or disposal of all the shares acquired (Article 53 of the PRCA-1). The Office may annul a decision declaring the concentration to be compatible with competition rules or a decision referred to in Article 46/2 of the PRCA-1, and in the same decision decide on the compatibility of the concentration with competition rules if an undertaking acts contrary to the obligations referred to in the second indent of Article 51/3 of the PRCA-1.

B. Timing

526. The notifying parties may propose corrective measures in both stages of the appraisal of concentrations. It is, however, unlikely to expect the notifying parties to propose structural remedies (e.g., divestiture) immediately upon the notification, as this would just about eliminate the fundamental structural goal of concentrative action. However, pre-emptive proposals of behavioural remedies can be anticipated at this stage, as the undertakings concerned strive for a timely positive decision by the SCPA (forty working days). In both stages of the appraisal procedure a proposed remedy extends the decision-making period of the SCPA for fifteen working days.

§4. Relations with Other Merger Control Authorities

I. Other Authorities within the Local Jurisdiction

527. Although the SCPA is the sole authority entrusted with the implementation of merger control and thus represents a sort of a one-stop shop for the undertakings involved in a concentration of national dimension, there are certain other bodies and institutions that are to have their own part in the broader appraisal procedure. Thence, the Ministry of Culture is empowered to issue consent decrees regarding transactions that result in a high concentration of ownership of printed media, radio or TV. The threshold for its consent is 20% in the assets of a broadcaster, or a share of the voting rights of 20%. As such a consent decree is mandatory if the threshold of 20% ownership/management/voting rights in the capital or assets of the media publisher is met, it can play a pivotal role in cases where 20 or more percent of transferred assets would also result in a change of control thus triggering the need for a notification and consequent appraisal by the SCPA. Without the consent decree, the SCPA's potentially positive appraisal result would be of no avail. The Insurance Supervision Agency is an independent regulatory body empowered with issuance of consent decrees in events of mergers of insurance companies. Its role, however, is limited by the 'monopoly' over merger control, vested in the SCPA, as Article 60a of the Insurance Act provides that the Insurance Supervision Agency cannot issue a consent decree had the SCPA found the concentration incompatible with the competition rules.

II. International Coordination

528. As regards the SCPA's potential collaboration with foreign institutions, it is important to point out its cooperation with the European Commission and national competition authorities from other Member States within the system of referrals as set out in the EU Merger Regulation (Regulation 139/2004).

Chapter 4. Challenging of the Administrative Decision

§1. Competent Courts

529. Decisions of the SCPA are administrative decisions issued in administrative proceedings as set out in the PRCA-1 and subsidiarily in the GAPA.[731] They can be challenged in judicial review proceedings before the Administrative Court of RS at its seat in Ljubljana (being the first instance court in administrative dispute proceedings) and the Supreme Court of RS (having a position of a court of second instance deciding on appeals and revisions).[732] No appeal against the SCPA's decision to any administrative body within the administrative proceedings is available, the plaintiff wishing to attack the SCPA's decision must thus file a lawsuit initiating administrative dispute proceedings directly to Administrative Court of RS.

530. It must be underscored that a separate set of proceedings take place and a separate set of rules apply with regard to setting fines for breaches of competition law. As has been elaborated in detail in Part I, Chapter 5, §1, I C and Part I, Chapter 5, §1, IV A of this monograph, the fines are set by the SCPA in separate minor offences proceedings performed in accordance with provisions of the PRCA-1 and the MOA-1. The SCPA's orders imposing fines are reviewed as priority by the Local Court in Ljubljana. Appeal and other remedies against the court's decision are also available.

531. Administrative judicial review proceedings in competition law cases are regulated in Articles 54–61a of the PRCA-1 that provide only for a couple of specific provisions as to the administrative dispute proceedings in competition law cases. As set out in Article 54/2 of the PRCA-1, the ADA-1[733] is to be applied mutatis mutandis with regard to all other procedural aspects of the administrative dispute (be it before the Administrative Court of RS or the Supreme Court of RS). The ADA-1 further states that in case the ADA-1 itself does not provide for a certain procedural solution, the CPrA will apply.[734]

532. The PRCA-1 provides for the following competition law specific rules on the court review proceedings: as a rule, the review court is to decide without a hearing;[735] cases subject to judicial review procedure are to be considered urgent and

731. For details on the rules on administrative decisions, see Kerševan & Androjna, *Upravno procesno pravo*, 304–342.

732. Article 14 of the ADA-1. For details on administrative dispute proceedings, see Kerševan & Androjna, *Upravno procesno pravo*, 501–630.

733. Sl. *Zakon o upravnem sporu (ZUS-1)*, Official Gazette RS, No. 105/06, with further amendments. For further details see Kerševan in Grilc et al., *PRCA-1 Commentary*, 462–475.

734. Article 22 of the ADA-1. Article 22 of the ADA-1 states which rules of the CPrA do not apply in administrative dispute proceedings. For further details, see Kerševan & Androjna, *Upravno procesno pravo*, 544.

735. Article 59 of the PRCA-1. This rule has been criticized by Žuber, *The Slovenian perspective of a main hearing in an administrative dispute*.

are to be handled by the court as priority;[736] the plaintiff may not introduce new facts or present new evidence;[737] the court is to test a decision of the SCPA (in some cases also its orders)[738] within the limits of the claim and within the limits of the grounds stated in the action, and is to pay attention ex officio to essential infringements of procedure;[739] acccss to case file documents before the court is allowed under the same ground as before the SCPA;[740] as of 2013, the CPA must publish all review judgments on its webpage.[741]

533. Between 2008 and 2013, the only available legal remedy against the decisions[742] of the SCPA was the initiation of an administrative dispute before the Supreme Court of the RS that decided competition law cases in a panel of three judges.[743] Between 1999 and 2008 (i.e., as of entry into force of the PRCA of 1999 and up until the enactment of the PRCA-1 of 2008), judicial review in administrative dispute was performed by the Administrative Court of RS,[744] while the Supreme Court of RS reviewed the decisions of the Administrative Court of RS. Such system was re-introduced in 2013 when the PRCA-1 was amended. An unusual judicial review mechanism was established by the PCA of 1993 (in force until 1999 when the PRCA came into force) which provided for judicial review by filing an action in civil proceedings.[745]

534. Between 2008 and 2013, the Supreme Court of RS had sole jurisdiction to assess the SCPA's decisions and orders. As no complaint, appeal, revision or any other legal remedy was available against the decisions of the Supreme Court,[746] there was only one stage in these judicial review proceedings. Perceiving such system as unconstitutional, the Supreme Court of RS asked the Constitutional Court of RS to assess whether the judicial review proceedings in force are in line with the Slovenian Constitution. It was the Supreme Court's position that the rules set out in

736. Article 55/5 of the PRCA-1.
737. Article 57 of the PRCA-1.
738. Article 55/2,3,4 of the PRCA-1.
739. Article 58 of the PRCA-1.
740. Article 60 of the PRCA-1 referring to Art. 18 of the PRCA-1 regulating the right of parties to review the SCPA case file.
741. Article 61a the PRCA-1.
742. As well as against some of the orders issued by the SCPA. See Art. 55/2,3,4 of the PRCA-1.
743. Articles 56 and 61 of the PRCA-1 that were repealed in 2013 by the latest amendment of the PRCA-1.
744. Article 42 of the PRCA of 1999.
745. Article 25 of the PCA of 1993. Such system enabled three-stage judicial proceedings in contrast to two-stage judicial proceedings in force between 1999 and 2008, and as of 2013, and to merely single-stage judicial proceedings in force between 2008 and 2013.
746. While appeals were expressly excluded by Art. 61 of the PRCA-1, the non-availability of a revision ensues from the following decisions of the Supreme Court: III Ips 111/2009, III Ips 117/2009, III Ips 118/2009, III Ips 116/2009, and III Ips 115/2009, available at (in Slovene): http://www.sodisce.si/znanje/sodna_praksa/.

Articles 54–61 of the PRCA-1 as valid at the time, are in breach of Article 23[747] of the Constitution guaranteeing the right to judicial protection.

535. On 25 January 2012, the Supreme Court stayed the judicial review proceedings in the 'skiing tickets cartel' cases[748] (in which the CPO determined a breach of Article 6 of the PRCA-1 (Article 5 of the previous PRCA) as well as (from 2004 onwards) Article 101 TFEU (Article 81 TEC prior to 1 December 2009) in the form of (agreed or concerted) price fixing of daily skiing tickets for adults that has allegedly taken place since 2000 by the majority of Slovene skiing undertakings),[749] and asked the Constitutional Court for constitutional review of two sets of provisions of the PRCA-1 as in force at the time – first, the provisions enabling the SCPA to perform inspections in undertakings and to examine communications without court orders (Articles 28 and 29 of the PRCA-1 as in force at the time),[750] and second, the provisions providing for one-stage judicial review of the SCPA's decisions by the Supreme Court of RS (Articles 54 to 61 of the PRCA-1 as in force at the time).[751] As the same questions had arisen also in the 'construction cartel' case pending before the Supreme Court on the initiation of major Slovene construction undertakings, taking, as substantiated by the SCPA, part in the cartel (by way of sharing projects, bid rigging and exchanging information on bid prices before submission of bids),[752] the Supreme Court has stayed the proceedings in that case, too.[753] In fact, the Supreme Court decided to continue to assess those and all other competition law related disputes only after the Constitutional Court would decide on the matter. That led to an approximately sixteen months' blockade in review of the SCPA's decisions. Due to the lengthy deadlock situation that had emerged, many undertakings, their attorneys and other competition law professionals perceived such decision of the Supreme Court (as well as the long-lasting assessment by the Constitutional Court) as a negative and unnecessary impact on effective assessment of complex competition law related cases.

---

747. *Everyone has the right to have any decision regarding his rights, duties and any charges brought against him or her made without undue delay by an independent, impartial court constituted by law. Only a judge duly appointed pursuant to rules previously established by law and by judicial regulations may judge such an individual.*
748. See Orders Nos. G 23/2010 and G 18/2010 of 25 Jan. 2012, issued by the Supreme Court in the proceedings initiated by the skiing undertakings (available at: http://www.sodisce.si/znanje/sodna_praksa/vrhovno_sodisce_rs/2012032113046277/ (in Slovene only)).
749. Decision No. 306-95/2009-62 of 11 May 2010, not available online.
750. See *supra* Pt. III, Ch. 1, §2, II.
751. It acted in accordance with Art. 156 of the Constitution and Art. 23/1 of the Constitutional Court Act (Sl. *Zakon o ustavnem sodišču (ZUstS)*, Official Gazette RS, No. 15/94, with further amendments). The order of the Supreme Court is available at http://www.sodisce.si/znanje/sodna_praksa/vrhovno_sodisce_rs/2012032113046277/ (in Slovene only).
752. CPO's decision No. 306-25/2010 of 23 Mar. 2012, operative part of the decision is available at (in Slovene): http://www.varstvo-konkurence.si/zakonodaja-in-dokumenti/ostali-dokumenti/arhiv-odlocb/odlocba232/.
753. See Orders Nos G 10/2011 and G 13/2011 of 25 Jan. 2012, available at (in Slovene): http://www.sodisce.si/znanje/sodna_praksa/.

536. The Constitutional Court issued the decision in April 2013.[754] It did not follow the reasoning of the Supreme Court and did not find the review system unconstitutional. Slovenian legislator has nevertheless amended the system (plausibly on petition of the Supreme Court judges wishing to be relieved of jurisdiction in first instance competition review proceedings,) so that the Administrative Court of RS has regained jurisdiction in first instance judicial review proceedings, while the Supreme Court is again merely the last instance court assessing the Administrative Court's decisions (as is generally the case in other cases of judicial protection in administrative cases[755]).

537. Between 2008 (when the Supreme Court was vested with jurisdiction of judicial review of the CPO's decisions as the first instance court in administrative dispute proceedings) and 2012 (when the Supreme Court of RS stayed all competition law related cases until the decision of the Constitutional Court of RS), the Supreme Court had issued only one important substantive judgment (copy-pasted mutatis mutandis in three other judgments dealing with the same CPO's decision)[756] in the well-known case of the so-called electricity cartel of four electricity undertakings concerting their electricity prices.[757] One of the interesting features of these judgments was that the Supreme Court dismissed the actions in all but one aspect: it shared the applicants' view that the CPO had not proven in its decision that beside national, European antitrust was also violated.[758] In essence, however, it confirmed the CPO's reasoning. The main notions analysed by the Supreme Court were concerted practices, economic unity, negative effect on competition, and effect on trade between Member States where it referred directly to the relevant case law of the CJEU. The case was a massive breakthrough of antitrust importance in Slovenia as it had direct impact on almost every Slovenian household and business. After the judgments had been issued, a Society for the refund of electricity overcharges[759] was established that campaigned for the follow-on private enforcement in order to give effect to the judgment in everyday life. Under pressure from the

754. Decision No. U-I/40-12 of 11 Apr. 2013, available at (in Slovene): http://odlocitve.us-rs.si/usrs/us-odl.nsf/o/6CB088ECD3674541C1257B5C003BC66A.

755. See Art. 12 of the ADA-1.

756. In contrast to some forty orders and judgments regarding more or less procedural issues, such as the availability of separate judicial review against certain SCPA's orders; the referral to the Constitutional Court of certain PRCA-1's provisions to assess their constitutionality; the Supreme Court's jurisdiction; the party status in administrative proceedings before the SCPA, etc.

757. Cases Nos U 5/2008, 2/2008, U 9/2008, U 4/2008, and U 6/2008 of 30 Jun. 2009, reviewing the CPO's decision of 6 Aug. 2008, available at (in Slovene): http://www.sodisce.si/znanje/sodna_praksa/.

758. As has already been stressed, according to Art. 25 of the PRCA-1, in cases of proceedings involving violations of Arts 101 or 102 TFEU, the SCPA must also conduct proceedings involving violations of Arts 6 or 9 of the PRCA-1. If during the proceedings it should be determined that there is no basis to conduct the proceedings under Arts 101 or 102 TFEU of since there is no effect on trade between the Member States, the SCPA is to issue an order terminating the proceedings in this segment. No legal remedy may be invoked against such order terminating the proceedings.

759. It was later renamed Society for the Rule of Law (www.dzp.si).

Society and the media, the undertakings have decided to refund a certain amount of the overcharges before any suits were filed with the courts.[760]

538. After the Constitutional Court's decision of 11 April 2013, of which the Supreme Court was notified on 6 May 2013, the Supreme Court continued assessing pending cases in which it stayed the proceedings for the time of the Constitutional Court's assessment of the PRCA-1 constitutionality. Several of these cases were of utmost importance to business and the citizens.

539. For example, Telekom Slovenije was challenging the CPO's decision on the abuse regarding the mobile phone package Itak Džabest.[761] In November 2013, the Supreme Court of RS acting as a review court set aside the CPO's decision concluding that the decision was burdened by incorrect application of the substantive law, significant procedural irregularities, and incomplete finding of facts, and returned the case to the CPA for reassessment in accordance with the Supreme Court's guidelines laid down in its judgment.[762]

540. A decision setting aside the CPO's decision and returning the case to the CPA was issued by the Supreme Court also in the GEN-I electricity cartel case in January 2014. In August 2012, the CPO issued a decision finding that GEN-I d.o.o. and GEN Energija d.o.o. concluded a cartel agreement fixing electricity prices in breach of Article 6 of the PRCA-1 and Article 101 TFEU. The Supreme Court followed the plaintiffs' argument that the CPO did not give the plaintiffs the possibility to elaborate on the question of existence of economic unity as the CPO analysed this concept and decided that there was no economic unity only in its decision, and not already during the proceedings breaching thereby the principle of adversarial procedure.[763]

541. In the following cases, the Supreme Court of RS dismissed the action and thereby upheld the CPO's decision: in the driving schools' cartel case[764] in June 2013; in the *Pro Plus* case[765] in December 2013; and in *Gasilska oprema*[766] case and in the *SAZAS* case[767] in January 2014.

---

760. The society has obtained over 73,000 authorizations from the citizens to address to the undertakings the claims in their names for refund of the overcharges (amounting to approx. EUR 30–EUR 300 per household). A law office was also engaged in the project in case actions had to be filed with the court.
761. For detailed analysis of the case, see Pt. II, Ch. 2, §2, I and V of this monograph.
762. Judgment No. G 9/2012-28 of 26 Nov. 2013. http://seonet.ljse.si/Default.aspx?doc=SEARCH&doc_id=53393.
763. Judgments Nos G 32/2012 and G 33/2012 of 14 Jan. 2013, available at (in Slovene): http://sodnapraksa.si/?q=g%2032/2012&database[SOVS]=SOVS&_submit=i%C5%A1%C4%8Di&page=0&id=2012032113062485 and http://sodnapraksa.si/?q=g%2033/2012&database[SOVS]=SOVS&_submit=i%C5%A1%C4%8Di&page=0&id=2012032113062447.
764. Judgment No. G 27/2011 of 11 Jun. 2013, available at (in Slovene): http://sodnapraksa.si/?q=omejevanje%20konkurence&database[SOVS]=SOVS&_submit=i%C5%A1%C4%8Di&order=date&direction=desc&page=0&id=2012032113055533.
765. See Pt. I, Ch. 5, §1, IV A; and Pt. II, Ch. 2, §2, III of this monograph. Judgment No. G 7/2013 of 3 Dec. 2013, available at (in Slovene): http://sodnapraksa.si/?q=g%207/2013&database[SOVS]=SOVS&_submit=i%C5%A1%C4%8Di&page=0&id=2012032113061544.

542. In the *Pro Plus* case (sic! where provisions as to judicial review proceedings as in force prior to the August 2013 amendment applied), the plaintiff filed on 16 January 2014 a request with the Supreme Court of RS for revision of the Supreme Court's judgment of 3 December 2013 dismissing the plaintiffs action. The plaintiff claimed that the Supreme Court made procedural errors as well as errors in the application of substantive law. On 7 April 2014, the Supreme Court dismissed the request for revision[768] stressing that the remedy of revision against the Supreme Court's judgments in competition law cases is not possible under Slovenian law. On 27 January 2014, the plaintiff motioned also for the opening of the proceedings which the Supreme Court dismissed on 15 April 2014[769] already due to formalities (partly due to the fact that it was not filed within the prescribed time-limit and that the plaintiff lacked legal interest, partly due to the fact that the plaintiff provided new facts what is prohibited by Article 57 of the PRCA-1[770]).

543. Further, disputes in the 'skiing tickets cartel'[771] and the 'construction cartel'[772] cases have also been solved. In the majority of the 'construction cartel' cases,[773] the Supreme Court dismissed the action and upheld the CPO's decision, save for the part where the CPO found that in addition to the Slovenian antitrust, the cartel breached European antitrust also. The Supreme Court stated in several of its judgments of December 2013, January 2014 and February 2014 (review proceedings were initiated by different undertakings taking part in the cartel and providing different arguments in their favour, and thus fourteen judgments dealing with the same 'construction cartel' was issued by the Supreme Court) that effect on trade between the Member States was not proven adequately by the CPO and thus returned the case with this regard to the CPO for reassessment. The Supreme Court thereby stressed that the cartel with the effect of higher prices would in its opinion, to the contrary of the CPO's argumentation, if anything, invite foreign competitors to bid for the project (in reality, however, it can be presumed that foreign investors being informed of the low ethical standards in construction tender proceedings in

766. See Pt. II, Ch. 2, §2 IV of this monograph. Judgment No. G 47/2010 of 11 Jun. 2013, available at (in Slovene): http://sodnapraksa.si/?q=omejevanje%20konkurence&database[SOVS]=SOVS&_submit=i%C5%A1%C4%8Di&order=date&direction=desc&page=0&id=2012032113061464.
767. See Pt. II, Ch. 2, §1, II of this monograph. The Supreme Court Judgment No. 24/2011 of 27 Jan. 2014 is available (in Slovene) at: http://sodnapraksa.si/?q=g%2024/2011%20&database[SOVS]=SOVS&_submit=i%C5%A1%C4%8Di&page=0&id=2012032113063758.
768. Decision No. III Ips 6/2014.
769. Decision No. G 7/2013, available at (in Slovene): http://sodnapraksa.si/?q=varstvo%20konkurence%20&database[SOVS]=SOVS&_submit=i%C5%A1%C4%8Di&order=date&direction=desc&page=0&id=2012032113066402.
770. See Pt. III, Ch. 4, §3 of this monograph.
771. See *supra* in this chapter.
772. See *supra* in this chapter.
773. Judgment No. G 27/2012 of 11 Feb. 2014, Judgment No. G 22/2012 of 11 Feb. 2014; Judgment No. G 18/2012 of 27 Jan. 2014; Judgment No. G 21/2012 of 27 Jan. 2014; Judgment No. G 17/2012 of 27 Jan. 2014; Judgment No. G 23/2012 of 27 Jan. 2014; Judgment No. G 26/2012 of 14 Jan. 2014; Judgment No. G 25/2012 of 14 Jan. 2014; Judgment No. G 19/2012 of 14 Jan. 2014; Judgment No. G 14/2012 of 14 Jan. 2014; Judgment No. G 24/2012 of 3 Dec. 2013; Judgment No. G 20/2012 of 24 Sep. 2013; Judgment No. G 13/2012 of 3 Dec. 2013; Judgment No. G 12/2012 of 3 Dec. 2013. All judgments are available at (in Slovene): http://sodnapraksa.si/search.php.

Slovenia were even not interested in taking part in them). In some of these cases, the plaintiffs petitioned the court to ask the CJEU for a preliminary ruling on the effect on trade concept but the Supreme Court (thus far – as stated by the court itself) did not opt for that as it returned the case for another assessment back to the CPA who is yet to present satisfactory argumentation as to the effect on trade.[774]

544. In the 'skiing tickets cartel', the Supreme Court of RS also upheld in its decisions of December 2013 and January 2014[775] the CPO's decision finding breach of Article 6 of the PRCA-1, whereas it quashed the decision in the part(s) where the CPO found (i) that the plaintiffs took part in the cartel in the seasons of 2004/5, (2005/6), 2006/7, 2007/8, and/or (ii) that the cartel breached also European antitrust.[776] In this regard, it returned the case to the CPA for detailed assessment that was lacking in the CPO's decision. This case is relevant also for the Supreme Court's application of the Constitutional Court's decision of April 2013 on unconstitutionality of the CPO's inspection system as set out in the PRCA-1 prior to its 2013 amendment. The Supreme Court emphasized that the Constitutional Court decided that until the unconstitutionality is abolished, the unconstitutional system further applies, meaning that the CPO had proper basis for conducting the inspection.

545. One of the interesting cases pending before the Supreme Court during the Supreme Court's stay of all cases where the PRCA-1 was to be applied, was also the Mercator merger case where the CPO had initiated proceedings against Mercator d.d. (a supermarket chain) and seven banks alleging that the banks have obtained joint control over Mercator,[777] and prohibited the Central Securities Clearing Corporation (KDD) to allow the realization of the sale until the case is assessed by the CPO.[778] Although the CPO had afterwards terminated the proceedings and declared the prohibitive decision void,[779] the applicants have, due to the importance of the matter, motioned the Supreme Court to assess the legality of the CPO's prohibition, and to issue a substantive decision despite the termination of the proceedings by the

774. Decree No. G 25/2012 of 14 Jan. 2014, available at (in Slovene): http://www.sodisce.si/znanje/sodna_praksa/search.php?q=sklep%20G%2030/2012&database%5BSOVS%5D=SOVS&_submit=i%EF%BF%BD%C3%A8i&order=changeDate&direction=desc&rowsPerPage=20&page=9&id=2012032113063757.
775. Judgment G 14/2012 of 14 Jan. 2014; Judgment No. G 24/2010 of 17 Dec. 2013; Judgment No. G 18/2010 of 17 Dec. 2013; Judgment No. G 22/2010 of 17 Dec. 2013; Judgment No. G 23/2010 of 17 Dec. 2013. All judgments are available at (in Slovene): http://sodnapraksa.si/search.php.
776. Different illegalities in the CPO's decision were found by the Supreme Court in these judgments as each judgment was issued on petition of different plaintiffs taking part in the cartel presenting different argument in their favour.
777. The CPO's decision No. 306-29/2011-2 of 30 Mar. 2011, not available online.
778. The CPO's decision No. 306-29/2011-4 of 26 Apr. 2011, not available online. For details as to Art. 45 of the PRCA-1 relevant with this regard, see Pt. III, Ch. 3, §1, IV B of this monograph.
779. The CPO's decision No. 306-29/2011-154 of 3 Oct. 2011, available at (in Slovene): http://www.varstvo-konkurence.si/fileadmin/varstvo-konkurence.si/pageuploads/informacija_javnega_znacaja/ijz116.pdf.

CPO. In spite of extreme importance of the case for further development of competition law in Slovenia, the case was pending up until October 2013.[780] Despite the termination of proceedings by the CPO, the Supreme Court found that the plaintiffs still show the legal benefit in petitioning the issuance of a declaratory judgment on the invalidity of the CPO's decisions. It agreed with the plaintiffs' arguments that the Supreme Court's decision on the matter is (in the absence of any precedent) of importance for preventing the CPO to issue such decisions in the future as well as for obtaining legal basis for claiming damages sustained by the CPO's conduct. The plaintiffs and other business as well as other professional public had high hopes for the Supreme Court's decision; unfortunately, the Supreme Court did not live up to their expectations as it stopped assessing the case and declared the CPO's decision illegal already by finding a jurisdictional mistake made by the CPO (it found that the CPO did not show that it was competent to assess the case according to the rules of Regulation 139/2004), whereas it did not dig into the heart of the problem of the CPO's decision, i.e., whether that really was a concentration or not.

546. All of the cases in which the Supreme Court had acted in revision of the Administrative Court's decisions pursuant to the PRCA of 1999, i.e., up until 2008, have been brought to an end. The one to be highlighted is the 'banking cartel' in the form of a concerted practice regarding the fees charged by four banks for withdrawal of money at other concerting banks' ATMs.[781] The Supreme Court has, inter alia, focused on analysing the definition of economic unity, referring thereby also on case law of the CJEU.[782] The Society for the Rule of Law that has in the recent years been active in promoting private out-of-court enforcement of competition law, has afterwards achieved (in cooperation with the Slovene Consumers' Association[783] and by intense media pressure) that the banks have unilaterally refunded almost EUR 4 million to almost 800,000 of their clients that had made more than 8 million ATM withdrawals.

780. Judgment and Decree Nos G 23/2011, G 29/2011, G 31/2011 and 32/2011 of 3 Oct. 2013, available at (in Slovene): http://sodnapraksa.si/search.php.

781. See Pt. II, Ch. 1, §1, II of this monograph. The banks started charging the fees on the same day (20 Feb. 2006) in the same amount of EUR 0.33 on the basis of the information they had leaked in the newspapers.

782. Case No. X Ips 113/2010 of 11 Oct. 2011, reviewing the Administrative Court's decision No. U 565/2007. The Administrative Court and the Supreme Court had dealt with three more cases resulting from the same CPO's decision (each of the banks challenged the CPO's decision by filing an individual action); No. X Ips 70/2010 of 15 Jun. 2010 reviewing the Administrative Court's decision No. U 581/2007; No. X Ips 114/2010 of 27 Sep. 2011 reviewing the Administrative Court's judgment No. U 582/2007; and No. X Ips 126/2010 of 11 Oct. 2011 reviewing the Administrative Court's decision No. U 584/2007.

783. See: https://www.zps.si/.

§2. TIME LIMITS

547. The PRCA-1 does not regulate the time-limit for challenging the SCPA's decision that established a breach of antitrust rules or incompatibility of a concentration. ADA-1 therefore applies in these cases.[784] According to Article 28 of the ADA-1, an action challenging the CPA's decision has to be filed with the Administrative Court of RS within thirty days after the CPA's decision had been served to the addressee. Formal prerequisites to be met for the action to be taken into review by the Administrative Court of RS are set out in the ADA-1.[785]

548. After the Administrative Court issues the decision in administrative review proceedings, the parties may make use of the following legal remedies: (i) an appeal to the Supreme Court of RS, (ii) a revision to the Supreme Court of RS, and (iii) re-opening of the proceedings.

549. The parties may appeal against the Administrative Court's judgment only in the case where the Administrative Court established different facts than the SCPA, and it itself changed the attacked act of the SCPA. The appeal must be lodged with the court that had issued the first instance judgment in fifteen days after the judgment was served to them.[786] The appeal is then forwarded to the Supreme Court in assessment.[787] The grounds for appeal are: (i) material breach of procedure before the Administrative Court of RS, (ii) erroneous application of the law, or erroneous assessment of the legality of the procedure before the SCPA, or (iii) erroneous or incomplete establishment of the facts. In competition law matters, such appeals are rare as it is rarely the case that – as far as the assessment of competition law breaches is concerned – the Administrative Court itself changes the attacked agency's act.[788] In practice, the court rather annuls the act and refers the case back to the agency for another assessment. In competition law matters, the remedy of revision presented in the next paragraph is thus the usual legal remedy before the Supreme Court of RS.

550. The remedy of revision may be filed for assessment of the final judgment by the Supreme Court of RS for grounds of (i) material breach of procedure before

784. For some of the SCPA's orders, e.g. on interim measures, the PRCA-1 itself sets out specific time-limits for filing an action. See, e.g., Art. 38 of the PRCA-1.

785. Articles 30, 31 and others of the ADA-1. For further details see Kerševan in Grilc et al., *PRCA-1 Commentary*, 468–469; Kerševan & Androjna, *Upravno procesno pravo*, 550; Dobravec Jalen in Kerševan, *Zakon o upravnem sporu s komentarjem*, 191–211

786. Articles 73–82 of the ADA-1. See also Kerševan & Androjna, *Upravno procesno pravo*, 603–610; Kerševan in Kerševan, *Zakon o upravnem sporu s komentarjem*, 414–419, 458–471; Domjan Pavlin in Kerševan, *Zakon o upravnem sporu s komentarjem*, 419–119; Golob in Kerševan, *Zakon o upravnem sporu s komentarjem*, 436–457.

787. Kerševan & Androjna, *Upravno procesno pravo*, 551.

788. See, e.g., order of the Supreme Court of RS No. I Up 174/2018 of 17 Oct. 2018, where the Supreme Court amended the agency's order on interim measures. See also the order of the Supreme Court of RS, No. I Up 31/2017 of 16 Mar. 2017 where the Supreme Court dismissed the appeal against the Administrative Court's order denying the searched undertaking a legal remedy in administrative dispute proceedings against the agency's search activities.

the Administrative Court of RS or (ii) erroneous application of the law.[789] Revision may be lodged in accordance with the CPrA, i.e., in fifteen days after being served with the Supreme Court's decision to allow the revision. The Supreme Court will allow the revision only if its decision is important for ensuring legal certainty, uniform application of the law, or the development of law through case-law.[790] In competition law matters, the Supreme Court often allows revision. A lodged revision does not prevent the enforceability of the judgment.

551. Further, the motion for re-opening of the proceedings may be lodged with the Administrative Court of RS in thirty days after the party has discovered one of the grounds for such motion or after it could have referred to it (e.g., relevant new facts or new evidence arise; the judicial senate was not established in accordance with the law; the party could not take part in the administrative dispute) but was – where relevant – unable to do so for reasons outside their guilt. In any event, the opening of the proceedings cannot be requested after five years as of the moment in which the judgment became final.[791]

§3. SCOPE OF JUDICIAL REVIEW

552. The PRCA-1 regulates judicial review in competition law cases in Articles 54–61a. It provides only for a couple of specific provisions as to the administrative dispute proceedings in competition law cases. As set out in Article 54/2 of the PRCA-1, the ADA-1 is to be applied mutatis mutandis with regard to all other procedural aspects of the administrative dispute (be it before the Administrative Court of RS or the Supreme Court of RS). The ADA-1 further states that in case the ADA-1 itself does not provide for a certain procedural solution, the CPrA will apply.[792]

553. The 2013 PRCA-1 amendment brought by one of the laws amending the Courts Act,[793] set aside Articles 56 and 61 of the PRCA-1 that stated that the Supreme Court of RS has jurisdiction in the review proceedings (Article 56), and that there is no legal remedy against a decision or an order issued within judicial review proceedings (Article 61). Deletion of these provisions was in line with the reorganization of judicial review proceedings shifting jurisdiction in first instance review proceedings back to the Administrative Court of RS leaving the Supreme Court of RS to be merely an appellate review court in competition law matters. As

789. Articles 84–95 of the ADA-1 and the relevant general rules of the CPrA on revision. See also Perševan & Androjna, *Upravno procesno pravo*, 610–625.
790. Articles 367–384 of the CPrA. Kerševan & Androjna, *Upravno procesno pravo*, 615. See, e.g., decision of the Supreme Court of RS, No. X Ips 58/2015 of 15 Jul. 2015.
791. Articles 96–101 of the ADA-1.
792. Article 22 of the ADA-1. The older version of the ADA-1 stated that the CPrA applies *mutatis mutandis*. This is no longer the case and the CPrA applies directly, not merely *mutatis mutandis* with regard to all those questions that are not regulated in the ADA-1. See Kerševan & Androjna, *Upravno procesno pravo*, 554.
793. See General Introduction, §§ 3 and 4 of this monograph.

a consequence of redrafting of the system of the CPA's powers of inspection, the 2014 PRCA-1 amendment also deleted one line in Article 55/3 of the PRCA-1 regarding the order of inspection.[794] The following analysis focuses on the currently valid regime of judicial review proceedings in competition law matters that was reinforced in August 2013.

554. According to Article 55/1 of the PRCA-1, judicial protection is available against all decisions of the CPA issued in accordance with the PRCA-1. As set out in Article 55/2 of the PRCA-1, judicial protection is available also against orders of the CPA issued in accordance with the PRCA-1, unless judicial protection against a particular type of order is expressly excluded.[795] Article 55/3 of the PRCA-1 further states that orders for request for information from an undertaking regulated in Article 27 of the PRCA-1 can be challenged only within the ambit of judicial review of the final CPA's decision. Additionally, Article 55/4 of the PRCA-1 provides for judicial protection available to contest all other orders of the CPA against which an appeal may be lodged according to the provisions of the GAPA (which broadens the possibility of contesting orders in comparison to the ADA-1 which would otherwise apply).[796]

555. Article 57 of the PRCA-1 provides that the plaintiff may not introduce new facts or present new evidence. This provision is stricter from the one in the general rules of the ADA-1 as it does not enable the plaintiffs to show that at the time of the first instance administrative proceedings it was justifiably impossible for them to submit certain facts and evidence that had existed already at that time.[797] It follows that the review court as well cannot gather evidence on its own motion in order to clarify and solve the case correctly.[798] This, however, does not mean that the court is bound by the CPA's factual findings regarding the case. The court must rely on the facts and the evidence put forward before the CPA, but it is not prevented from establishing a different factual state of the case on the basis of these facts and evidence.[799]

556. According to Article 58 of the PRCA-1, the review court is limited to testing the CPA's decision/order within the limits of the claim and within the limits of the grounds stated in the action, and must, ex officio, pay attention to essential

---

794. See Pt. III, Ch. 1, §2, II of this monograph.
795. As, for example, in cases of orders terminating the proceedings (Art. 40 of the PRCA-1), orders regarding the CPA's consent to performance of commitments (Art. 39/4 of the PRCA-1), etc.
796. Terševan in Grilc et al., *PRCA-1 Commentary*, 474–475. See also Terševan & Androjna, *Upravno procesno pravo*, 420–422.
797. Articles 20 and 52 of the ADA-1. The party informed of such new facts and evidence after the CPA's decision was issued will have the possibility to open of the proceedings before the CPA in accordance with the general rules of the GAPA. Terševan in Grilc et al., *PRCA-1 Commentary*, 477. See also Smrekar in Terševan, *Zakon o upravnem sporu s komentarjem*, 113–119, 308–314.
798. Terševan in Grilc et al., *PRCA-1 Commentary*, 476–477.
799. *Ibid.*

infringements of procedure.[800] The court cannot, therefore, deliberate on other infringements, albeit existent, were they not claimed by the applicant.

557. As set out in Article 59 of the PRCA-1, the case is as a rule decided without the hearing. This provision which has been much criticized in Slovenian legal theory,[801] encroaches upon the general regime prescribed by Article 51 of the ADA-1 which clearly provides for a hearing as the common manner of deciding administrative disputes (with the exceptions enumerated in Article 59 of the ADA-1).[802] The wording of Article 59 of the PRCA-1 is extremely vague as it does not provide the reasons for the explicit exclusion of the hearing in competition matters, and is thus to be interpreted as directing the review court to, first and foremost, always analyse whether the general conditions to omit the hearing set out in Article 51 of the ADA are met.[803]

558. Referring to Article 18 of the PRCA-1 regulating the right of parties to review the CPA case file, Article 60 of the PRCA-1 states that access to case file documents before the court is allowed under the same ground as before the CPA.[804] Therefore, specific rules on access to file as set out in Article 18 of the PRCA-1 (and not as set out in the ADA-1 and the CPrA) apply.

559. The lawsuit in administrative dispute review proceedings may be filed by (i) a person claiming that the CPA's act (i.e., a decision or an order) interfered with their legal status and is thus protecting their rights or legal benefits (such a person has legal standing only if he or she was a party or an intervener in the proceedings before the CPA), or by (ii) the public interest representative nominated by the Government of RS if the latter detected illegality in the CPA's act on the detriment of public interest.[805] To the author's knowledge, the Government has so far not opted for this legal possibility. The defendant in the dispute is the Republic of Slovenia represented by the CPA.[806] Any person showing that the revocation or amendment of the CPA's decision in the administrative dispute proceedings would cause direct harm to it may also take part in the proceedings.[807]

800. See also Arts 27/3 of the ADA-1 and 237 of the GAPA. See also Dobravec Jalen in Krševan, *Zakon o upravnem sporu s komentarjem*, 153–172.
801. See Žuber, *The Slovenian perspective of a main hearing in an administrative dispute*.
802. See Steinman in Kerševan, *Zakon o upravnem sporu s komentarjem*, 331–343.
803. For further details see Kerševan in Grilc et al., *PRCA-1 Commentary*, 479–480.
804. See Pt. III, Ch. 1, §3, II C of this monograph.
805. Articles 16–18 of the ADA-1. See Steinman in Kerševan, *Zakon o upravnem sporu s komentarjem*, 93–106.
806. The Government of RS could authorise another state body to represent it, but in practice, it is always represented by the CPA. The CPA can, of course, have its own representative, but it usually takes part in the proceedings on its own. See Arts 17 and 22 of the ADA-1. See also Steinman in Kerševan, *Zakon o upravnem sporu s komentarjem*, 97–103, and Smrekar in Kerševan, *Zakon o upravnem sporu s komentarjem*, 122–126.
807. Article 19 of the ADA-1. See Steinman in Kerševan, *Zakon o upravnem sporu s komentarjem*, 107–113.

560. The grounds for review, as set out in the ADA-1, consist of errors in application of substantive law, fundamental errors in procedural law, errors in the finding of facts, and reasons for annulling administrative acts. Instituting review proceedings does not suspend enforcement of the CPA's decision or order, but when filing the action, the plaintiff may request the court to grant interim measures if it shows that (i) enforcement of the CPA's decision or order would cause the plaintiff hardly repairable harm and that (ii) granting interim measures would not affect disproportionally the public interest and the interests of the opposing parties.[808] One of such cases was the *Geoplin* case where in 2015, the Supreme Court rejected Geoplin's appeal against an order issued by the Administrative Court of RS denying granting interim measures as requested by Geoplin,[809] who has attacked the CPA's decision finding an abuse through the Administrative Court of RS.[810]

561. Disputes before the competent court in judicial administrative review proceedings are, in principle, so-called disputes on the legality of the CPA's decision or order meaning that the review court must refer the case back to the CPA after it has set the decision or order aside. Only in extraordinary circumstances as set out in the ADA-1 may the review court set aside the CPA's decision or order and amend the decision or order by itself (the so-called dispute of full jurisdiction).[811] The court is not bound by the type of relief sought by the plaintiff and may decide which kind of decision to issue (it may, however, decide in the dispute of full jurisdiction only if so requested by the plaintiff).[812]

562. After the Administrative Court of RS issues the judgment in administrative review proceedings, the parties taking part in these proceedings may lodge a revision against the judgment to the Supreme Court of RS in accordance with the general provisions of the ADA-1 and the CPrA on the remedy of revision As has already been explained,[813] the remedy of revision is the typical remedy in competition law related administrative disputes.

563. The re-opening of the proceedings may also be filed. General provisions of the ADA-1 regulating administrative dispute proceedings apply[814] in addition to the specific rules set out in the PRCA-1.

---

808. Article 32 of the ADA-1. See Dobravec Jalen in Kerševan, *Zakon o upravnem sporu s komentarjem*, 212–227.
809. See the CPA's press releases of 24 Mar. 2015 (in Slovene): http://www.varstvo-konkurence.si/medijsko-sredisce/novica/?tx_ttnews%5BbackPid%5D=1465&tx_ttnews%5Btt_news%5D=5361&cHash=9216915e2ba8984a5c27b53603fd6e1f, and of 16 Feb. 2015 (in Slovene): http://www.varstvo-konkurence.si/medijsko-sredisce/novica/?tx_ttnews%5Bpointer%5D=1&tx_ttnews%5BbackPid%5D=1465&tx_ttnews%5Btt_news%5D=5360&cHash=e7e45a810c9584c9c21eb632e96219a8.
810. Operative part of the CPA's decision is available (in Slovene) on the CPA's website: http://www.varstvo-konkurence.si/zakonodaja-in-dokumenti/ostali-dokumenti/arhiv-odlocb/odlocba306/.
811. Kerševan in Grilc et al., *PRCA-1 Commentary*, 464–466.
812. Articles 7, 33, 65, 69 of the ADA-1.
813. See *supra* paras. 549 and 550.
814. Revision is regulated in Arts 84–95 of the ADA-1, while opening of the proceedings is regulated in Arts 96–101 of the ADA-1.

Selected Bibliography

Books or Parts Therein

In English

Allendesalazar Rafael. 'Oligopolies, Conscious Parallelism and Concertation'. In *European Competition Law Annual 2006: Enforcement of Prohibition of Cartels*, Hart Publishing (referred to as: Allendesalazar, *Oligopolies, Conscious Parallelism and Concertation*).

Brezigar Masten Arjana, Gregorič Aleksandra & Zajc Katarina. 'Power Struggle: Cooperation or Competition?: Post-Privatization Ownership Changes in Slovenian Corporations'. In *Papers from 22nd Annual Conference of European Association for Law and Economics, September 15–17, 2005*, Ljubljana, Slovenia, Pravna fakulteta: = Facultas Iuridica, [2005], 23 (referred to as: Brezigar Masten, Gregorič & Zajc, *Power Struggle: Cooperation or Competition?...*).

Buccirossi Paolo. 'Facilitating Practices'. In *Handbook of Antitrust Economics*, edited by Buccirossi. MIT Press, 2008 (referred to as: Buccirossi, *Facilitating Practices*).

Bugarič Bojan. 'Law and Development in Central and Eastern Europe: Neoliberal Development State and Its Problems'. In *Law and Development of Middle-Income Countries: Avoiding the Middle-Income Trap*, edited by Peerenboom Randall P. & Ginsburg Tom. New York: Cambridge University Press, 2014, 131–155 (referred to as: Bugarič, *Law and Development in Central and Eastern Europe* ...).

Bugarič Bojan. 'The Europeanization of National Administrations in CEE'. In *Apres Enlargement, Legal and Political Responses in Central and Eastern Europe*, edited by Sadurski Wojciech, Ziller Jacques & Zurek Karolina. European University Institute, Robert Schuman Centre for Advanced Studies, Florence, 2006 (referred to as: Bugarič, *The Europeanization of National Administrations in CEE*).

Craig P. Paul P. & de Búrca Gráinne. *EU Law: Text, Cases, and Materials*. 5th edn. Oxford University Press, 2011 (referred to as: Craig & de Búrca, *EU Law* ...).

Ehrlich Isaac & A. Posner Richard. 'An Economic Analysis of Legal Rulemaking'. *Journal of Legal Studies* 3 (1974): 257 (referred to as: Ehrlich & Posner, *An Economic Analysis of Legal Rulemaking*).

Selected Bibliography

Fatur Andrej & Podobnik Klemen. *Competition Law in Western Europe and USA, SI/C, Slovenia/Commentary*, Suppl. 318 (February 2011), Kluwer Law International, 2011 (referred to as: Fatur & Podobnik, *Competition Law in Western Europe and USA: Slovenia*).

Galič Aleš. 'Reshaping the Role of Supreme Courts in the Countries of the Former Yugoslavia'. In *Nobody's Perfect, Comparative Essays on Appeals and other Means of Recourse against Judicial Decisions in Civil Matters*, Intersentia, Cambridge, 2014, 289–316 (referred to as: Galič, *Reshaping the Role of Supreme Courts ...*).

Galič Aleš. 'Slovenia'. *International Encyclopaedia of Laws, Civil Procedure*, suppl. 49, The Hague, Kluwer Law International, 2008 (referred to as: Galič, *Civil Procedure, Slovenia*).

Galič Aleš & J.S. Hodges Christopher. 'Slovenia'. In *Consumer ADR in Europe*, edited by J.S. Hodges Christopher, Benöhr Iris & Creutzfeldt-Banda Naomi. Hart Publishing, 2012 (referred to as: Galič & Hodges, *Consumer ADR in Europe, Slovenia*).

Galič Aleš. '(In)compatibility of Procedural Preclusions with the Goals of Civil Justice: An Ongoing Debate in Slovenia'. In *Goals of Civil Justice and Civil Procedure in Contemporary Judicial Systems*, edited by Uzelac Alan. Ius Gentium. Comparative Perspectives on Law and Justice, vol. 34, Springer (2014): 221–243 (referred to as: Galič, *(In)compatibility of Procedural Preclusions ...*).

Galič Aleš & Ana Vlahek. 'Challenges in Drafting and Application of the New Slovenian Collective Actions Act. In *Class Actions – The Holy Grail for (European) Civil Procedure?*, edited by Uzelac Alan, Van Rhee Cornelis Hendrik (Remco). Springer, to be published (referred to as: Galič & Vlahek, *Challenges in Drafting and Application ...*).

Grilc Peter. 'Competition Law'. In *Business Transactions in Eastern Europe.* New York; San Francisco: Matthew Bender, Pub. 273, 1999 (referred to as: Grilc, *Competition Law*).

Grilc Peter & Juhart Miha. 'Slovenia'. In *International Privatization.* London: The Hague: Boston, Kluwer Law International, 1996 (referred to as: Grilc & Juhart, *Slovenia, Privatization*).

Grilc Peter & Juhart Miha. 'Slovenia'. In *International Franchising Law*, edited by Campbell Dennis. LexisNexis, 2004 (referred to as: Grilc & Juhart, *Slovenia, International Franchising*).

Hovenkamp Herbert. *Antitrust.* 3rd edn. West Group, 1999 (referred to as: Hovenkamp, *Antitrust*).

Juhart Miha. 'Currency Regulation'. In *Business Transactions in Eastern Europe.* New York, San Francisco: Matthew Bender, Pub. 273, 1999 (referred to as: Juhart, *Currency Regulation*).

Kramberger Jerca & Vlahek Ana. 'Slovenia'. *International Encyclopaedia of Laws, Property Law*, suppl. 11. The Hague: Kluwer Law International, 2010 (referred to as: Kramberger & Vlahek, *Property Law, Slovenia*).

Možina Damjan & Kovač Mitja. *Commercial and Economic Law Slovenia*, International Encyclopaedia of Laws. The Hague: Kluwer Law International, 2014 (referred to as: Možina & Kovač, *Commercial and Economic Law Slovenia*).

Pleskovic Boris & Sachs Jeffrey D. 'Political Independence and Economic Reform in Slovenia'. In *The Transition in Eastern Europe*, edited by Blanchard Olivier Jean & A. Froot Kenneth & D. Sachs Jeffrey. Vol. 1. University of Chicago Press, 1994 (referred to as: Pleskovic & Sachs, *Political Independence and Economic Reform in Slovenia*).

Podobnik Klemen & Vlahek Ana. 'Slovenia'. In *Die Modernisierung des EG-Kartellrechts: ersteErfahrungenmit der VO 1/2003: Initial Experiences with Regulation 1/2003: premières expériences avec le règlement no 1/2003*, edited by Koeck Heribert Franz & Karollus Margit Maria. (Kongress-Publikationen, 23, Bd., vol., tome 2). 1. Aufl. [Baden-Baden]: Nomos; Wien = Vienna = Vienne: Facultas. WUV, 2008, pp. 281–288 (referred to as: Podobnik & Vlahek, *Slovenia, Initial Experiences with Regulation 1/2003*).

Podobnik Klemen & Vlahek Ana. 'Chronology of Development of Private Law in Slovenia'. In *Private Law Reform*, edited by Lavický, Hurdík et al. Acta Universitatis Brunensis, Iuridica, Editio Scientia, No. 501, Masaryk University, Brno, 2014, 283–329 (referred to as: Podobnik & Vlahek, *Chronology of Development of Private Law in Slovenia*).

Posner Richard A. *Antitrust Law, An Economic Perspective*. The University of Chicago Press, 1976, 55 (referred to as: Posner, *Antitrust Law, An Economic Perspective*).

Schulze Reiner (ed.). *Common European Sales Law (CESL)*. C.H. Beck, Hart, Nomos, 2012 (referred to as: Schulze (ed.), *Common European Sales Law (CESL)*).

Tridimas Takis. *The General Principles of EU Law*. 2nd edn. Oxford EC Law Library, 2006 (referred to as: Tridimas, *The General Principles of EU Law*).

Van den Bergh Roger & Camesasca Peter. *European Competition Law and Economics*. Intersentia, 2001 (referred to as: Van den Bergh & Camesasca, *European Competition Law and Economics*).

Vlahek Ana. 'Challenges of Private Enforcement of Antitrust in Slovenia'. In *EU Competition Law, Economic Evidences and the National Enforcement Problems*. Intersentia Publisher*s, 2015 (referred to as:* Vlahek, *Challenges of Private Enforcement of Antitrust in Slovenia*).

Vlahek Ana & Podobnik Klemen. 'Slovenia'. In *Implementation of the EU Damages Directive in Central and Eastern European Countries*, edited by Piszcz Anna. (Centre for Antitrust and Regulatory Studies, Warsaw, 2017 (referred to as: Vlahek & Podobnik, *Slovenia*).

Zajc Katarina. 'Removing Obstacles: The Competition Law regime of Slovenia'. In *Removing Obstacles: A Mutual Learning Experience Towards Good Practices in Competition Law Enforcement*, edited by Gerbrandy Anna & Berends Wouter-Jan. Europa Instituut Utrecht, 4, The Hague: Eleven International Publishing, cop. 2012, 183–187 (referred to as: Zajc, *Removing Obstacles: The Competition Law Regime of Slovenia*).

In German

Grilc Peter & Podobnik Klemen. *Das Wettbewerbsrech in Slowenien*, in: Ekey Friedrich L. & Klippel Diethelm & Kotthoff Jost & Meckel Astrid & Grilc Peter

& Podobnik Klemen & Brämer Antje: *Heidelberger Kommentar zum Wettbewerbsrecht*, (Heidelberger Kommentar), 2., neubearbeit. Auflage, Heidelberg, C.F. Müller, cop. 2005. XXV (referred to as: Grilc & Podobnik, *Das Wettbewerbsrech in Slowenien*).

In Slovene

Barlič Jelka, et al. *Zakon o varstvu konkurence s komentarjem, Zakon o trgovini s komentarjem*, Gospodarski vestnik, Ljubljana, 1993 (referred to as: Zabel et al, *PCA of 1993 Commentary*).

Galič Aleš, et al. *Zakon o preprečevanju omejevanja konkurence (ZPOmK) s komentarjem*, Gospodarski vestnik, Ljubljana, 2000.

Grilc Peter, et al. *Zakon o preprečevanju omejevanja konkurence (ZPOmK-1): s komentarjem*, (Nova slovenska zakonodaja), 1st edition, Ljubljana, GV Založba, 2009 (referred to as: Grilc et al., *PRCA-1 Commentary*).

Grilc Peter & Bajec Tomaž. *225. člen*, in: Korošec Damjan & Filipčič Katja & Zdolšek Stojan: Veliki znanstven komentar posebnega dela Kazenskega zakonika (KZ-1), 2. knjiga, Uradni list, Pravna fakulteta Univerze v lJubljani, Ljubljana, 2019, pp. 732–755 (referred to as: Grilc & Bajec, *225. člen*).

Juhart Miha & Plavšak Nina (eds). *Obligacijski zakonik s komentarjem (splošni del)*, GV Založba, Ljubljana, 2003 (referred to as: Juhart et al., *CO Commentary*).

Krševan Erik & Androjna Vilko. *Upravno procesno pravo*, GV Založba, Ljubljana, 2017 (referred to as: Kerševan & Androjna, *Upravno procesno pravo*).

Kerševan Erik (ed.). *Zakon o upravnem sporu s komentarjem*, GV Založba, Ljubljana 2019 (referred to as: Kerševan, *Zakon o upravnem sporu s komentarjem*).

Možina Damjan. *Kršitev pogodbe*, GV Založba, Ljubljana, 2006 (referred to as: Možina, *Kršitev pogodbe*).

Nešović Branimir & Prunk Janko. *20. stoletje*, DZS, Ljubljana 1993 (referred to as: Nešović & Prunk, *20. stoletje*).

Podobnik Klemen. *Pravo in politika konkurence v Evropski uniji*; in: Seliškar Toš Mojca (ed.): *Mednarodna konferenca Slovensko pravo in gospodarstvo ob vstopuSlovenije v Evropsko unijo, Portorož, 21.-23. april 2004*, (LitteraScriptaManet, Zbirka Manet), Ljubljana: Pravna fakulteta: = Facultas iuridica, 2004, pp. 435–447.

Štajnpihler Tilen. *Precedenčni učinek sodnih odločb pri pravnem utemeljevanju*, Zbirka Scientia iustitia, 20, Ljubljana: GV založba, 2012, 288 pp. (referred to as: Štajnpihler, *Precedenčni učinek sodnih odločb pri pravnem utemeljevanju*).

Štajnpihler Tilen. *Sodna praksa kot dejavnik pri sodnem odločanju: sociološki vidik*, in: Novak Aleš, Accetto Matej, Pavčnik Marijan (Eds.): *(Ustavno)sodno odločanje*, (Zbirka Pravna obzorja, 45, GV založba, Ljubljana, 2013, pp. 183–223 (referred to as: Štajnpihler, *Sodna praksa kot dejavnik pri sodnem odločanju* …).

Vlahek Ana. *Nova Direktiva 2014/104 o nekaterih pravilih glede odškodninskih zahtevkov in postopka zaradi kršitev evropskega in nacionalnega antitrusta*, in: Grilc Peter: *Izbrani vidiki razvoja slovenskega gospodarskega in civilnega prava od srede 20. stoletja do danes: (liber amicorum Bojan Zabel)*, Ljubljana: Pravna fakulteta, 2015, pp. 171–200 (referred to as: Vlahek, *Nova Direktiva 2014/ 104 ...*).

Zabel Bojan. *Tržno pravo*, Gospodarski Vestnik, Ljubljana, 1999 (referred to as: Zabel, *Tržno pravo*).

Zabel Bojan. *Uvod v gospodarsko pogodbeno pravo*, ČGP Delo – TOZD Gospodarski vestnik, Ljubljana 1987 (referred to as: Zabel, *Uvod v gospodarsko pogodbeno pravo*).

Articles

In English

Axinn, Stephen M. 'A Practical Approach to the New Merger Practice'. *Antitrust Law of Journal* 50 (1981–1982): 205, 206 (referred to as: Axinn, *A Practical Approach to the New Merger Practice*).

Bugarič Bojan. 'Courts as Policy-Makers: Lessons from Transition'. *Harvard International Law Journal* 42, no. 1 (Winter 2001): 247–288, ISSN 0017-8063 (referred to as: Bugarič, *Courts as Policy-Makers: Lessons from Transition*).

Dimitrova-Grajzl Valentina, Grajzl Peter & Zajc Katarina. 'Understanding Modes of Civil Case Disposition: Evidence from Slovenian Courts'. *Journal of Comparative Economics* (2014), available at: http://www.sciencedirect.com/science/article/pii/S0147596714000316 (referred to as: Dimitrova-Grajzl, Grajzl & Zajc, *Understanding modes of civil case disposition* ...).

Dimitrova-Grajzl Valentina, et al. 'Court Output, Judicial Staffing, and the Demand for Court Services: Evidence from Slovenian Courts of First Instance'. *International Review of Law and Economics* 32, no. 1 (2012): 19–29, ISSN 0144-8188. [Print ed.] http://dx.doi.org/10.1016/j.irle.2011.12.006 (referred to as: Dimitrova -Grajzl & Grajzl & Šušteršič & Zajc, *Court Output, Judicial Staffing, and the Demand for Court Services* ...).

Elzinga Kenneth G. & Mills David. 'Leegin and Procompetitive Resale Price Maintenance'. *Antitrust Bulletin* 55 (2010): 349 (referred to as: Elzinga & Mills, *Leegin and Procompetitive Resale Price Maintenance*).

Galič Aleš. 'The Role of the Supreme Court in Creating Precedents in Slovenian Civil Procedure'. In *Los recursos ante los tribunales supremos en Europa = Appeals to supreme courts in Europe, Difusión Jurídica*, edited by Ortelis Ramos Manuel. Madrid, 2008, 261–274 (referred to as: Galič, *The Role of the Supreme Court* ...).

Galič Aleš. 'Legal Remedies for the Protection of the Right to Trial within a Reasonable Time in Slovenia'. In *The Right to Trial within a Reasonable Time and Short-Term Reform of the European Court of Human Rights: Round Table Organized by the Slovenian Chairmanship of the Committee of Ministers of the Council of Europe.* Bled, Slovenia, 21–22 September 2009, Ministry of Justice, Ministry of Foreign Affairs, 2009, 71–87 (referred to as: Galič, *Legal Remedies for the Protection of the Right to Trial within a Reasonable Time in Slovenia*).

Gregorič Aleksandra, Zajc Katarina & Simoneti Marko. 'Agents' Response to Inefficient Judiciary: Social Norms and the Law in Transition'. *European Journal of Law and Economics* 34, no.1 (2012): 147–172, ISSN 0929-1261, http://

www.springerlink.com/content/47247566t1740552/fulltext.pdf, doi:10.1007/s10657-010-9215-6 (referred to as: Gregorič, Zajc & Simoneti, *Agents' Response to Inefficient Judiciary* ...).

Gregorič Aleksandra, Brezigar Masten Arjana & Zajc Katarina. 'From Social to Private Ownership Firms: Multiple Blockholders in Slovenian Unlisted Firms'. In *Emerging Markets Finance & Trade* 47, no. 5 (September/October 2011): 27–51, ISSN 1540-496X, doi: 10.2753/REE1540-496X470502 (referred to as: Gregorič, Brezigar Masten & Zajc, *From Social to Private Ownership Firms* ...).

Grillo Michele. *Collusion and Facilitating Practices: A New Perspective in Antirust Analysis*, IUE working paper 2002 (referred to as: Grillo, *Collusion and Facilitating Practices* ...).

Janežič Aleksandra. 'Slovenia'. In *Getting the Deal through – Dominance, Global Competition Review, Chapter 31*, 2007 (referred to as: Janežič, *Getting the Deal through – Dominance, Slovenia*).

Koponen Jonas. *Joint Purchasing Agreements*, presentation at the *Half-Day Conference: The New Legal Framework for Horizontal Cooperation Agreements,* College of Europe, 16 February 2011, https://www.coleurope.eu/content/gclc/documents/J.%20Koponen%20-%20Joint%20purchasing%20agreements%20%282%29.pdf (referred to as: Koponen, *Joint Purchasing Agreements*).

Mitić Aleksandra & Rogl Marko (Kavčič, Rogl & Bračun). 'Slovenia'. In *The European Antitrust Review 2013*, A Global Competition Review Special Report, Global Competition Review, 2012.

Možina Damjan. *Slowenisches Schuldrecht zwischen Jugoslawien und Europa am Beispiel des Leistungsstörungsrechts*, Jahresheft (Int. Juristenver. Osnabr.), 2009/2010 (referred to as: Možina, *Slowenisches Schuldrecht* ...).

Podobnik Klemen. 'Framing a New Competition Law for Slovenia'. *Global Competition Review*, August/September 1999, 20–21 (referred to as: Podobnik, *Framing a New Competition Law for Slovenia*).

Ridyard Derek. 'The Commission's New Horizontal Merger Guidelines – An Economic Commentary'. *The Global Competition Law Centre Working Papers Series GCLC Working Paper* 02/05, https://www.coleurope.eu/system/files_force/research-paper/gclc_wp_02-05.pdf?download=1 (referred to as: Ridyard, *The Commission's New Horizontal Merger Guidelines – An Economic Commentary*).

Röller Lars-Hendrik & de la Mano Miguel. 'The Impact of the New Substantive Test in European Merger Control'. *European Competition Journal* (April 2006) (referred to as: Röller & de la Mano., *The Impact of the New Substantive Test in European Merger Control*).

Röller Lars-Hendrik, Stennek Johan & Verboven Frank. *Efficiency Gains from Mergers*, Research Institute of Industrial Economics, Working Paper Series, no. 543 (referred to as: Röller, Stennek & Verboven, *Efficiency Gains from Mergers*).

Savage David, G. 'Paging Dr. Miles: Antitrust Law Examined'. American Bar Association Journal 93 (2007): 14, http://www.abajournal.com/magazine/article/paging_dr_miles_antitrust_law_examined (referred to as: Savage, *Paging Dr. Miles* ...).

Slaughter & May. *The EU Competition Rules on Horizontal Agreements*, May 2012, https://www.slaughterandmay.com/media/64578/the-eu-competition-rules-on-horizontal-agreements.pdf (referred to as: Slaughter & May, *The EU Competition Rules on Horizontal Agreements*).

Vlahek Ana & Podobnik Klemen. *Provisions of the damages directive on limitation periods and their implementation in CEE countries*, in: Yearbook of Antitrust and Regulatory Studies (2017), 147–175, http://www.yars.wz.uw.edu.pl/yars2017_10_15/147.pdf, DOI: 10.7172/1689-9024.YARS.2017.10.15.8. (referred to as: Vlahek & Podobnik, *Provisions of the Damages Directive* ...).

Žuber Bruna. *The Slovenian perspective of a main hearing in an administrative dispute*, in: Admìnìistrativne pravo ì process (2019), 57–66 (referred to as: Žuber, *The Slovenian perspective of a main hearing in an administrative dispute).*

In German

Pogorelčnik Vogrinc Neža. *Der Zivilprozess in Slowenien*, in: Jahrbuch für Ostrecht, 2018, bd. 59, hb. 1, pp. (referred to as: Pogorelčnik Vogrinc, *Der Zivilprozess in Slowenien*).

In Slovene

Ahtik Meta & Vlahek Ana. *Določanje odškodnin v primeru kršitev antitrusta*, in: Dnevi slovenskih pravnikov 2011 od 13. do 15. oktobra, Portorož, Podjetje in delo, Y. 37, No. 6/7, Ljubljana, GV Založba, 2011, pp. 1344–1359 (referred to as: Ahtik & Vlahek, *Določanje odškodnin v primeru kršitev antitrusta*).

Ahtik Meta & Vlahek Ana. *Kartelni dogovor o višini Euriborja?*, in: Pravna praksa, GV Založba, ISSN 0352-0730, 15 March 2012, Y. 31, No. 10, pp. 13–15.

Betetto Nina. *Vzorčni postopek*, in: Pravni letopis, ISSN 1855-5861, 2011, pp. 231–241, 404–405 (referred to as: Betetto, *Vzorčni postopek*).

Bugarič Bojan. *Neodvisne regulativne agencije v Evropi: analiza agencij na področju varstva konkurence*, in: Javna uprava, ISSN 1318-2277, 2010, Y. 46, No. 3/4, pp. 139–169 (referred to as: Bugarič, *Neodvisne regulativne agencije v Evropi* ...).

Damjan Matija. *Množični zahtevki zaradi posegov v zdravo življenjsko okolje*, in: Pravni letopis, ISSN 1855-5861, 2011, pp. 243–270, 406–407 (referred to as: Damjan, *Množični zahtevki zaradi posegov v zdravo življenjsko okolje*).

Damjan Matija. *Učinek mediacije na tek rokov*, in: Pravnik, ISSN 0032-6976, 2008, Y. 63, No. 1/3, pp. 37–62 (referred to as: Damjan, *Učinek mediacije na tek rokov*).

Galič Aleš. *Skupinske tožbe na področju potrošniškega prava*, in: Pravni letopis, Inštitut za primerjalno pravo pri Pravni fakulteti v Ljubljani, 2011 (referred to as: Galič, *Skupinske tožbe na področju potrošniškega prava*).

Galič Aleš & Vlahek Ana. *Zakon o kolektivnih tožbah*, in: Pravosodni bilten, 2018, Y. 39, No. 2, pp. 25–48 (referred to as: Galič & Vlahek, *Zakon o kolektivnih tožbah*).

Grilc Peter. *Konkurenčno pravo EU po reformi – evolucija, redefinicija ali stagnacija?*, in: Zbornik znanstvenih razprav, Pravna fakulteta v Ljubljani, 2004, Y. 64, pp. 157–179.

Grilc Peter. *Zaveze podjetja po novem zakonu o preprečevanju omejevanja konkurence*, in: Dnevi slovenskih pravnikov 2008 od 16. do 18. oktobra, Portorož, Podjetje in delo, Y. 34, No. 6/7, Ljubljana, GV Založba, 2008, pp. 1442–1450 (referred to as: Grilc, *Zaveze* ...).

Grilc Peter. (*Razvoj) razmerja med temeljnimi pravicami in svoboščinami ter temeljnimi ekonomskimi svoboščinami ter pravili o konkurenci v pravu EU*, in: Zbornik znanstvenih razprav, ISSN 1854–3839, 2011, Y. 71, pp. 117–141.

Grilc Peter. *Cenovne zlorabe in razvoj doktrine pri predatorstvu*, in: Zbornik znanstvenih razprav, ISSN 1854-3839, 2009, Y. 69, pp. 83–109.

Grilc Peter. *Meje konkurence, konkurenčne politike in konkurenčnega prava*, in: Javna uprava, ISSN 1318-2277, 2007, Y. 43, No. 1, pp. 117–143.

Grilc Peter. *Koga varuje konkurenčno pravo in pred kom*, in: Juren Peter (Ed.): Dnevi slovenskih pravnikov, od 17. do 19. oktobra 1996 v Portorožu, Podjetje in delo, ISSN 0353-6521, Y. 22 (1996), No. 5/6, Ljubljana, Gospodarski vestnik, 1996, pp. 781–792.

Grilc Peter. *Pogledi na ekstrateritorialne učinke konkurenčnega prava EGS*, in: Dnevi slovenskih pravnikov 89 od 12. do 14. oktobra 1989 v Portorožu, Združeno delo, ISSN 0350-7327, 1989, Y. 15, No. 5, Ljubljana, Gospodarski vestnik, 1989, pp. 614–631.

Grilc Peter. *Konkurenčno pravo v obdobju gospodarske krize (antitrust in koncentracije)*, in: Dnevi slovenskih pravnikov 2010 od 14. do 16. oktobra, Portorož, Podjetje in delo, ISSN 0353-6521, Y. 36, No. 6/7, Ljubljana, GV Založba, 2010, pp. 1343–1354.

Grilc Peter. *Reforma konkurenčnega prava v EU*, in: Zbornik znanstvenih razprav, ISSN 1854-3839, 2000, Y. 60, No. 2, pp. 51–75.

Grilc Peter. *Kršitev prava Skupnosti in posledice v primerih kršitve 86. člena PES*, in: Dnevi slovenskih pravnikov 2007 od 11. do 13. oktobra, Portorož, Podjetje in delo, ISSN 0353-6521, Y. 33, No. 6/7, Ljubljana, GV Založba, 2007, pp. 1113–1124.

Grilc Peter. *Reforma konkurenčnega prava v EU in vpliv na slovensko pravo* in: Juren Peter (Ed.): Dnevi slovenskih pravnikov 2000: od 12. do 14. oktobra v Portorožu, Podjetje in delo, ISSN 0353-6521,. 26, No. 6/7, Gospodarski vestnik, Ljubljana, 2000, pp. 849–857.

Grilc Peter. *Javna podjetja in konkurenčno pravo: nekateri vidiki po Zakonu o preprečevanju omejevanja konkurence in pravu EU*, in: VI. dnevi javnega prava, Portorož, 5.-7. junij 2000, Izobraževanje in usposabljanje v javni upravi, ISSN 1408-0427, Ljubljana, Inštitut za javno upravo, 2000, pp. 111–120.

Grilc Peter. *Združitve in konkurenčno pravo*, in: Dnevi slovenskih pravnikov, od 14. do 16. oktobra 1999 v Portorožu, Podjetje in delo, ISSN 0353-6521, Y. 25, 1999, No. 6/7, Ljubljana, Gospodarski vestnik, 1999, pp. 1128–1138.

Grilc Peter. *Varstvo konkurence v postopkih prevzema*, in: Prelič Saša (Ed.): Gospodarski subjekti na trgu, Maribor, Inštitut za gospodarsko pravo, 1999, pp. 43–60.

Hojnik Janja & Vlahek Ana. Promocija slovenskih živilskih proizvodov in enotni trg EU, in: Pravna praksa, ISSN 0352-0730, 17. March 2011, Y. 30, No. 10, pp. 12–14 (referred to as: *Hojnik & Vlahek. Promocija slovenskih živilskih proizvodov in enotni trg EU*).

Jakulin Vid. *Odgovornost pravnih oseb za kazniva dejanja v državah, nastalih iz nekdanje Jugoslavije*, in: Zbornik za Alenko Šelih: kazensko pravo, kriminologija, človekove pravice, Inštitut za kriminologijo pri Pravni fakulteti, Pravna fakulteta Univerze v Ljubljani, Slovenska akademija znanosti in umetnosti, Ljubljana, 2013, pp. 213–224 (referred to as: Jakulin, *Odgovornost pravnih oseb* ...).

Podobnik Klemen. *Program prizanesljivosti – novost v slovenski konkurenčnopravni ureditvi*, in: Pravni letopis, Inštitut za primerjalno pravo, 2009, pp. 205–223.

Podobnik Klemen. *Možnosti in spremenjena paradigma; razmejitev EU/SLO pravo*, in: V. Dnevi civilnega prava: Portorož, 19. mar. – 20. apr. 2007, Ljubljana, Inštitut za primerjalno pravo, 2007, pp. 116–122.

Podobnik Klemen. *Nova ekonomija in novi trendi v konkurenčnem pravu*, in: Dnevi slovenskih pravnikov 2002: od 10. do 12. oktobra v Portorožu, Podjetje in delo, Y. 28, No. 6/7, Ljubljana, Gospodarski vestnik, 2002, pp. 1486–1493.

Podobnik Klemen. *Javna podjetja v EU tekmujejo.*, in: Finance, ISSN 1318-1548, 22 May 2003.

Podobnik Klemen. *Sistem distribucije motornih vozil v EU*, in: Finance, ISSN 1318-1548, 25 September 2003, pp. 185.

Podobnik Klemen. *Javni sektor in evropsko (konkurenčno) pravo*, in: Pravna praksa, ISSN 0352-0730, July 1998, Y. 17, No. 13, pp. 5–6.

Podobnik Klemen. *Pravo in politika konkurence v Evropski uniji*, in: Seliškar Toš Mojca (Ed.): Mednarodna konferenca Slovensko pravo in gospodarstvo ob vstopu Slovenije v Evropsko unijo, Portorož, 21–23 April 2004 = International Conference Slovene Law and the Economy upon EU Accession, Portorož, 21st–23rd April 2004, Littera Scripta Manet, Zbirka Manet Ljubljana: Pravna fakulteta: = Facultas iuridica, 2004, pp. 435–447.

Podobnik Klemen. *Vpliv ameriškega antitrusta na konkurenčno pravo Evropske skupnosti in kontinentalnega pravnika*, in: Dnevi slovenskih pravnikov 2001: od 11. do 13. oktobra v Portorožu, Podjetje in delo, ISSN 0353-6521, 27, No. 6/7, Ljubljana, Gospodarski vestnik, 2001, pp. 1213–1220.

Podobnik Klemen. *Reforma in Komisija ter Sodišče prve stopnje*, in: Dnevi slovenskih pravnikov 2004: od 14. do 16. oktobra v Portorožu, Podjetje in delo, ISSN 0353-6521, Y. 30, No. 6/7, Ljubljana, Gospodarski vestnik, 2004, pp. 1300–1306.

Podobnik Klemen: *Izzivi za Slovenijo ob reformi evropskega konkurenčnega prava*, in: Evropsko gospodarsko pravo: strokovno gradivo: 4. in 5. marec, Portorož 2004, Ljubljana, GV Izobraževanje, 2004.

Rosina Aleš. *Samoupravni sporazumi in družbeni dogovori o cenah*, in: Pravnik, 1975, Y. 30, No. 7/9, pp. 236–250 (referred to as: Rosina, *Samouporavni sporazumi in družbeni dogovori o cenah*).

Rosina Aleš. *Sporazumi o vertikalni delitvi trga in izključitvene pogodbe*, in: Pravnik, 1973, Y. 28, No. 4/6, pp. 114–126 (referred to as: Rosina, *Sporazumi o vertikalni delitvi trga in izključitvene pogodbe).*

Rosina Aleš. *Monopolski dogovori in zloraba dominantnega tržnega položaja*, in: Pravnik, 1969, Y. 24, No. 1/3, pp. 33–55 (referred to as: Rosina, *Monopolski dogovori in zloraba dominantnega tržnega položaja*).

Vlahek Ana. *Reforma antitrusta v Evropski uniji*, in: Podjetje in delo, 2004, Y. 30, No. 2, pp. 230–272 (referred to as: Vlahek, *Reforma antitrusta v Evropski uniji*).

Vlahek Ana. *Amicus curiae, sodelovanje med slovenskimi sodišči, UVK in Evropsko komisijo v konkurenčnopravnih zadevah*, in: Pravosodni bilten, 2009, Y. 30, No. 4, pp. 301–330 (referred to as: Vlahek, *Amicus curiae ...*).

Vlahek Ana. *Oris odškodnin na področju skupnostnega antitrusta*, in: Evro PP, Y. 28, No. 11, Ljubljana, GV Založba, 2009, pp. 44–46.

Vlahek Ana. *Kolektivno varstvo v EU*, in: Pravna praksa, 31 May 2012, Y. 31, No. 21, GV Založba, Ljubljana, pp. 16–17 (referred to as: Vlahek, *Kolektivno varstvo v EU*).

Vlahek Ana. *Množični (odškodninski) zahtevki zaradi kršitev konkurenčnega prava (antitrusta)*, in: IX. dnevi civilnega prava, 20–21 April 2011, Ljubljana, Inštitut za primerjalno pravo, 2011.

Vlahek Ana. *Reforma konkurenčnega prava v Evropski uniji*, University of Ljubljana diploma thesis, Ljubljana, 2003, 126 pp.

Vlahek Ana. *Novosti na področju odškodninskih tožb zaradi kršitev evropskega antitrusta*, in: Pravnik, 2016, Y. 71, No. 7/8, pp. 547–590, 620–621 (referred to as: Vlahek, *Novosti* ...).

Vlahek Ana & Lutman Karmen. *Ureditev zastaranja odškodninskih terjatev zaradi kršitev konkurenčnega prava v Direktivi 2014/104/EU in njena implementacija v pravne rede držav članic*, in: Pravnik, 2017, Y. 72, No. 1/2, pp. 41–70, 135–136 (referred to as: Vlahek&Lutman, *Ureditev zastaranja* ...).

Vogrinec David. *Oviranje preiskave po ZPOmK-1*, in: Pravna praksa, Y. 33, No. 21, pp. 8–10 (referred to as: Vogrinec, *Oviranje preiskave po ZPOmK-1).*

Index

The numbers here refer to paragraph numbers.

Index

Index

www.ingramcontent.com/pod-product-compliance
Lightning Source LLC
Chambersburg PA
CBHW071439230926
51846CB00001B/282
* 9 7 8 9 4 0 3 5 2 6 9 0 4 *